GETTING OVER EQUALITY

CRITICAL AMERICA

Richard Delgado and Jean Stefancic
General Editors

Global Critical Race Feminism: An International Reader
Edited by Adrien Katherine Wing

Law and Religion: Critical Essays
Edited by Stephen M. Feldman

Changing Race: Latinos, the Census, and the History of Ethnicity in the United States
Clara E. Rodríguez

From the Ground Up: Environmental Racism and the Rise of the Environmental Justice Movement
Luke Cole and Sheila Foster

Nothing but the Truth: Why Trial Lawyers Don't, Can't, and Shouldn't Have to Tell the Whole Truth
Steven Lubet

Critical Race Theory: An Introduction
Richard Delgado and Jean Stefancic

Playing It Safe: How the Supreme Court Sidesteps Hard Cases
Lisa A. Kloppenberg

Why Lawsuits Are Good for America: Disciplined Democracy, Big Business, and the Common Law
Carl T. Bogus

How the Left Can Win Arguments and Influence People: A Tactical Manual for Pragmatic Progressives
John K. Wilson

Aftermath: The Clinton Impeachment and the Presidency in the Age of Political Spectacle
Edited by Leonard V. Kaplan and Beverly I. Moran

Getting over Equality: A Critical Diagnosis of Religious Freedom in America
Steven D. Smith

STEVEN D. SMITH

GETTING OVER EQUALITY

*A Critical Diagnosis of Religious Freedom
in America*

New York University Press • *New York and London*

NEW YORK UNIVERSITY PRESS
New York and London

Library of Congress Cataloging-in-Publication Data
Smith, Steven D. (Steven Douglas), 1952–
Getting over equality : a critical diagnosis of religious freedom in
America / Steven D. Smith.
p.   cm. — (Critical America)
Includes bibliographical references and index.
ISBN 0-8147-9794-6
1. Religious tolerance—United States. 2. Protestantism—United
States.   I. Title. II. Series.
BR526 .S63 2001
323.44'2'0973—dc21   2001001906

New York University Press books are printed on acid-free paper,
and their binding materials are chosen for strength and durability.

Manufactured in the United States of America

10 9 8 7 6 5 4 3 2 1

Contents

Acknowledgments

Several of the essays in this book are adapted (sometimes beyond ready recognition) from papers published or presented elsewhere. As a result, the various essays have benefited from comments by and conversations with friends, colleagues, and critics too numerous and diverse to mention here. But I cannot forbear from acknowledging the persistent help of my former colleagues from the University of Colorado, Paul Campos and Bob Nagel, and of my friends Larry Alexander and Michael Perry. As always, I appreciate the less direct but even more important help and support of my wife, Merina, and my family. Debbie Sumption provided valuable secretarial assistance in readying the manuscript for publication. Hope Durant squeezed preparation of the index into cramming for finals. And I thank the following journals for permission to use and adapt the following articles:

Steven D. Smith, "Blooming Confusion: Madison's Mixed Legacy," 75 *Indiana Law Journal* 61 (2000) (Copyright 2000 by the Trustees of Indiana University Press). Reprinted by permission).

Steven D. Smith, "Unprincipled Religious Freedom," 7 *Journal of Contemporary Legal Issues*. Copyright (1996). Reprinted with the permission of the *Journal of Contemporary Legal Issues*.

Steven D. Smith, "Is a Coherent Theory of Religious Freedom Possible?" 15 *Constitutional Commentary* 73 (1998). Reprinted by permission of *Constitutional Commentary*.

Steven D. Smith, "Religion, Democracy, and Autonomy: A Political Parable," 42, no. 3, *William and Mary Law Review* (2000). Reprinted by permission of *William and Mary Law Review*.

Steven D. Smith, "Free Exercise Doctrine and the Discourse of Disrespect," 65 *University of Colorado Law Review* 519 (1994). Reprinted by permission of the *University of Colorado Law Review*.

Introduction

Beyond Failure

IF THE OLD joke is right—the joke about how everyone talks about the weather but nobody *does* anything about it—the reason, obviously, is that nobody knows *how* to do anything about the weather. And the same might be said about the familiar ways in which we talk and think about religious freedom. Nearly all scholars—and, in less judicious moments, many judges and Justices—complain that the constitutional doctrines of religious freedom elaborated by the Supreme Court make little sense, and that the decisions rendered under these doctrines are chaotic. Calls for "rethinking religious freedom" proliferate. Yet no one seems to know *how* to think about religious freedom in a way that really departs from our established modes of thought. So efforts at "rethinking" nearly always turn out to be variations on a set of familiar themes.

Often, in fact, they are not really even variations. A colleague who wrote some impressive essays on religious freedom in the 1980s told me that he rarely reads new scholarly literature on the subject. "Why waste my time? It's all just the same old stuff."

More specifically, despite strident disagreements on issues like graduation prayer or school vouchers or public postings of the Ten Commandments, and even despite what appear to be deeper disagreements about history and constitutional doctrine, nearly everyone who participates in debates about religious freedom seems to honor certain virtually sacred assumptions governing what can and cannot be said. We might notice three such assumptions. First, it is assumed that some "principle" of religious freedom is embedded in the Constitution, and that debates about specific issues must be grounded in that constitutional principle. Just how the principle (whatever the particular advocate thinks it is) gained its status as *the Constitution's* principle is often less than clear. Probably the most commonsensical view is that "the framers" put the principle into the Constitution; and both in scholarly

I

literature and even more so in popular debates—television talk shows featuring representatives of the ACLU or Americans United for the Separation of Church and State, for example—advocates often talk as if this is what they mean. But because "framers' intent" theories have well-known difficulties, sophisticated advocates are often more coy on this point. They may discreetly omit to explain just how a particular principle became the Constitution's principle, or what it means for a principle to be the Constitution's principle; they may thereby create the impression that "the Constitution" is some sort of entity with a mind and meaning of its own—a mind and meaning, of course, to which we are required to defer.

A second common assumption, especially in more scholarly discussions of religious freedom, is that the Constitution's principle can be equipped for active use only with the help of a substantial amount of theorizing. Such theorizing is required in part because the various candidates for "the Constitution's principle" are too unrefined, standing alone, to be able to provide solutions to concrete disputes, but also because the preferred principle itself needs to be justified and defended. Scholarly advocates understand, it seems, that constitutional principles can lose their cogency, and that in order to retain their vigor they must be reinforced with theoretical supplements.

Finally, and perhaps most importantly, advocates take it for granted that whatever principle they happen to find in the Constitution and whatever results they may derive from that principle in specific controversies, their position needs to comply with the unrelenting requirement that all religions are to be regarded as equal. For many, of course, religious equality (or its corollary, official religious neutrality) simply *is* the core constitutional principle. But even for those who describe some other principle as *the* meaning of the Constitution's religion clauses— liberty or "autonomy," perhaps—equality is still at least an important and imperative side constraint: a position that treated religions unequally would be ipso facto out of court. In this spirit, Michael Perry reports that it is "constitutional bedrock"—not a point of contention, evidently—that government may not treat any religion as religiously "better along one or another dimension of value than one or more other religions or than no religion at all," and that government may not treat any religious practices as religiously "better—truer or more efficacious . . . or more authentically American—than one or more other religious or nonreligious practices or than no religious practice at all."[1]

So despite differences and disagreements, advocates approach religious freedom questions in basically similar ways. They appeal to the principle of religious freedom contained in some nebulous sense in the Constitution. If they are scholars, they try to elaborate this principle into a more full-blown theoretical position; and they expend considerable effort in defending their favored theories, attacking the theories of their opponents, and drawing out the implications of their own theories for specific controversies. And advocates argue that contrary positions treat different religions unequally—or perhaps, varying the terminology to gain rhetorical power, that these positions "discriminate" in favor of some religions and against others—while insisting that their own positions are benignly egalitarian, "neutral," and nondiscriminatory toward the variety of religious and nonreligious positions that Americans hold.

In describing the prevailing discourse in this way, I am hardly saying anything novel or surprising. This is simply the way the people who participate in debates about religious freedom—the lawyers and judges and politicians and scholars—routinely talk. *Of course* they approach the issues in this way. How else *could* they deal with the hot, sensitive issues of religious freedom?

Despite present appearances, however, we are not predestined to follow the prevailing approach to questions of religious freedom. Reading a little history, for example, we can see that in earlier times the daunting questions arising from the interplay of religion and conscience and government have often been addressed in very different ways. The questions have been addressed *without* assuming that debate is circumscribed by some "principle" supposedly entrenched in a written Constitution, *without* assuming that the answers to the questions must be derived from a "theory," and *without* requiring participants to assume for purposes of public debate what no one believed (and what, even in our own latitudinarian and antitheological and egalitarian times, no one can truly affirm without falling into incoherence)—that is, that all religions are "equally" true and virtuous and "authentically American." So our ways of talking and thinking are not the only possible ways. Moreover, there is reason to suspect that our standard approaches to religious freedom—approaches governed by the contestable assumptions described above—are unproductive, or even counterproductive.

Still, I admit that it is difficult to see our way clear of the current mode of discourse. Several years ago I wrote a book called *Foreordained Failure: The Quest for a Constitutional Principle of Religious Freedom*. The book contained a historical section arguing that the Constitution and the Bill of Rights, as originally composed and understood, did not contain any substantive principle of religious freedom: the First Amendment religion clauses were intended to do no more than confirm in writing the widely shared commitment to leaving jurisdiction over religion questions with the states.[2] In a more theoretical section, the book tried to show that it is impossible to articulate a satisfactory theory of religious freedom, because any theory will of necessity violate its own premises and betray its own objectives. I had hoped that the book might work in a small way to disrupt the prevailing, unsatisfactory discourse of religious freedom. But with the benefit of hindsight, I must also acknowledge that in one sense the title—*Foreordained Failure*—might describe the book itself. The book was foreordained to fail, in a practical sense at least, *not* (in my humble opinion, of course) because its arguments were wrong, but rather because it did not offer any other way of addressing religious freedom questions.

With regard to the historical argument that the Constitution contained *no* substantive principle of religious freedom, for example, a scholar at another school remarked to me off the record, "Your argument might be right—in fact, it probably is—but no one in the field is going to admit it, because we'd all be out of business." Another prominent constitutional law scholar made a similar point in conversation. After saying some complimentary things about the largely critical work reflected in my book and also in the related work of some of my former colleagues at the University of Colorado, he abruptly qualified his praise with a damning conclusion: "But what you people at Colorado don't seem to realize is—*life has to go on*."

I accept this objection, though only in part. The objection is overdrawn, I think, insofar as it fails to recognize that criticism—figuring out what isn't working and why—*is* a necessary part of the way in which life goes on. In addition, this sort of objection—the objection, that is, which complains that some legal scholarship is excessively critical—is typically quite complacent and unselfconscious about some other dubious assumptions. It tends to assume, for example, that *courts* must necessarily play the central role in defining the meaning of religious freedom (or of the constitutional order generally), and also that courts act legitimately only when they act on the basis of something usually described as "principle." Legal scholars in particular often seem constitutionally incapable of questioning these revered but highly contestable premises—an incapacity which would explain why they so easily conclude that scholarship not eventuating in a "principled" prescription telling courts what to do is without practical value. So my view continues to be that in general, constitutional law scholarship—and religious freedom scholarship in particular—suffers far more from being too complacent than from being unduly critical. I hope to avoid this error, including in this book. (But of course I am in part a product of the current culture, and of the current legal culture, and I frankly doubt that I have succeeded in avoiding inordinate complacency.)

Having said this, I must also admit that the "life has to go on" objection states an important truth. Life *does* have to go on. Religious freedom questions will continue to arise, and people will have to find ways to talk about them. Often the questions will be taken before courts, for better or worse, and then courts will have to have ways of talking about the questions. Consequently, if a critic merely proclaims, "This isn't working" or "This way of talking doesn't make sense" but suggests no other way of working or talking, then it is to be expected that people will go on as before. What else *could* they do?

So the chapters in this book try to be constructive as well as critical. Or at least some of them do. The chapters in Part I are still largely critical in nature; they challenge the basic approach to religious freedom reflected in modern religion clause discourse. Two central values (equality, autonomy) come in *not* for repudiation—it would be merely immature and overdramatic to purport to renounce values so venerable—but for a close, skeptical examination; and the third essay argues more generally that a "principled" theoretical account of religious freedom is—even in principle—impossible. The essays in Part II have a critical dimension as well; but they also try to deal constructively with the questions that academic lawyers are obsessed with. Did the Court "get it right" in *Wisconsin v. Yoder* (the Amish school case), or in *Employment Division v. Smith* (the peyote case), or in *Church of the Lukumi Babalu Aye v. Hialeah* (the animal sacrifice case), or in the dozens of sundry parochial school aid cases whose disparate results have become an open scandal? How do we know, or what criteria should we bring to bear, in deciding whether the Court "got it right"? And, most importantly, *what should "we"* (meaning, typically, the courts) *do*?

For the impatient, I can give a capsule preview of my responses to this last (and, for most lawyers, ultimate) question. What *should* the courts do? Although I confess to having no detailed program or agenda, and although I am estopped by past writings and current beliefs to offer any governing "principle" from which right answers could be deduced, in these essays I argue that the courts can and should promote prudence over principle and tolerance over equality (or neutrality). I also argue that courts should be more deferential to the nonjudicial institutions of society than they often have been in our ongoing collective effort to craft a regime of religious freedom. To be sure, this is messy counsel; it does not pretend to supply the kind of elegant prescriptions that legal scholars typically offer or embrace—and that sometimes seem to be the only kind of prescriptions that are cognizable at all within the legal academy. So after reading my responses to the question, "What should we do?" some readers are likely to react with "That's all fine, but *what should we do?*" In these essays, though, I try to show not only that judges *could* act deferentially in ways that would promote prudence and tolerance, but indeed that judges *have*, in their occasional better moments, been guided by such counsel.

One who advocates tolerance ought to be prepared to defend that suspect virtue not only against the familiar modern criticism which holds that tolerance is too insipid or unambitious a goal for a "liberal" society, but also against the opposite and older (but, I think, more formidable) objection which insists that tolerance is a political or psychological or even logical impossibility. In a variety of provocative recent writings, Stanley Fish has renewed this objection and, in his typically ferocious way, has applied the objection to a variety of more "liberal" views (including mine, though the label "liberal" fits awkwardly). In a different spirit, "liberals" themselves may wonder whether the rash of recent efforts, arising in places from Mississippi courtrooms to the United States Congress, to promote public prayer as well as public postings of the Ten Commandments, demonstrates that Fish is right: tolerance seems to be beyond the capacity of our society. In Part III, I consider this question. I conclude that tolerance *is* possible—though hardly easy, much less inevitable. But contrary to both Fish and his "liberal" opponents, it is precisely our theistic heritage and commitments that make tolerance an achievable virtue (as our wisest and most influential public theologian, Abraham Lincoln, appreciated).

PART I

HOW FIRM A FOUNDATION?

THE "PRINCIPLES" OF equality and autonomy compose the foundation of modern understandings—and, perhaps, modern misunderstandings—of religious freedom. Each of these terms is at the core of a cluster of closely related notions or near synonyms: "equality" is a sort of alter ego to what is sometimes called "the antidiscrimination principle" and it is the virtual twin of "neutrality" (and each comes in a variety of shapes and sizes), while "autonomy" is the more pretentious kin of notions like "freedom of conscience" or "freedom of choice" or "voluntarism" or simply "liberty." Modern debates about religious freedom generally, or about particular controversies such as school prayer or Christmas displays or aid to religious schools, nearly always invoke one or more of these ideas as the general premises from which specific conclusions are then argued for.

Some readers may wonder why I do not give "separation" equal billing among the foundational principles of American religious freedom. After all, we sometimes declare with evident pride that the "separation of church and state" is the distinctive American contribution to the centuries-old controversies about religious freedom. Although I have no wish to understate the significance of the "separation" theme, it becomes increasingly clear that "separation" in our tradition is more superstructure than foundation—more a conclusion, or perhaps an institutional implementation, than a basic premise. Even self-styled "strict separationists" will likely acknowledge that people can sensibly and legitimately ask (and people sometimes do ask): "Why separation?" or "What makes separation a good thing?" These are questions that separationists can understand—and that they think they can answer. Their answers are likely to invoke deeper values or "principles" like "religious equality" or "individual autonomy" (or "freedom of conscience," or "freedom of choice"). But if someone asks, "Why equality?" or "What's so good about freedom of conscience?" the very question may seem obtuse. "Well, if you don't understand that," we may be tempted to respond, "there isn't much I can say."

Questioning equality or autonomy or freedom of conscience may seem almost like asking, "What's so good about happiness?" Some things are "properly basic," as the philosophers say, and it seems a misunderstanding to demand that basics be justified by anything *more* basic. In our current constitutional culture, the notions of religious equality and individual autonomy appear to enjoy this "properly basic" quality to a much greater degree than "separation" does.

This situation is not inevitable; it is not, as far as I can see, foreordained as a matter of logic. But Supreme Court decisions over the last decade or so increasingly reflect some such ordering; they treat equality (or "neutrality") and autonomy (or freedom of conscience, or of choice) as more basic notions than "separation." The Court either uses those more basic notions instead of separation, or (perhaps more accurately) it uses them as a way of interpreting the meaning of separation. And this seems sensible. After all, the notion of "separation," in the abstract, is not actually our invention; predecessors whom we typically classify as theocrats—the Massachusetts Puritans, for instance, or the popes of the High Middle Ages—also emphasized the importance of a separation of church and state. Our distinctive achievement, if there has been one, comes from interpreting "separation" in accordance with the more basic principles of "equality" and "autonomy."

So in considering "foundations," these are the principles we will reflect on—equality and autonomy. Conveniently, each of these ideas is also associated with an influential American political thinker—with James Madison and Immanuel Kant, respectively. It may seem odd to call Kant an "American political thinker"; after all, he never actually set foot on these shores. But modern theorists like John Rawls and Ronald Dworkin routinely explicate the Constitution, including its implications for religious freedom, in accordance with liberal democratic theory dominated by ideas traceable to Kant—in particular by the idea of "autonomy." In such discussions, as Michael Zuckert observes, "[o]ne is far more likely to find Kant cited as an authority than the Declaration of Independence. Indeed, one is nearly certain to find the one and not the other."[1] So it seems that Kant has become an American thinker by adoption. Consequently, the first two chapters in this part use Madison and Kant as focal points for considering, and reassessing, the principles that dominate modern thinking about religious freedom. The third chapter moves beyond these particular principles with their associated theories and invokes a still older and not very American thinker—Augustine—in wondering whether any coherent theory of religious freedom is achievable.

1

Blooming Confusion

Religious Equality in the "Age of Madison"

"FOR THOSE WHO like to speak of an 'Age of Constantine' that began in the fourth century," Martin Marty observes, "there is reason to regard [Jefferson's Virginia Bill for Religious Liberty] as the key moment of the end of that age and the beginning of a new age."[1] And even more than Jefferson, James Madison was the principal prophet of that new age. Madison authored perhaps the most powerful brief for religious disestablishment that has ever been written, he pushed Jefferson's bill through the Virginia legislature, and his common sponsorship of that measure and of the First Amendment provided the pretext on which the modern Supreme Court read the Virginia provision into the Constitution. If the era before the 1780s was the "Age of Constantine," then the period since then can with even greater justification be called the "Age of Madison."

And what *is* the condition of religious freedom in the Age of Madison? Here we encounter a paradox. On the one hand, no society in history has afforded greater scope and protection for a diverse range of religious belief and conduct. Or at least so we like to suppose; and I have no intention of disturbing that supposition here. On the other hand, there is something approaching unanimity on the proposition that the prevailing *discourse* of religious freedom—or the official framework and language within which issues of religious freedom are argued about and judicially resolved—is deeply incoherent. Our situation is just the reverse, it might almost seem, of that of earlier periods in which apologists and theorists could argue about questions of church and state in forceful, cogent, substantive terms,[2] even while actual respect for and protection of religious freedom was comparatively feeble. As our practice has improved, it seems, our understanding and discursive facility have deteriorated.

How to explain this curious development? And for which part of our current paradoxical situation does Madison deserve the credit, or the blame? In this chapter I want to argue that Madison—as symbol and to an impressive extent as actor—is the source of both the happy and unhappy parts of our current situation. Moreover, this is not a case in which Madison's positive contributions were partially marred by unfortunate extraneous mistakes, or in which our inheritance includes both a valuable estate and some regrettable independent debts. On the contrary, the two aspects of our situation are interrelated; we probably could not have one without the other. So in both our virtues and our vices we are Madison's faithful heirs.

THE FIRST BEQUEST: THE PRINCIPLE OF RELIGIOUS EQUALITY

Probably the most visible part of Madison's legacy is the principle—by now regarded as a sort of central and self-evident truth—that all religions should be treated as equal before the law. For two-and-a-half centuries before Madison, from the time in which the Protestant Reformation had fractured Western Christendom, European states and their colonies had struggled to find a satisfactory principle for regulating the conflicts among competing faiths. The earliest principle had favored monolithic religious establishment. Thus, the Peace of Augsburg had decreed that the religion of the prince should be the religion of the realm—*cujus regio ejus religio*. That principle had been challenged—but only in part—by proponents of a different approach, which we might call the principle of toleration, and which was perhaps most importantly advocated by John Locke. But *toleration* was still offensive to some because it implied that some religions were favored over others. "Toleration is not the *opposite* of intoleration," fumed Thomas Paine, "but is the counterfeit of it. Both are deceptions." To borrow a modern expression, toleration meant that even if people were allowed to practice their various religions, some religions were still "insiders" while others were "outsiders."

So a few visionaries like Madison favored a more radical principle—a principle of religious equality—that aimed to eliminate the remaining invidious distinctions. The discourse of religious freedom as it has evolved in this country has come to regard the equality principle as axiomatic, and credit for perceiving and promoting that principle is often given to Madison.[3] The honor is deserved. Madison was ahead of his time in emphasizing—again and again—that all religions should be treated equally. Thus, in 1776, when Virginia was adopting a bill of rights for itself as a state, George Mason offered a provision ensuring the "toleration" of diverse religions. Mason may have thought he was expressing the enlightened or progressive sentiment of his time, but Madison wanted—and got—more: The provision was amended to say that the free exercise of religion extended to all *equally*. William Lee Miller comments that "everything that was to come in the American arrangement of these matters [of religion and government] was already present in Williamsburg, Virginia, in June of 1776, in the proposals of young James Madison."[4]

Later, in his famous *Memorial and Remonstrance*, written in opposition to Patrick Henry's "Assessments Bill" that would have renewed a state subsidy to Christian churches, Madison argued eloquently in behalf of religious equality. "If 'all men are by nature equally free and independent,'" he reasoned, then it followed that

all men are to be considered as entering into Society on equal conditions. . . . Above all are they to be considered as retaining an *"equal* title to the free exercise of Religion according to the dictates of conscience." Whilst we assert for ourselves a freedom to embrace, to profess and to observe the Religion which we believe to be of divine origin, we cannot deny an *equal* freedom to those whose minds have not yet yielded to the evidence which has convinced us.[5]

Later, in the First Congress, Madison proposed a constitutional amendment providing that "[n]o state shall violate the equal rights of conscience."[6] Nitpickers may point out that this "equality" proposal was defeated in the Senate, and so was never presented to the states for possible ratification. But Madison was posthumously vindicated when, using the notion of "incorporation," the modern Supreme Court construed the Constitution *as if* it contained the provision that Madison had favored. Consequently, the equality principle (along with the corollary notion that government must be "neutral" in matters of religion) has provided the major premise under which modern religion clause controversies have been debated and decided.

So if there is cause to question Madison's legacy in this respect, it is not because of any uncertainty about his zeal or skill in championing the equality principle. Questions, if there are any, would have to concern the *value* of that principle.

EQUALITY AND OBFUSCATION

And in fact there *is* room to wonder whether the equality principle has been entirely beneficent in its influence. Suppose, for example, that we were to reflect on Madison's favored principle immediately after reading an essay by Michigan law professor Peter Westen that caused a stir in the legal academy when it was published in the Harvard Law Review almost two decades ago. The thrust of Westen's subversive essay, called "The Empty Idea of Equality,"[7] was that equality is a purely formal notion, devoid of substantive content, and hence useless for resolving real controversies. Equality simply means that like cases should be treated alike—a proposition with which no one really disagrees. What people *do* disagree about is whether some particular case really *is* like some other case in relevant respects. But the notion of equality does nothing to help resolve that sort of disagreement.

To put the point more generally, every person is in different ways both like and unlike every other person. Every situation is like every other situation in some respects but not in others. Political and legal controversies turn on whether particular similarities and differences are relevant for a particular purpose. Blindness, for example, is a characteristic of some people but not others, and it matters for some purposes (eligibility to *drive*, for instance) but not for other purposes (eligibility to *vote*). The crucial point is that the "principle of equality" does nothing to tell us whether particular similarities or differences are relevant. If we independently know that blindness is relevant to driving but not to voting, we will know how to treat blind people without appealing to equality; and if we *don't* know whether blindness is relevant, invoking equality ("Treat people equally." "Treat like cases alike.") won't help us. Either way, the notion of equality does no useful work, Westen suggested: the notion is simply "empty."

Westen's argument does *not* mean that equality is a "bad thing," of course; nor does it necessarily mean that we should drop the word "equality" from our vocabulary. But the argument *does* imply that claims about equality are conclusions to be *argued for*, not premises to be *argued from*. Westen's criticism suggests that whenever the concept or principle of equality seems to be doing any significant intellectual work on a controversial question (as opposed to merely expressing a conclusion), on closer inspection it will probably become apparent that this is "illegitimate" work—illegitimate in the sense that the language of equality is being used to smuggle in (or, more often, to exclude) some more substantive values or criteria without any careful attempt to provide justification. If we see controversial issues being debated mainly in terms of what "equality requires," in short, we will have reason to suspect in advance that some kind of cheating—or deception, or self-deception—is going on.

Equipped with this suspicion inspired by Westen, let us revisit the principle of religious equality. Can we detect any of the problems described by Westen in Madison's use of the principle?

EGALITARIAN QUESTION-BEGGING IN
MADISON'S MEMORIAL

We might start with a small point. The Assessments Bill which Madison opposed in his *Memorial and Remonstrance* had provided that each taxpayer could designate which Christian denomination should receive his or her contribution, and the bill had then limited the churches' use of this money to the purposes of paying ministers or constructing and maintaining buildings for worship. But Quakers and Mennonites (or "Menonists," as both the bill and Madison called them) were exempted from these restrictions—presumably on the assumption that these faiths did not believe in or support a paid, professional ministry. Though still requiring Quakers and Mennonites to pay the tax, the bill provided that they might place the money "in their general fund, to be disposed of in a manner which they shall think best calculated to promote their particular mode of worship."[8] The manifest purpose of this exception was to treat these religions "equally" by allowing them to use the money in a way consistent with their own religious beliefs and practices. But Madison quarreled with the exemption; he argued that the bill *violated* the principle of religious equality by granting Quakers and Mennonites a legal privilege not enjoyed by other faiths.[9]

We see here an early version of the "free exercise exemption" controversy (to be discussed in more detail in Part II), in which advocates appeal to the same principle—equality (or "neutrality")—to argue, variously, that free exercise exemptions are constitutionally forbidden, or permitted, or required. Should religious pacifists such as Quakers be excused from military conscription, for example, if nonreligious objectors are drafted? That question hinges on whether there is some relevant substantive difference between a *religious* objection and a conscientious but *nonreligious* objection. Both today and in the past, some people have thought there is a relevant difference; others have disagreed.[10] But the important point is that the formal principle of equality simply does not speak to that substantive question at all. So the language of equality at best offers a tempting way of *begging* the real question.

And that is just what Madison did in his *Memorial*. If the Assessments Bill treated Quakers and Mennonites differently from other Christians, presumably it did so because its sponsors believed Quakers and Mennonites *were* different from other Christians—and different in a way that warranted different legal treatment. Madison evidently disagreed. Perhaps he could have supported his contrary view with substantive arguments. But he didn't. Instead, he chose to beg the question—to smuggle his more substantive judgments into the debate under the innocent guise of "equality."

The fudginess in Madison's treatment of Quakers and Mennonites points to a larger problem that afflicted Madison's *Memorial* at all levels. Though he insisted that all religions should be treated equally, an inspection of the *Memorial* reveals that in an important sense Madison's argument pervasively depended on treating religions differently. His first and central argument, one on which much of the rest of the *Memorial* depended, was explicitly theological in nature. You may find the argument appealing—I do—or even self-evidently correct; but the crucial point for now is that the argument plainly discriminated among faiths by accepting and endorsing some religious views while rejecting other religious views. Here is Madison's primary argument:

> [W]e hold it for a fundamental and undeniable truth, "that Religion or the duty which we owe to our Creator and the Manner of discharging it, can be directed only by reason and conviction, not by force or violence." The Religion then of every man must be left to the conviction and conscience of every man. . . . It is the duty of every man to render to the Creator such homage, and such only, as he believes to be acceptable to him. This duty is precedent both in order of time and degree of obligation, to the claims of Civil Society. Before any man can be

considered as a member of Civil Society, he must be considered as a subject of the Governor of the Universe: And if a member of Civil Society, who enters into any subordinate Association, must always do it with a reservation of his duty to the general authority; much more must every man who becomes a member of any particular Society, do it with a saving of his allegiance to the Universal Sovereign.[11]

Given its explicitly theological content, this argument plainly will not speak to an atheist (even if the conclusion is welcome). But neither will it speak to everyone who happens to be "religious": as would have been even more evident at the time it was offered, the argument has a definite "sectarian" quality. We might roughly describe the religious beliefs in which Madison's argument was grounded as theistic—and not merely theistic but Christian, and not merely Christian but Protestant, and not merely Protestant but reflective of a sort of nonstatist voluntarist Protestantism akin to that of the Baptists whom Madison had earlier defended against persecution and who later provided the votes to elect Madison to Congress. Indeed, throughout the *Memorial* Madison made arguments and drew conclusions with which not only atheists but also Catholics and Protestants in the mainstream Lutheran and Reformed and Anglican traditions would surely have taken issue—and on the basis of their own, different religious beliefs and commitments.

Both in its premises and in the conclusions to which those premises led, in short, the sort of "equality" that Madison wanted to build into law was compatible with some religious beliefs and incompatible with others. It would be a bit severe but not inaccurate to say that under the heading of "equality," Madison was in effect seeking to have some central tenets of a particular and controversial version of Christianity adopted as the official position of the government.

Lest I be misunderstood, let me emphasize that although Madison's use of the equality principle was in some respects question-begging and perhaps a bit deceptive, it was *not* hypocritical or inconsistent in its practical consequences. All citizens *would* be treated equally under the substantive views and criteria favored by Madison, just as they would be treated equally—albeit equally in a very different way—under the substantive beliefs and criteria favored by Madison's opponents (or, for that matter, under the substantive beliefs and criteria that had guided the Massachusetts Puritans, or the Inquisition). Madison and the Puritans both believed that like cases should be treated alike, and they both made judgments on the basis of their overall understandings of the world—understandings that were in important part "religious"—about what cases were and were not alike. In that sense, they both worked to have their substantive views—views that were often religious in nature—embodied in the law.

Insofar as their substantive religious views differed, of course, the results of the equal application of these views would also differ. We might say that both the Madisonian and the Puritan positions rejected some religious beliefs as heretical, and both positions also imposed legal burdens on heretics; they differed in the specific content of their heresies and in the specific legal sanctions they would impose. Under the Puritans' religious views, someone like Roger Williams would be deemed heretical and legally sanctioned—perhaps, as in Williams's case, by being banished from the community. Under Madison's religious views, someone like Williams's old antagonist, the Puritan divine John Cotton, or Madison's own opponent, Patrick Henry, or for that matter any religiously motivated proponent of the religious establishment would be deemed in error and legally sanctioned—by being constitutionally prohibited from implementing his more establishmentarian religion. But both the Puritans' and Madison's positions aspired to treat "like" cases alike.

So in many respects, James Madison and the Massachusetts Puritans were similar. But there were two crucial differences. Most obviously, as I have just said, they differed in their substantive religious views. But they also differed in the rhetorical strategies they adopted to promote those views: the Puritans were in a sense up-front about their efforts to embody their religious beliefs in law, while Madison's more deliberate use of the language of equality tended to conceal the legal adoption of his own religious beliefs and the legal rejection of incompatible religious beliefs.

Since Madison was working in a transition period in which the new regime still had to be actively argued for, the concealment was less complete than it would later become: as discussed, Madison's religious premises and his reliance on those premises in shaping the law were still readily visible. We might say that Madison had only begun to glimpse the rhetorical possibilities opening up with the new nation's commitment to "equality." In the ensuing two centuries, those possibilities would be extravagantly exploited.

EQUALITY IN THE MODERN DISCOURSE OF RELIGIOUS FREEDOM

Rhetorical exploitation of the idea of equality, or of related concepts like neutrality, pervades the modern discourse of religious freedom. Consider (to take an example almost at random*) NYU professors Christopher Eisgruber's and Lawrence Sager's argument about the still controversial issue of free exercise exemptions. In addressing this and other issues of religious freedom, Eisgruber and Sager start from a principle much like Madison's, which they call the principle of "equal regard." In general, "equal regard" means that "the interests and concerns of every member of the political community should be treated equally"; and in the context of religion this principle implies, they say, that "the government is obliged to treat the deep religious commitments of members of minority religious faiths with the same regard as it treats the deep commitments of other members of the society."[12]

The notion of "equal regard" has a tone of fairness, benevolence, sagacity. It is hard to imagine anyone—anyone in our society, at least—*opposing* such a notion (and I certainly do not intend to oppose it here). But notice how the inevitable question-begging is already being committed in the corollary. That corollary smuggles in (without actually declaring or defending) substantive criteria under which "deep" commitments are relevantly like each other and unlike other commitments—shallow commitments, perhaps?—but in which "religious" commitments are *not* relevantly different from nonreligious commitments. What matters, in other words, is the "depth" of a commitment, not its religious character. Eisgruber and Sager have not yet come to the question of free exercise exemptions, but once the notion of "equal regard" has been tilted in this way, the answer is foreordained: the distinctiveness of religion *as religion* has already been tacitly denied as part of the very definition of equality. So you hardly need to read any further to know that Eisgruber and Sager will go on to conclude that specifically religious exemptions are constitutionally offensive: minority religious believers can be excused from general laws only to the extent that nonreligious citizens with "comparable commitments" are likewise excused.[13]

One might have thought that whether religious and nonreligious

---

* It is purely a coincidence that I pick an example from a review criticizing my work.

objections *are* "comparable" for exemption purposes is precisely the question at issue. But that is a hard and controversial question. Rather than addressing the question, Eisgruber and Sager circumvent it by resorting to the obliging rhetoric of "equality."

This example is simple and stark. Often scholars and jurists (including, in other writings, Eisgruber and Sager themselves) offer more complicated and sophisticated treatments. As a substitute for the vocabulary of "equality" or "equal regard," scholars may use essentially equivalent notions, such as "antidiscrimination." And advocates usually do not rely *solely* on the rhetoric of equality; they often mix appeals to equality with more substantive argumentation (as Madison himself did in his *Memorial* as a whole). The challenge in all such cases is to extract the substantive claims from their packaging in the beguiling language of equality, and then to examine the substantive positions on their own merits. Sometimes the positions will be able to stand on their own. But often a position will seem quite feeble when denuded of the trappings of equality or nondiscrimination.[14]

My assessment of these efforts by leading legal scholars may seem harsh, so let me quickly make some disclaimers. To begin with, I emphatically do not mean to suggest that the scholars I have mentioned are uniquely guilty of equivocation or question-begging. Their equality-based arguments reflect the predominant character of modern discourse about religious freedom, which routinely purports to deduce answers to difficult substantive questions from the notion of equality, or from its companion notion of neutrality. They are only doing what Supreme Court Justices have been doing, and what virtually everyone in this field has been doing. Indeed, one might argue that the discourse of religious freedom is itself merely an example in miniature of the modern discourse of "liberal democracy," which a critic might view as a massive project in question-begging based on the empty notions of equality[15] or, sometimes, neutrality.

Neither do I think that the practitioners of this rhetorical art are being insincere or consciously manipulative, any more than I think that Madison (as admirable a figure, probably, as any in our constitutional tradition, with the possible exception of Lincoln) was being insincere or manipulative. The magical rhetoric of equality, especially when employed in support of positions that "reasonable" or right-thinking people regard as axiomatically correct, seems able to beguile the rhetoricians at least as effectively as it beguiles their audiences.

Finally, I do not even mean to suggest that the question-begging rhetoric of equality is a bad thing, or that it is something necessarily to be regretted or avoided. Whether or not such rhetoric is desirable presents a question that cannot be decided in the abstract. And so we need to return to that question after first considering the other major part of Madison's legacy.

THE SECOND BEQUEST: RELIGIOUS PLURALISM

Madison's less celebrated but perhaps more important contribution to religious freedom lay in his recognition, carefully and eloquently presented in Federalist 10 and again in Federalist 51, that the best way to maintain a condition of religious freedom in a religiously pluralistic society is not to subject the pluralism to some legally enforceable substantive principle, but rather to permit the pluralism to flourish—and to maintain institutional structures in which pluralism *can* flourish. We might call this Madison's "positive pluralism" theme: unlike so many other people who saw pluralism only as a *problem*—as a source of civil strife possibly culminating in tyranny—Madison recognized that pluralism could also be a solution to an array of potential problems. To be sure, Madison proposed pluralism as an answer to the problem of faction in general, not just religious faction. But he explicitly included religion in his analysis. "In a free government," he insisted, "the security for civil rights must be the same as that for religious rights. It consists in the one case in the multiplicity of interests, and in the other in the multiplicity of sects."[16]

It might be argued that Madison deserves less credit for the religious pluralism theme than he receives for the equality theme. After all, Madison obviously did nothing to originate religious pluralism in this country; it grew up on its own, perhaps with the aid of more providential nurturing. It may also be that, unlike the religious equality theme, which Madison articulated repeatedly and with conviction, this "positive pluralism" theme was something that Madison stumbled onto almost by accident as he tried to defend the Constitution against the argument, taken from Montesquieu, that republican governments must necessarily be small. Robert Wiebe suggests that Federalists like Madison were not initially committed to a strongly federalist system at all, and indeed were opposed to it in the constitutional convention: they came to favor federalism only by necessity when their preferred arrangements were rejected. "Unrepentant they simply lost the vote, and in the process they became federalists in spite of themselves."[17] But regardless of how he came to the view, Madison did in the end recognize and articulate the positive function of pluralism more clearly than anyone else seems to have done, and he worked energetically for a Constitution that would maintain it.

So pluralism was a direct and intended consequence of the federalism that was at least *an* original purpose—or, in my view, *the* original purpose[18]—of the First Amendment religion clauses. And it seems clear that this pluralism deserves most of the credit for the elimination of religious establishments in this country and for the spectacular growth of a diversity of religions and faiths. For example, within a half-century after the adoption of the Constitution, all states had eliminated their official religious establishments—wholly without prodding, we should note, from the Supreme Court. During this same period a large number of religious movements and experiments sprang up throughout the country. Some of these, such as revivalism, were outgrowths of the more traditional faiths. Others were more exotic. Most of the new movements, such as the Kingdom of Matthias,[19] were short-lived; others, such as Mormonism, proved to be more enduring.

I don't mean to suggest, of course, that pluralism was an entirely happy, harmonious affair. Judged by conventional standards, many of the new movements (and some old ones, such as Roman Catholicism) were heretical, or in bad taste—or downright immoral, or even traitorous. In the rough-and-tumble world of expanding America, consequently, unpopular faiths were forced to endure persecution, sometimes to relocate against their will: the Mormon migrations from New York to Ohio to Missouri to Illinois and finally to the Great Basin were the most dramatic example.

The important point, though, is that the ferment that caused religious diversity to flourish—and that is largely responsible for the condition of religious freedom we enjoy today—was a product of pluralism; it owed little or nothing to judicial review, or to the legal elaboration and enforcement of any constitutional "principle of religious freedom." And if anyone deserves credit for recognizing the function of this pluralism and for crafting a Constitution that would preserve it, Madison does.

PLURALISM AND THE LANGUAGE OF EQUALITY

My discussion so far has suggested that James Madison's religious legacy had two principal parts: his promotion of a legal principle of religious equality, and his recognition of the value of pluralism in promoting religious freedom. Though the first of these bequests is more often celebrated in the literature of religious freedom, I've also suggested that the second bequest has been more important in promoting actual religious freedom. If the argument thus far is persuasive, then it might almost seem that we could have dispensed altogether with the equality principle—which after all has mostly been a source of deceptive and question-begging rhetoric—and trusted our fate entirely to pluralism.

But this conclusion would overlook some crucial complications. It would overlook the ways in which the language of equality and the conditions of pluralism have been mutually complementary, and also the ways in which they are potentially antagonistic. Consider first how the language of equality can complement and support pluralism. Religious pluralism in itself is a sort of cultural fact or condition; it is not initially a theory, or a way of talking and thinking. Still, pluralism does not just automatically and silently work itself out. In practice, pluralism results in innumerable questions and conflicts that are provisionally worked out only through a process of talking and thinking. Of course, the conflicts are more decisively worked out through processes like politicking and litigating, but these processes depend in part on talking and thinking. In short, pluralism generates issues that governments at all levels, as well as public entities like school boards and private entities like business corporations, are forced to address. Should we start the meeting (or the class, or the football game) with prayer—and if so, what kind of prayer? Should work cease on religious holidays? Which holidays? What books should the library stock? And so forth.

A pluralistic society has to find viable ways in which these questions can be raised and debated. So what language should we use in discussing the issues of religious pluralism? There is no easy or obvious answer to that question (which we will consider at greater length in later chapters). For now, though, we can notice some broad general strategies.

One possibility—we might call it the sectarian approach— is for everyone to talk in his or her own religious (or perhaps devoutly secular) language. I might urge that questions of public prayer be answered in terms of my understanding of scripture. You could respond by arguing that I have misconstrued the scripture, or that what I regard as scripture is not really scripture at all, or that the very idea of authoritative scripture is implausible or oppressive. There is a bracing forthrightness to this approach. There are also obvious risks. We might never reach agreement on many issues. Debates might become overheated, or even violent. Consequently, pluralism—and civil peace, and thus religious freedom itself—might be jeopardized by this approach.

Given these risks, it may seem that we should find or develop a substantive language that transcends the more specific religious belief systems that together make up a pluralistic society. Stephen Toulmin explains how, in the aftermath of the seventeenth-century wars of religion, thinkers like Leibniz dreamed of a universal language in which all controversies could be discussed and resolved.[20] The modern liberal notion of a discourse of "public reason" can be viewed as a sort of pale, latter-day descendant of this dream.

Not surprisingly, the dream has proven illusory. If such a universal language could be developed, it would not merely transcend our specific religious languages; it would replace them. Why talk in narrowly parochial terms if a universal discourse is available that is both efficacious and satisfactory to people of different faiths and traditions? The dream of a universal language in which profound substantive questions could be satisfactorily answered is in essence the dream of a universal religion to which everyone will be converted. Short of the millennium, when lions will munch grass with lambs, that dream is unlikely to be realized.

So, if the sectarian approach seems too explosive but a more encompassing language is unavailable, what is the alternative? In matters of diplomacy, or in everyday contexts involving colleagues or neighbors or family members, we often confront something like this same problem; and we often deal with it by finding ways of talking that allow us to express substantive disagreements allusively, or indirectly, or in code, thereby softening the force of our disagreements and criticisms. "A *charming* idea," one of the professors I knew as an undergraduate used to say, and those who knew him understood the condemnation that was intended. Even so, the effect was still a little different—and more gentle—than it would have been if the teacher had simply said "A *stupid* idea" or "A truly *idiotic* idea."

Just how this sort of diplomatic double-talk works is a bit of a mystery to me. If we didn't understand what the code meant, then it wouldn't work. Students who presented papers that were pronounced "charming" would feel encouraged, and they would work to produce more of the same. On the other hand, if we understood the code so immediately that it ceased to be a code, or if the code vocabulary came to be exactly synonymous in its denotations and connotations with a more ordinary vocabulary, then again it wouldn't work: calling an idea "charming" *would* have exactly the same belittling consequences as calling it "really stupid." Like legal fictions, diplomatic codes seem to work at two levels, and to require a subtle double-mindedness on the part of both speaker and listeners. So we manage to understand the speaker's real meaning by picking up on his actual assessment of an idea, but then we shift back to the more conventional meaning for the limited purpose of avoiding offense.

But however it works, this sort of use of language is perfectly familiar, and it might provide an alternative to both the "sectarian" approach and the "universal language" approach in dealing with the issues generated by religious pluralism. To a significant extent, it seems, the language of religious equality and religious neutrality has served just this purpose. And its very question-begging quality, or its propensity to let substantive values and criteria be smuggled in without explicit acknowledgment, is what allows it to serve this function. When it works well, this language allows issues of religious conflict to be debated and resolved, while at the same time reassuring the parties to the conflict that they are equally valued—that no one is an "outsider." Even as an adverse decision is reached and announced, the losers are told that their faith is held in equal esteem as the faith of the winners. And the winners are reminded that their victory should not be taken as blanket approval for their faith.

From a detached perspective, no doubt, it will seem that a good deal of deception is going on. At least for the moment and for the issue at hand, the faith of the winners *has* been preferred, and the faith of the losers has been rejected. Couching the decision in the language of equality tries to conceal this fact. But then diplomatic double-talk always involves a degree of concealment.

I don't quite mean to endorse this diplomatic deception, which to me is troublesome, especially when used by academics who have no very plausible claim to diplomatic immunity. I only mean to observe that as a historical matter the language of equality and neutrality *has* provided the dominant vocabulary by which religious pluralism has worked itself out, and also to suggest a reason why pluralism may have found this question-begging vocabulary attractive and perhaps necessary.

With this approach, as with the "sectarian" approach, however, there are also serious risks. One obvious risk can be noted quickly: the losers in any particular dispute may not be fooled by assurances that their faith has not been disfavored, and they might even feel more offended or alienated by such false assurances than they would feel if a decision were honestly presented as reflecting at least a limited and local rejection of their religious beliefs. In my experience, it is the winners—or those who belong to classes that are not burdened by government policies and decisions affecting religion—who seem most easily convinced that an outcome is merely a necessary consequence of "equality" or "neutrality." But perhaps there is value even in this. Who knows? Maybe it is better to have a governing class that operates under the illusion that it can and should avoid making judgments about the merits or truth of conflicting religions than a class that realizes that such judgments are inevitable and then confidently proceeds to make them. Maybe a brutal candor in this context would eventually lead to more brutal results and policies.

The other side of this point, though, as various sorts of Critical studies have pointed out, is that this sort of reassuring illusion can blind governors to the harmful consequences of their decisions; and this observation points to the greater risk posed by a discourse centered on the principle of equality. The risk is that this discourse will fall into the hands (or into the mouths and pens) of people who combine a sort of overearnestness with either of two quite opposite qualities: either a kind of innocence that would lead someone to suppose that equality or neutrality just automatically has a particular meaning, period, or conversely a kind of shrewdness that understands equality or neutrality as rhetorical resources to be manipulated to secure the ends favored by the rhetorician. In either case, the risk is that equality will become the banner for an aggressive campaign—naively aggressive or shrewdly aggressive— to bring the diverse and wayward practices of the nation's multitude of communities into line with the requirements of "equality." Such a campaign would turn equality from being pluralism's ally—admittedly a somewhat unsteady ally—into pluralism's nemesis.

CONCLUSION

My own observation is that over at least the last half-century there have been many such earnest people in this country. Some of them are called "Professor." Some wear black robes. It is hard to tell, of course, whether someone falls into the "innocent" aggressive category or the "shrewd" aggressive category, since both types will talk in pretty much the same way. And though it ought to be impossible, a person might in fact belong to both categories; this is one of the many ways in which human nature scoffs at crude rationality. But in any case, Madison's legacy will continue to have value for us, I think, only to the extent that his first bequest does not manage to overwhelm his second.

2

Religion, Democracy, and Autonomy

A Political Parable

SHOULD LEGISLATORS FEEL free to rely on their religious beliefs in deciding how to vote on, say, an abortion regulation, or a same-sex marriage bill? Should citizens be encouraged to resort to their religious faith as they vote in elections? Should judges consult their religious convictions in deciding how to rule in a difficult case? Or does such reliance on religion in public decision making somehow violate, if not the Constitution itself, at least the meaning or spirit of democracy?

For a decade or so, these and similar questions have provoked a fierce dispute within the academy that I will call the "religion-and-democracy" debate. I call it that in part because *democracy* provides the fundamental premise from which virtually everyone argues. Professors on one side of the debate may contend, that is, that *citizens*—or maybe even *legislators*—have a right to invoke the Bible or appeal to theology in debating and deciding political issues. But the professors themselves typically do not exercise any such right in debating *this* issue: they would not think of approaching the question, for instance, by asking whether *God would want* people to rely on faith in making their political decisions. Or even if such a question does occur to the professors, the conventions of academic discourse prevent it from being raised and considered, at least in any straightforward way. So instead, law professors and political theorists argue about whether it is *more consistent with democracy* for people to debate and vote on public matters on whatever grounds (religious or secular) appeal to them or, conversely, to check their faith at the door before entering the public domain.

In effect, academics treat the issue they are arguing about with respect to *the broader political culture* (is it permissible to rely upon religious grounds?) as one that has already been resolved—in the negative—for purposes of *the academy* itself. This treatment gives the debate a somewhat peculiar quality, to say the least; and of course it limits what can be said (at least in any straightforward way) in, for example, an essay like this one.

To be sure, framing the question as one about democracy does not lead inexorably to the conclusion that religious beliefs are an inappropriate basis for political decisions. On the contrary, when the debate is understood as one about the implications of democracy, perhaps the more obvious answer is an affirmative one: Wouldn't democracy imply that "the people" can act on any grounds they see fit to act on? The puzzlement is reflected in Sanford Levinson's question: "Why doesn't liberal democracy give everyone an equal right, without engaging in any version of epistemic abstinence, to make his or her arguments, subject, obviously, to the prerogative of listeners to reject the arguments should they be unpersuasive?"[1]

THE DEMOCRACY OF KANT

There is an important, even portentous answer to that question, I think, but it is not the most familiar answer, which I believe to be a "red herring." The familiar answer—within academic debates, at least—suggests that democratic deliberation, or perhaps even democratic legitimacy, requires that public decisions be made on the basis of reasons "accessible" to all citizens. But this position has been effectively criticized, and I doubt that it fully captures democracy-based resistance to religion in public discourse. One major reason for this doubt is that the accessibility position, taken at face value, does not faithfully serve the purposes of its own proponents. If "accessible" is taken to mean something like "intelligible" or "understandable," then the constraint excludes the wrong things. Many complicated scientific and philosophical analyses will not be "accessible" in this sense to many or most of us; conversely, many of the most controversial religious rationales will be readily understandable. "God prohibits homosexual conduct" is a highly debatable proposition, no doubt; but it is not especially hard to figure out what people who assert this proposition are basically claiming. (A possibly sacrilegious billboard that I passed recently on the Indiana Turnpike reads: "WHAT PART OF 'THOU SHALT NOT' DIDN'T YOU UNDERSTAND?"—*GOD*) Conversely, if "accessible" is taken to mean something more like "believable" or "generally accepted," then the "accessibility" requirement would become unduly severe. Disagreements are likely to arise precisely because people differ about the believability of the premises or rationales that support different conclusions; if such differences are enough to make a premise or rationale inadmissible in democratic deliberation, then there will be precious little to base our deliberations on.

So the argument about "accessibility," I believe, is artificial, and it has distracted us from the deeper and more far-reaching reason for resistance to the use of religion in democratic politics. And what is that deeper reason? It was hinted at by Alexander Hamilton during the constitutional convention. At one contentious point in the proceedings, Benjamin Franklin proposed that daily sessions be opened with prayer. The proposal was rejected, and Hamilton is said to have wisecracked that the convention had no need of "foreign aid." Hamilton was no great democrat, but in this remark (if he actually made it) I think he was ahead of his time in anticipating the implications of a modern conception of democracy. The basic thought is that democracy means self-government, and self-government means government *of and by ourselves*. We should make our own decisions, without outside assistance or interference.

In this respect, modern democracy is merely an extension to the political level of what "autonomy" is thought to mean on the individual level. Theorists may associate this position with Kant. Kant, after all, was a major proponent of a highly influential view of the autonomous, rational person which holds that enlightened autonomy means "thinking for yourself," and that an "inability to make use of one's own understanding without the guidance of another" is a form of "immaturity" reflective of "[l]aziness and cowardice."[2] Autonomy entails "not submitting to groundless authorities," or to "'alien' authorities"—a contestable category, no doubt, but one that at least includes "state, church, majority, tradition, or dictator."[3] This commitment to autonomy supports a cluster of intertwined Kantian propositions that have become virtually axiomatic in much modern liberal democratic theorizing—that "autonomy is the supreme good,"[4] that only obligations that we legislate for ourselves are binding on us,[5] that autonomy is the essential basis of human dignity,[6] and that "[t]here is no place for others to tell us what morality requires, nor has anyone the authority to do so—not our neighbors, not the magistrates and their laws, not even those who speak in the name of God."[7]

It is clear enough, even on the face of these assertions, that projecting this notion of *individual* autonomy onto the *political* level will raise some delicate questions. Robert Paul Wolff argues enthusiastically, for instance, that if the concept of autonomy is carefully considered, it leads us inexorably to embrace anarchism.[8] Setting aside that sort of question, though, it is not hard to see how someone with this general orientation would look with suspicion on the resort to religion in democratic decision making—not necessarily because of any singular hostility to religion per se but because religion typically includes something like deference to God, and God (if there is a God) is an "alien authority." Doing what God wants because God wants it is not the same as thinking and acting "for yourself." So deferring to God's will is a way of submitting to "foreign aid," as Hamilton put it.

At this point, professors of philosophy might eagerly launch into a discussion about what Kant really meant, or about how some of his pronouncements should be understood in light of others, or about which among modern positions that invoke the authority of Kant in opposing deference to authority correctly understand his views and which do not; and of course the professors would disagree about those matters (as professors of philosophy always do).[9] I do not want to get into that kind of discussion here, however, for several sufficient reasons. In the first place, I lack the training (and probably the kind of mind) needed to contribute much to that kind of debate. More importantly, for our purposes it doesn't make much difference what Kant really meant, or what he would or should have said with regard to our issues. Like other great thinkers, Kant released some potent ideas into the world, and thereafter they no longer belonged to him. Others may have misapprehended those ideas—or they may have apprehended them more clearly than Kant himself did; but in any case what matters for practical purposes is what Kant's ideas came to mean, not what he meant. Or, probably more realistically, it may be that Kant was not so much originating new ideas as articulating (in his own idiosyncratic and ponderous way) notions that were (and *are*) "in the air." So for some purposes the more cogent question might ask *not* how well others understood Kant but how well *he* understood *them*. (Perhaps not all that well, I suspect, in either case.)

In any event, for purposes of the present discussion what matters is not what Kant meant, but instead what the ideas (or sentiments, or slogans) often associated with him and lumped under the heading of "autonomy" mean for us, and whether "autonomy" is incompatible with the use of religion in public deliberation and, if so, whether "autonomy" as it has come to be understood is a coherent and attractive ideal. In short, *is the introduction of religion into public deliberation inappropriate because it offends a justified commitment to human autonomy?* This is the real question, I think, that runs through the religion-and-democracy debate.

It is a difficult question; I for one am not completely sure about my views on some aspects of the question. In addition, as a law professor and not a professional philosopher, I hardly feel competent to address this sort of question directly. So instead I want to explore the question in a way more fitting to a law professor—that is, by posing a hypothetical story.

THE PARABLE

Imagine that with the onset of a new millennium and the spiritual exhaustion of conventional, Clintonesque politics, our political culture experiences a series of dramatic and unexpected developments. Among other things, a virulent nostalgia (or perhaps a yearning for the "reenchantment" of the world) generates surprisingly widespread support for a new political party that calls itself the "Democratic Royalist Party," or the DRP, led by a charismatic figure named James ("Jimmy") Stuart.

Like many historic figures, Stuart is a complex and perhaps contradictory personality—passionate but also thoughtful, pure-hearted and strong-willed. Born in one of the few remaining domestic log cabins and largely self-tutored, Stuart is a quintessential man of the people. But he also exudes a sort of innate nobility, and this quality has surfaced in a surprising way in his political thought. It happened in this way: somewhere in his self-education, Stuart stumbled upon some faded seventeenth-century monarchical tracts, and these led him to the conclusion that the British monarch does indeed possess the right of rulership, and that all English-speaking people owe allegiance to the crown.

Stuart also continues to believe in democracy, however, and so he goes to Washington with a novel proposal: adhering scrupulously to the procedures of the Constitution, Americans should cede all political power to the Queen of England for a ten-year term. At the end of that term, another election will be held to determine whether the benevolent despotism will be renewed for a second term, and so on. In this way, Stuart claims, the Queen's right to rule will be respected, but the system will remain fundamentally democratic.

As you might expect, this platform provokes fierce opposition. Some of Stuart's opponents attack his ideas on the merits. They criticize his monarchical assumptions on theoretical grounds; they protest his proposal on pragmatic grounds. A few go so far as to argue that the British royal line does not even exist. These critics contend that the current so-called "royal family" is nothing more than a sort of fraudulent facade; consequently, modern political philosophy must cast off all vestiges of monarchical thought and proceed with a constant awareness that "the Queen is dead."

However, one of Stuart's most sophisticated critics—a descendant of a long line of opponents of monarchy (or at least of English monarchy) with the improbable name of Ronald the Bruce—adopts a different perspective. Instead of criticizing the DRP platform on its merits, Ronald asserts that what Stuart offers is not even a bad political philosophy; it is no philosophy at all. That is because monarchical ideas are inherently incompatible with democratic assumptions: one cannot coherently maintain *both* that the British crown has a right to rule *and* that democracy is the correct form of government. So Stuart's views cancel themselves out, so to speak. And the proper conclusion, Ronald sometimes says, is not merely that Stuart's royalist views are wrong, but that Stuart himself does not really hold those views (even though he may *think* he does). In fact, as Ronald sometimes puts the point, monarchism is by now not even "a thought to be had."

Though Stuart complains that this last claim overreaches, he is brought by these criticisms to reconsider his views. Upon further thought, he concludes that monarchy and democracy are indeed incompatible if viewed *as basic accounts of political authority.* But he still thinks there is something valuable and valid in his royalist notions— something that needs to be articulated in a better, more coherent way. Seeking to achieve reflective equilibrium between his general democratic assumptions and his particular royalist judgments, Stuart comes to the conclusion that the Queen should be deferred to—*not* because the royal line has any "right to rule," as he had inaptly put the point, but rather because the Queen is quite simply the wisest and most benevolent person in the world. So we in this country should freely choose to defer to her decisions, not because she has "authority" over us exactly, but because this course of deference is most conducive to our own welfare.

This revised view leads to a revised platform for the DRP, but one that still lets the party keep its name. As modified, the platform no longer calls for any official cession of political authority to the Queen. In form, politics and lawmaking in this country will continue as they have always done: elections will be held, the bicameral Congress will meet, bills passed in both houses will be presented to the President, and so forth. But the party pledges that if it gains a dominant position in government, it will solicit and defer to the Queen's judgments, categorically and on all matters. Technically, the Queen's judgments will be advisory only, but in practice they will be more than that; the party will treat them as dispositive. It would make little sense to follow the Queen only when she recommends what we would have independently chosen anyway. The reason for deferring to the Queen, after all, is that she is the wisest and most benevolent person in the world; and if that is true then it is precisely in cases of disagreement that deference to a wiser source is most imperative.

Stuart maintains that this new position is thoroughly democratic, while also possessing the virtues of royalism. Again, of course, many of his critics attack the platform on its merits, arguing that the Queen is a fool, that she knows next to nothing about this country, that deferring to her judgment would be practically disastrous, and that she is not even a real queen. But as it happens, conditions in the country are such that many citizens—indeed, a majority—are drawn to Stuart's exalted opinion of the Queen; a view that many thought had passed irretrievably from the world has turned out to have surprising vitality after all. So Ronald the Bruce does not challenge that view directly; he concedes—for purposes of argument, at least—that the Queen is the Queen and that she is the veritable incarnation of wisdom and benevolence. Nonetheless, Ronald still argues that the DRP platform is deeply undemocratic. Indeed, he now adds that the platform is unconstitutional because it violates the "republican form of government" clause (which applies to the national government, he explains, through incorporation into the Fifth Amendment's due process clause).[10]

Stuart and his supporters are at first incredulous: how can their program be undemocratic if it carefully preserves all the central democratic features—elections, majority rule, and so forth—and if a majority of citizens choose to vote for it? Wouldn't it be *more* undemocratic to prevent the citizens from adopting the program that most of them prefer? But Ronald patiently explains that the self-styled democratic royalists still have not thought through their position carefully enough. Democracy, Ronald points out, is not just whatever a majority endorses: if the electorate voted overwhelmingly for the proposition that "Democracy means the dictatorship of Napoleon," their vote would not make it so. Nor is democracy merely a set of *forms*, or *procedures*—hoops to jump through in making public decisions. There is nothing sacred about democratic procedures for their own sake; in fact, the forms in themselves are manifestly inefficient, expensive, and often downright unseemly. We nonetheless adhere to those forms only because they implement a deeper, more substantive political and moral value or commitment.

And what is that value? Ronald maintains that the value underlying democracy is the ideal of self-rule, or self-determination, or "autonomy"—of thinking and making decisions for ourselves, or of being the authors of our own lives. The only duties or moral obligations that are truly obligatory for us are the product not of outside forces or authorities, but of *self-legislation*. And it is only by virtue of possessing and exercising such autonomy that human beings have a unique dignity and worth. Moreover, the ideal of self-rule or autonomy cannot be realized through forms alone, devoid of substance. In order to be responsible and autonomous human beings, rather, we ourselves must actually think through and then make our own decisions. If instead we delegate those decisions to some outside authority, we sacrifice our autonomy, our dignity—indeed, our very humanity.

In more familiar situations, Ronald patiently explains, we readily understand this point. In a marriage, for example, it sometimes seems that one of the partners always does whatever the other partner says should be done. Suppose we cross-examine the submissive spouse about this practice, and he or she responds, "No, you don't understand. I'm fully autonomous. It's true that I always and unquestioningly obey my spouse, but *I freely choose* to do that. So there's no conflict between complete autonomy and total submission." We would easily see the delusion in this stance. Similarly, we do not allow people to sell themselves into slavery—even if that's what they say they want. We understand that such a condition would in reality be a forfeiture of autonomy; and so we would promptly reject the argument that by allowing and enforcing voluntary contracts to enter into slavery we would better facilitate the exercise of people's autonomy. On similar reasoning, we don't allow a legislature to bind itself in the future because, as old sages like Dicey and Blackstone explained, to allow the legislature to do this would be to infringe on the legislature's own sovereignty.

So even though the current DRP platform retains the outward forms of democracy, Ronald concludes, the platform effects a wholesale forfeiture of autonomy by entrusting all real thinking and decision making to the Queen. But autonomy—self-rule—is the central value supporting democracy. Indeed, democracy is little more than autonomy writ large—autonomy projected onto the political stage. Consequently, the DRP philosophy remains incoherent (not really a philosophy at all, as Ronald sometimes says) and deeply undemocratic in the most fundamental sense.

Let us suppose that Ronald succeeds in convincing the electorate on this point; consequently, the once vigorous DRP fades into oblivion. Even Jimmy Stuart eventually concedes his error: convinced by Ronald that his underlying commitment has been to autonomy all along, Stuart resolves to follow the path of autonomy faithfully, wherever it may lead. The democracy-autonomy argument will also have the effect of discrediting several DRP offshoots. For example, one splinter faction wants to adopt a policy of total deference, not to the Queen of England, but rather to the Queen of Sheba (who is said to have acquired tremendous wisdom somewhere along the line). This faction hopes to avoid the rhetoric (which proved highly effective in getting Ronald's main point across to the philosophically innocent public) that the DRP program would in essence rescind the Declaration of Independence and the Revolutionary War, so that American patriots would have bled and died in vain. After all, the Sheba party argues, we never fought a war for independence *from Sheba*. Another faction, influenced by Plato, proposes that deference be given to Jürgen Habermas on the grounds that he is the smartest philosopher in the world; and still a third group proposes to confer the honor on Richard Rorty because he is not only a really smart guy (though perhaps not *quite* as smart as Habermas) but an American citizen to boot.

Although these proposals gain a smattering of initial support, political theorists and citizens in general quickly realize that the distinctions offered by these splinter parties are spurious. The autonomy argument means that we should not delegate our decision making responsibilities to *anyone*. It doesn't really matter whether the delegee is a monarch, or British, or a philosopher, or a foreigner: the critical fact is that she or he is not *us*. What is objectionable, in other words, is that we give decisional responsibility away—*not* to whom we give it.

In fact, it doesn't really matter whether the recipient of deference is a "who" or a "what." The point becomes important because still another new political party—the AI Party—proposes that political decisions be made by a new, staggeringly powerful supercomputer dubbed "Shepherd." Shepherd has been programmed to make decisions based on consulting all the political philosophies ever devised and then applying those philosophies to a wealth of data far surpassing the information that could be assimilated by any human, or any discrete body of humans. The autonomy rationale proves crucial here because the arguments on the merits are more touch-and-go than they were for some of the other proposals. Scientists and philosophers are still arguing, that is, about the precise nature of Shepherd's intellectual qualities—does Shepherd really "think"? how does Shepherd choose among competing philosophies? and so forth—but no one denies that in some sense Shepherd has vastly greater cognitive capacities than even the smartest human beings. Moreover, with the other proposals there was always the nagging concern that the recipient of deference might be corrupted; he or she might use this newly conferred power for his or her own interests—and thus against ours. But Shepherd is incorruptible and has no "self-interest," having been programmed to act solely for the public good. Nonetheless, the AI Party is voted down—mostly, it seems, on autonomy grounds. After all, an opponent explains (in what has become a familiar refrain), it is only autonomy that gives us dignity—that makes us, as humans, distinctively valuable. Maybe Shepherd *would* consistently make sounder, better informed decisions than we do. But so what? What would it profit us to gain the whole world and lose our own autonomy?

Ronald the Bruce feels the flush of success as one opponent of autonomy after another goes down to defeat. But his satisfaction turns to frustration when his own arguments come to be used against him. It happens in this way: A new political movement has given rise to a political party that calls itself "the Party of Principle." This party proposes that all public decisions be made in accordance with what have come to be known as "the two-and-a-half principles." These principles have been developed and defended through intricate and abstruse argumentation by an all-star team of philosophers. The merits of this political philosophy are very much in dispute, of course, and it seems safe to predict that the dispute will end only if and when people finally just lose interest in the subject (or rather when political philosophers lose interest, since they are the only people who manifest any interest in the philosophical issues even now). Ronald the Bruce, though, is a perennial pick for the philosophers' all-star team, and he heartily supports the Party of Principle.

But critics of the party object that, regardless of the substantive merits of the formidable philosophical issues, the Principle Party's platform should be rejected because it is undemocratic. Ironically, it is Jimmy Stuart, chastened by his earlier dialectical defeats, who now offers himself as the champion of autonomy. Stuart makes this argument: "Ronald the Bruce said we couldn't defer to the Queen, even if she is the embodiment of wisdom and benevolence, because this would forfeit our autonomy, which is what gives us dignity and worth. On the same reasoning, we couldn't defer to Habermas, or Rorty, or even to Shepherd (a machine). So I want to know: why is it any less a sacrifice of our autonomy to let our decisions be determined by some set of *principles?* If is cowardly and belittling to let your life be governed by a *person,* isn't it even more demeaning to turn your life over to a *formula?** Indeed, what's the difference between Shepherd and a set of principles? Shepherd is just a set of principles embodied in circuitry rather than ink; the main difference is only that Shepherd is a lot more sophisticated and less simple-minded than the two-and-a-half principles. Or what if Shepherd were programmed *only* with the two-and-a-half principles: *then* would it be okay to make a dumbed-down Shepherd our effective dictator? That in essence is what the Party of Principle proposes."

* Though Stuart himself reads philosophers only occasionally, a bookish friend points out that in enjoining "thinking for oneself" and condemning the "[l]aziness and cowardice" that lead most people to trust themselves to the "guidance of another," the philosopher Immanuel Kant did not seem to distinguish between deferring to *personal* or *impersonal* authorities. It was objectionable to defer to a "pastor who has a conscience for me" but also to "a book that has understanding for me"; and "[r]ules and formulas" could be the "fetters of an everlasting immaturity" as much as kings or bishops could. See Immanuel Kant, An Answer to the Question: What Is Enlightenment? reprinted in What Is Enlightenment? Eighteenth-Century Answers and Twentieth-Century Question 58–59 (James Schmidt ed. 1996).

Angered by this abuse of his ideas, Ronald agrees to debate Stuart on national television. It would be tedious to report the full debate, but I need to recite one of the pertinent exchanges:

RONALD: You completely misunderstand. When we act on a principle we don't sacrifice autonomy, because we ourselves have willed—have *legislated for ourselves*—the principle. Acting on a principle is not a violation of autonomy; on the contrary, it is precisely the way we realize and exercise our autonomy.

STUART: Well, of course, most of us *haven't* approved the two-and-a-half principles. We don't even understand them—or at least we don't accept the logic of the arguments you give for those principles. So *we* aren't legislating for *ourselves*; and you want to adopt the principles anyway.

But set that problem aside: even if every last one of us did understand and approve those principles, we'd still be turning our future decisions over to them—letting a formula or a set of principles determine our decisions in the same way we'd have been letting Shepherd determine our decisions if the AI Party had been elected.

RONALD: It isn't the same thing at all. If *you* approve the principles, then *you* choose to follow them. You're still legislating for yourself.

STUART: That's just what I said about the Queen. It would have been *my* decision—*our* decision—to defer to her. And the decision would have been just as free as a decision to be governed by a set of principles. Even more free, maybe: aren't you always saying that if we are reasonable and rational, then we "have to" adopt the two-and-a-half principles because they are supported by "compelling" arguments? But you said that sort of decision was throwing away our autonomy.

RONALD: That was totally different. If we defer to the Queen, we won't be thinking about the merits—the substance—of individual decisions at all. If we adopt the two-and-a-half principles, on the other hand, we *will* have thought about the merits of our decisions. We'll have thought through the merits in advance, so to speak, in deciding to adopt the two-and-a-half principles.

STUART: Well, political views and philosophies have never stayed stagnant, you know. And I see no reason to suppose that the two-and-a-half principles will be the end of political thought. So wouldn't we need to think through the substance of those principles fresh for each new decision—to have the whole debate all over again in the circumstances surrounding each new issue and in light of our current views? If we really want to be autonomous, I mean?

RONALD: Why on earth would we need to do that?

STUART: Because otherwise we might be turning our lives over to principles that we once found attractive but that, if we were to rethink them in light of further experience and new considerations, we wouldn't even agree with.

RONALD: I don't understand. Nothing in the party's platform says that in adopting the two-and-a-half principles, we have to adopt them irrevocably and for all time. If the principles turn out to be deficient, we can always revise or replace them.

STUART: But how will we know whether we would think they are deficient, in any given case, unless we rethink them in *every* case—have the full debate in light of current considerations and current views?

RONALD: This makes no sense. You seem to want a sort of perpetual rethinking and rearguing of first principles. Obviously that wouldn't be feasible; but there's an even more serious problem. What you want would actually eviscerate the meaning of living by a principle altogether. What would it even mean to commit yourself to a principle, or to have the sort of integrity that comes from living by a principle, if you intend in every situation to consider the matter from scratch and to follow the principle only if it happens to dictate doing what seems best to you anyway?

Besides, nothing in our constitutional system works like that. Take the privilege against self-incrimination. We don't reexamine that privilege in every case; we may not even remember for sure why it was adopted in the first place. If we

were to start from square one, *maybe* . . . , just maybe, we'd
still choose to adopt a privilege against self-incrimination.
Maybe we wouldn't. You could say the same for any other
basic constitutional principle. And of course sometimes we
do abandon old principles, or adopt new ones. But until we
decide to do that, we treat ourselves as bound. That's what it
means to be a "community of principle."

What you want, on the other hand, seems to be a sort of
perpetual, radical "ad hocery." That would destroy our constitutional system.

STUART: Maybe it would. But so far as I can see, that's where
the logic of autonomy leads. And remember—it's autonomy
that gives us dignity. Autonomy is the source of human
worth. So if our constitutional order is inconsistent with the
logic of autonomy, then I think we will just have to relinquish our constitutional order.

At this point the debate reached an impasse. In postdebate inter-
views, Ronald insisted that Stuart had misunderstood the meaning and
implications of autonomy. Most mainstream political philosophers
agreed. But a few more adventurous political thinkers and actors took
just the opposite view; in fact, they thought that Stuart had not taken
the logic of autonomy far enough. So in the aftermath of the debate,
new political factions emerged.

For instance, the Anti-Formalist Party argued that the very notion
of constitutionalism was undemocratic, because the Constitution
clearly placed a whole variety of limits on the people's right of self-rule.
This party started with a small insight: somebody noticed that the cum-
bersome amending procedures spelled out in the Constitution itself severely limit "We the People" from expressing and implementing their—
or should it be "our"?—will. So democratic Anti-Formalists started saying that constitutional amendments should be allowed outside the
bounds of the procedures described in the text. Amendments shouldn't
even have to be written out and voted on at all if "We the People" don't
feel inclined to do that. (Ironically, this much of the Anti-Formalists' an-
ticonstitutional agenda was inspired by Ronald the Bruce himself, who
earlier in his career had devoted three entire books—admirers referred
to these books in hushed tones as "the trilogy"—to the development of
these ideas.) More far-sighted Anti-Formalists eventually realized that

the same logic applied to *all* the formalities that the Constitution places upon lawmaking—such as the requirements that statutes must be passed by both houses of Congress and submitted to the President.

Anti-Formalist Party conventions tended to be chaotic and a lot of fun, with a good deal of posing and shouting. Sadly, the party never managed to agree on any formal platform. Some Anti-Formalists advocated pure majority rule; others, who regarded themselves as "purists," favored spontaneous mass direct democracy. Perhaps the most attractive Anti-Formalist proposal—or at least the one most frequently and enthusiastically defended by the party's more respectable members— called for implementation of the general will of "We the People" by a small group of professors and jurists who would acquire an uncanny, almost mystical access to that will by attending conferences at Ivy League law schools.

An even more radical party, known as the Anti-Sociabilists, advanced a platform that was individualistic to the point of being anarchist. By contrast to the familiar sort of radicals who argue that the government is illegitimate because it is not truly representative, the Anti-Sociabilists argued that government should be overthrown because it *is* representative; after all, turning one's decision making responsibility over to a "representative" is a classic forfeiture of autonomy. Autonomy, they stressed, means *self*-rule, and the polity doesn't have a "self": only individuals have selves.

Jimmy Stuart initially sympathized with both these parties, but he soon concluded that the logic of autonomy was inconsistent with organized political action altogether—there was something faintly ridiculous about a *political party* of anarchists, or a formal organization of antiformalists—and so he retired from public activity, determined to lead a life of pure, solitary self-legislation. Consequently, what happened afterward is perhaps not strictly relevant to a *political* parable. But in case it matters, I can very quickly relate the rest of Stuart's curious career.

He happened to run into Ronald the Bruce one evening at a sidewalk café; and now that their political battles were over the old antagonists actually felt like sitting down for a cordial chat. At least it was cordial at the beginning. Stuart, who was wearing an old sport coat with a swimsuit but no shoes, explained his current thinking. In order to be autonomous, he said, he was adopting a policy of complete spontaneity— at least for the moment. "I do what I feel like doing. Go where I feel like going. Take what I feel like taking."

Unconsciously putting his hand on his wallet, Ronald explained that in a wholly nonjudgmental way he fully and equally respected Stuart's views about the good life—even though he felt obligated to add, with all due respect, that as a strictly philosophical matter Stuart was utterly confused, as usual. "Autonomy" most emphatically did not mean "doing whatever you *feel like* doing at the moment." On the contrary, Stuart ought to realize that he was a rational being, that doing what he *felt like* doing was a form of submitting to the heteronomy of desires and emotions, that he truly exercised his autonomy only by acting rationally, that acting rationally entailed acting only on principles that he could consistently will to be universally observed, and that it followed from this that he ought to treat all other rational beings with respect—as "ends" not "means."

Stuart replied that none of this made any sense. He *was* a rational being, to be sure, but he was also an emotional being, and an intuitive being, and a spiritual being. If "rationality" was what separated him from the beasts, as Ronald had argued, emotion and intuition and spirit were what distinguished him from Shepherd. So he didn't see how "autonomy" justified letting his "reason" enslave or subordinate the rest of him: to identify the rational part of him with his "self," or his "being," seemed arbitrary—even, paradoxically, irrational. Moreover, even insofar as he was a rational being it did not seem to follow that he must act only on universal principles—"You've heard of *instrumental* rationality, haven't you?"— and in any case he was quite sure he could craft universal principles that would faithfully support anything he truly felt like doing, and in this sense would capture his sincere motivation. "I take your drink," Stuart said, taking Ronald's drink, "on the universal principle that 'Jimmy Stuart gets whatever he wants.' I really, sincerely wish that everyone *would* accept and act on that principle. It's not going to happen, of course, but where's the rational inconsistency?" Finally, the part about all persons being "ends," not "means" seemed intolerably vague and a non sequitur to boot (though it *was,* Stuart conceded, a "charming sentiment"). "So I still don't see how being 'autonomous' doesn't mean doing whatever I choose to do."

At this point, Ronald lost patience and called Stuart a "philosophical moron." Stuart shot back that Ronald simply lacked the courage of his convictions, and hence was constantly resorting to sophistry to invent spurious limits on autonomy whenever the concept became troublesome. "When did philosophizing about 'autonomy' ever lead you to a conclusion you didn't like in the first place?" Stuart demanded. The conversation broke down, but rather than part as permanent enemies the pair agreed to meet again—same time, same place—one week later. At the appointed time, Ronald came to the restaurant prepared with a lucid presentation organized around three extremely subtle distinctions that Stuart (and nearly everyone else) had somehow overlooked. But he wasn't able to give the presentation, because Stuart never showed up.

Several weeks later the two happened to pass on the sidewalk. For a moment Ronald failed to recognize Stuart, who was shirtless, unshaven, and a bit wild-eyed; but Stuart grabbed Ronald by the arm and, in what Ronald charitably interpreted as a friendly gesture, gave him a vigorous slap on the back. Taken by surprise, Ronald stammered "hello" and then asked why Stuart had not appeared at the scheduled meeting. "Well, I know I had promised to come," Stuart said. "And I even intended to come. But at the last moment, I didn't feel like it. And I thought, . . .—let's see, what did I think?—oh, yes, I'm like, 'Jimmy, you're an autonomous self. I'm not sure whether you're the same autonomous self that was in the restaurant with Ronald last week . . . , but be that as it may, you're an autonomous self, and you can't be bound by old promises.' . . . 'Dead hand of the past,' 'Can't bind the sovereign,' and all that, you know. . . . So I'm like, 'Jimmy, you're only bound by obligations that you legislate for yourself, and keeping promises—or at least keeping *this* promise—isn't an obligation that you choose to impose on yourself.' So in the plenitude of my autonomy, I freely decided not to come." And he erupted in a roar of laughter that to Ronald sounded almost maniacal.

Realizing that the case was hopeless (or worse), Ronald shook his head sadly and walked on. An image of Frankenstein flashed through his mind, and he glanced nervously back over his shoulder once or twice. But Stuart did not follow; indeed, he seemed to have already forgotten the whole encounter, and was gazing in apparent fascination at a flashing neon sign in a store window.

That was the last time the two ever met. Years later, though, Ronald heard reports about what had happened to Stuart. The reports were second- or third-hand, and they seemed to contradict each other. So Ronald wasn't sure which of the reports, if any, was correct.

According to one story, Stuart ended up in a mental institution, suffering from severe schizophrenia. A different report had it that Stuart, consumed with dread and sick to death of autonomy, finally resolved to act on his original inclination. So he took a vow of fidelity to the Queen. Since Stuart was not known to have had any personal audience with the Queen, it was not clear exactly what this vow might have meant. Stuart had believed, of course, that the Queen was the wisest and best person in the world, so maybe his vow meant that he would make decisions by reflecting, using a sort of "imaginative reconstruction," about what a truly wise and good person would recommend. Or maybe Stuart had gotten hold of information about the Queen's views and values (which were, as it happened, reported in a well-known if controversial book on the subject). In any case, according to this story, Stuart's vow of fidelity somehow helped him pull his fragmented self back together, so that in the end he achieved a kind of peace, and even self-mastery, that had previously eluded him. In trying to relinquish his autonomy, ironically, he had actually acquired it.

Nothing in these reports led Ronald to question his own entrenched commitment to autonomy—to "autonomy," that is, interpreted in the way that reasonable people would understand it. But he was moved to wonder whether autonomy was a concept (or possibly a conception) that could safely be entrusted to nonphilosophers. Maybe the mass of people would be better off exercising their freedom under the benign, watchful tutelage of the enlightened. In order to be effective, of course, this tutelage would need to be regularized and supported by the means typically used by the state; it would need to take the form of a sort of "freedom's law."

THE MORAL?

So much for the story: what is the moral? But as you perfectly well know, the Socratic code of the law professor prohibits me from answering that question for you. And in a Socratic spirit I am also constrained to say that I do not know the answer.

But I suppose it would not transgress the rules to say this much as a partial conclusion to the story: it seems that the fundamental modern concept of "autonomy"—the concept that pervades the religion-and-democracy debate, as well as modern political thought generally—is a problematic notion. Whether that notion offers a coherent and attractive ideal for guiding our moral and political deliberation seems very much open to question.

3

Is a Theory of Religious Freedom Possible?

FOR A COUPLE of generations or more, judges and especially scholars have been trying to articulate a satisfactory theory of religious freedom. If it seems that the task ought to have been completed long ago,
we need to remember that not just any collection of ideas or arguments
qualifies for consideration as a "theory." It's obvious, for example, that
we can and do *talk about* and *argue about* issues of religious freedom—
school prayer, aid to parochial schools, and so forth. But in the prevailing usage mere "talk," or ad hoc argumentation, does not rise to the dignity of being a "theory." Neither does a mere compromise or "modus
vivendi" count as a "theory." That is because a modus vivendi doesn't
do what a theory is designed to do: it doesn't give us an internally consistent set of principles capable of generating answers to questions of
religious freedom. Instead, it is more in the nature of a negotiated, and
perhaps messy, truce. Thus, even in a work calculated to propose a position that is supposed to be "political not philosophical," John Rawls
find a mere modus vivendi unacceptable.[1]

One last but crucial qualification needs to be noticed: even a position that might count as a "theory" does not qualify as a theory of religious freedom if it begins by preferring one (or some subset) of the
religious and secular positions that compete for adherence in society,
and then proceeds to spell out what that preferred position does and
doesn't allow. Suppose I contend, for example, that the law should permit teacher-led school prayer but not compulsory baptism; and when
asked to explain these conclusions I argue that they follow from the best
interpretation of Catholic theology, or perhaps Mormon or Muslim theology, and that this particular theology is the truest or best one available. Under current usage, we do not consider this sort of position to be
a theory of religious freedom (even though it *does* allow for a range of
choice in religious matters). On the contrary, this sort of position looks

more like the enforcement of a privileged orthodoxy. That approach to religion is as a historical matter entirely familiar, and it is just what religious freedom is supposed to save us from.

WHY THERE CAN BE NO THEORY OF RELIGIOUS FREEDOM

My view is that all argumentation about religious freedom will be disqualified from being a "theory of religious freedom" on one or another of these grounds: it will either fail to be a "theory," or else it will fail to be a theory of "religion freedom." I will give the reason for my view in summary form, and then elaborate.

The establishment and free exercise controversies that we are familiar with present one aspect of a more universal problem, which we might call the problem of "the spiritual and the temporal." "For the flesh lusteth against the Spirit, and the Spirit against the flesh: and these are contrary the one to the other."[2] Different people would use different vocabularies, of course; they might distinguish between the *soul* with its goods and the *body* with its appetites, or between our welfare in this life and in the next. But whatever terms we use, the enduring problem is to determine how these matters stand in relation to each other. Does the spiritual take priority over the temporal, or vice versa? Is the spiritual more real, or more authoritative, than the temporal—earth being merely a footstool for heaven? Or, conversely, is the spiritual merely derivative, or epiphenomenal, or perhaps merely a delusion?

Problems of religious freedom present one manifestation of this conflict within the realm of politics and law. These problems may involve competing claims to authority advanced by spiritual and temporal institutions. Or they may involve spiritual claims made by individuals that conflict with more general temporal interests. And when such spiritual-temporal conflicts arise, possible responses or resolutions can be understood as falling into three general categories, which I will describe as "spiritual primacy," "temporal primacy," and "dualism." The first two categories offer the possibility (at least in the abstract) of "theory," or of principled resolutions of conflicts—but not of resolutions that can usefully be described as respecting "religious freedom." The last category—dualism—is capable of recognizing a place for religious freedom, but it does not offer the possibility of principled resolutions of conflicts.

Spiritual Primacy

I want to try to clarify these general observations by considering a concrete example of each of these responses. So let me start with the category of "spiritual primacy." In this view, the temporal is subordinate to, or perhaps a subset of, the spiritual. And it seems to follow that spiritual-temporal conflicts should be resolved by applying *spiritual* criteria.

As an example of this approach, consider the medieval papacy's conception of government and law, as interpreted by Walter Ullmann. Ullmann explains that

> the papacy, in common with medieval doctrine and literature, held that the individual's activities cannot be separated into more or less well defined categories. . . . Christianity seized the whole of man— man was whole and indivisible: every one of his actions was thought to have been accessible to the judgement by Christian norms and standards.[3]

Those Christian norms and standards were ultimately directed toward a spiritual end: the salvation of the soul. But it did not follow that the affairs of this life were unimportant. On the contrary, "while the end of this [Christian] society and of its members was in the other world, the terrestrial life was nonetheless of fundamental importance in achieving this other-worldly aim, that is, salvation. The principle of indivisibility embraced the life in this as well as in the other world."[4]

Within this spiritual conception of life, the church was responsible for administering the Christian norms that governed all earthly activities.[5] Consequently, the papacy regarded the church and the pope as possessing jurisdiction to direct all the affairs of Christendom. Within this comprehensive jurisdiction, Ullmann argues, all other authorities (including both bishops and princes) were subordinate to papal authority. "Power, that is, jurisdiction, was concentrated in the pope, who handed part of it on to the bishops, part of it to kings and emperors, and so forth."[6] In sum, "the secular prince [was] a necessary, auxiliary organ . . . instituted by divinity to assist the pope in his government."[7]

This conception provided an intellectual framework within which conflicts between religious and secular authorities could be adjudicated.[8] To use our terms, that framework allowed for a "theory," I think, because it contained inclusive principles that were accepted by the competing interests as those interests were understood at the time. Of course, kings and emperors often resisted the popes' claims, and in the realm of power and politics their resistance was often successful. But in the realm of theory the secular rulers were severely handicapped because they themselves embraced the inclusive premises on which the papal claims rested.

Thus, Ullmann explains that "it would be wholly erroneous to think that these principles were, so to speak, imposed upon kings and princes."[9]

> No king or emperor ever objected to the papal theme that his kingdom was entrusted to him by God: on the contrary, it was the kings themselves who, quite independent of, and uninfluenced by, the papacy had adopted this standpoint.[10]

Of course, a king could claim that he received his power from God directly, rather than through the intermediary of the pope. In the eleventh century, the emperor Henry IV made just this claim in his famous dispute with pope Gregory VII. But in an officially Christian world this assertion seemed weak. The New Testament recorded Christ's conferral of power on Peter—and, by inference, on his successors—but what evidence was there of any independent divine conferral of authority on the king or the emperor? And what special competence could a worldly and perhaps illiterate prince claim in matters of scripture and Christian doctrine? Ullmann stresses that within the Christocentric worldview, papal claims to sovereignty were perfectly logical—indeed, virtually irresistible. We might put the point more generally: if the primacy of a spiritual position is accepted within a community, then it is natural that the office or institution responsible for preserving and interpreting that spiritual position should enjoy ultimate authority within the community.

Consequently, the possibility of a secular authority independent of the church awaited the emergence of a dualistic worldview in which the "temporal" was freed from its subordination to the "spiritual." Opponents of papal authority sometimes tried to develop this position. Ull-mann explains: "What the dualists aimed at in their opposition to the papacy was the ascription of autonomous and indigenous character to the 'temporal.' In this way it was believed that the monarchy of the king could be saved: in temporal matters the king was to be the monarch, in spiritual matters the pope."[11]

This dualist talk begins to sound familiar to modern ears accustomed to the theme of "separation of church and state." But in the medieval climate of opinion the dualist view made little headway, for the understandable reason that the spiritual and the temporal did not seem severable. Dualism, Ullmann explains, "contradicted not only the Pauline doctrine, which the papacy had made its own, but also the principle of totality or indivisibility, which in itself was the message of Christianity, seizing as it did the whole of man and the whole of his activities without splitting them up into different compartments."[12]

In sum, in a world in which competing parties concurred in accepting a set of premises that treated the temporal as subordinate to the spiritual, it was possible to develop a theory regulating the relations between, to use our terms, church and state. And this theory could contemplate—indeed, insist upon—a division of functions between "secular" officials such as kings and religious officials such as bishops. Still, it would seem a little strange to describe this theory as a theory of *religious freedom*. The label seems inappropriate not because the theory allowed secular authorities no freedom—in fact the popes never tried to dictate every decision made by kings and emperors—but because a system under which secular authorities are auxiliaries to the church and have just as much power as the church assigns to them is not the sort of arrangement we have in mind when we talk about "religious freedom." On the contrary, we would call such a system a "theocracy." And we are accustomed to treating "theocracy" not as a version of, but rather as the antithesis of, "religious freedom."

Temporal Primacy

I've been describing the medieval papacy's conception of government, as depicted by Ullmann, as an example of a system that gives priority to the spiritual. What might be an example of the opposite position—that is, of a system that treats the spiritual as subordinate to or a subdivision of the temporal? You might suspect that the answer is very close at hand—that as citizens of a secular public culture we actually inhabit just such a system. Maybe so, but to avoid controversial characterizations, let me adopt the law teacher's trick of describing a partly hypothetical culture that will illustrate my point—one that you can recognize in our situation, or not, as you choose.

Imagine, then, a community in which most people ultimately believe in and care only for the temporal. They believe, perhaps, that this life is all we have: "When we die, we die." This community also believes that there is no guiding intelligence or overall purpose or design in the cosmos. So the purpose of people—and hence of governments established of, by, and for the people—is to promote the welfare of human beings in this life. The community and most of its members are committed, that is, solely to the pursuit of temporal values and interests. Of course, this community might still care about "spiritual" or "sacred" things in a watered-down sense of the words—it might use such adjectives to describe things like opera and poetry, for example—but it has rejected religious entities or notions like God, the soul, grace, the supernatural, and life after death.

But lest we solve the problem of religious freedom too quickly simply by eliminating religion, we can suppose that a residual commitment to the spiritual lingers on in several ways. First, a few members of the community retain a genuine faith in God, the soul, life after death, and the divine authorship of scripture. These religious believers are widely regarded as peculiar and backward, and at least among the more educated their faith is viewed as "irrational superstitious nonsense."[13] Even so, they are capable of causing unpleasantness. Moreover, in view of the community's egalitarian pretensions these religionists are thought to be entitled in some ill-defined sense to "equal concern and respect."

In addition, some members of the community who do not actually believe in God or the soul still feel a degree of selective affection toward religious practices and traditions. They may think some traditions are useful in the upbringing of children. They expect that as adults these erstwhile children will come to understand the purely pragmatic function of the traditions—while of course continuing to pass on the traditions to their own children. Others may find religious practices soothing (Gregorian chants, maybe), or aesthetically attractive, or useful on special occasions for expressing emotions like hope or grief. There are also agnostics of an antiquarian bent who find that religious traditions and rituals help them to preserve their ties to the past, and perhaps to maintain a sense of personal or communal identity.

In short, "religion" continues to exist in various senses even in this devoutly temporal community. But would there be any room, or any reason, to give special honor or legal status to religious freedom? Of course, the community might recognize and in a sense respect practices that for some purposes are classified under the heading of "religion." The community might protect these practices, that is, because they implicate temporal interests. If government interferes with religious belief or exercise, the interference might injure people's peace of mind or sense of identity. Frustrated religionists might become uncivil or even violent. For reasons like these, the community conceivably might carve out an area of human activity called "religion" and afford it different or special legal treatment. And it's even conceivable, if unlikely, that this special treatment could be successfully codified in terms of some principle or theory. People who advocated such a position might claim that they had articulated a theory of religious freedom.

Still, there are good reasons to question both this possibility and this characterization. Notice first that although the hypothetical position *could* be called a "theory of religious freedom," it does not offer any protection to religion *as* religion, or *because* of its character as religion. Rather, the theory protects religion as a temporal human activity and because that activity is thought to affect temporal interests. To put the point differently, *from the community's standpoint* it is in a sense merely fortuitous that the activities and beliefs which affect the temporal interests in question happen to be religious activities and beliefs. So we might doubt that it is helpful, or accurate, to attach the label of "theory of religious freedom" to an account that does not even count the religious character of a belief or activity as relevant in itself or for its own sake.

This question about truth-in-labeling points to a related practical objection: the temporal interests invoked by the theory will probably not correlate cleanly with "religious" activities and beliefs, and so it will come to seem both illogical and imprudent to make the theory's application coextensive with what is for other purposes called "religion." Suppose, for example, that a theory is based on the value of "autonomy," or perhaps "self-realization." The theory holds, perhaps, that government should not interfere in religious choices because these choices are too closely linked to a person's sense of who she is, or to her very identity; and self-definition or self-realization are temporal interests that the community should respect.[14] The point about labeling suggests that it would be more accurate to call this a "theory of autonomy," or a "theory of self-realization"—not a "theory of religious freedom." The related practical point is that self-realization probably does not correlate precisely, or even very closely, with religion. For many people, choices that are not religious may be central to self-realization, while choices that involve religion may not always affect self-realization in any essential way. So the logic of the theory suggests that it should abandon its claim to being a theory of religious freedom not only in name but also in practical application.[15]

One response to this objection might argue that although "religion" is not identical to temporal interests like personal autonomy, still for practical purposes religion is a pretty good proxy for those interests. But this argument seems dubious at best. Particularly in a pluralistic culture where "religion" takes a variety of radically diverse forms, it seems prima facie implausible that the amorphous category of "religion" would correlate even approximately with any particular temporal interest or set of interests.

In this situation, how would we account for continuing efforts to theorize about religious freedom? If a given community already has a long-standing commitment to religious freedom derived from earlier events and other commitments (perhaps by now largely forgotten), then it would be tempting to interpret temporal arguments for religious freedom as post hoc (and less than persuasive) rationalizations for a commitment that the community has inherited but no longer fully grasps. And a prescription that might naturally follow from this interpretation is that the community should clean up its theory and practice in light of its current beliefs and values. One way to do this would be to dissolve religious freedom into other, more current theories and commitments—commitments to free speech, perhaps, or to equality.[16]

In this way the community conceivably might bring its practice into line with what is, for it, a plausible theory or set of principles. And under other headings, like "free speech" or "equality," the community might continue to give legal protection to some beliefs and practices that the believers and practitioners themselves regard as "religion."[17] But the purified temporal community would not now claim to have, or to operate according to, any "theory of religious freedom."

Dualism

The positions I've talked about thus far have been monistic in the sense that they have regarded either the spiritual or the temporal as primary and encompassing, with the subordinate term being viewed as a subdivision of the primary or preferred category. I have argued that at least in the abstract both perspectives offer the possibility of "theory" prescribing principled resolutions for some of the disputes that we treat under the headings of "religious freedom," or "church and state"; but neither perspective actually recognizes the value of "religious freedom" in a meaningful sense.

That value is more accurately associated, perhaps, with a dualist position—one that regards both the spiritual and the temporal as independently valuable. This sort of perspective, with both its promises and problems, is reflected in John Locke's "A Letter concerning Toleration." Locke acknowledges the importance of both spiritual interests—the salvation of the soul—and of temporal or "civil interests," or "things belonging to this life," such as "life, liberty, health, and indolence of body; and the possession of outward things, such as money, land, houses, furniture, and the like."[18] And spiritual and temporal values are independent of each other; property, for example, is a good not because it will contribute to our eternal salvation, but because it is valuable in the here and now.

Based on this dualistic view, Locke argues for a division of responsibility between the church and the state. The church's function is to care for the salvation of souls, and in such matters of salvation the state has no legitimate concern. The state's function, rather, is to protect and promote the civil interests of its citizens. In this way, Locke concludes that church and commonwealth are "perfectly distinct, and infinitely different from each other" and that "[t]he boundaries on both sides are fixed and immoveable."[19]

Of course, dualistic thinking and imagery have pervaded discussions of religious freedom in this country. The notion surfaces again and again: church is church and state is state, they are separated by a high and impregnable "wall," and both are happier for the split. The dualist view is attractive because it seems to recognize the value of religious freedom in a more meaningful sense than do either of the more monistic views.

In addition, presentations like Locke's even seem at first to allow for a *theory* of religious freedom. The task of theory is to determine which interests belong to the spiritual domain and which belong to the temporal, and in this way to draw a line of demarcation between the spheres. Once that line has been fixed, when questions of religious freedom arise we need only examine the interests closely to see which side of the line they fall on.

Upon closer examination, though, the pleasant prospects offered by the dualist view dissolve. One way to consider the problem is to ask *from whose perspective* it can be said that the church's concern is solely for the salvation of souls, while the state's responsibility is for this-worldly, "civil" interests. If this is the way the church itself and the state itself understand their respective domains, then a nice harmony of interests seems possible. Indeed, it becomes difficult to explain why religious freedom and church-state relations ever created such a ruckus in the first place. On the other hand, if the church or the state do *not* understand their roles in this way, so that Locke's description of roles is merely his own (or perhaps the state's, or the church's) view of what the division of responsibilities *ought to be,* then no principled resolution has been achieved. Instead, the pretense of such a resolution is in reality merely the imposition of terms by a dominant party employing a deceitful description of what the other party cares about.

In fact, churches historically have not understood their concern to be limited to the salvation of souls in the next life. For example, many churches have regarded the achievement of education, social justice, and civil rights as major religious objectives. Even more importantly, religions rarely separate the concerns of this life from those of the next; they have typically taught that the way a person lives here will powerfully affect the disposition of the soul after death. Indeed, later in his essay, Locke acknowledges that both religion and the state are vitally concerned with issues of morality.[20] The concession effectively negates his earlier claim that the spiritual and temporal spheres are "perfectly distinct, and infinitely different from each other"—a claim which is essential to the possibility of a dualistic or separation principle.

A different way of highlighting the false promise of dualism is to ask whether the different interests of the spiritual and the temporal are wholly different, or whether their respective spheres of interest are different but overlapping, as in a Venn diagram. If the spheres of interest were wholly different, then a principled resolution of conflicts should be easily attainable; indeed, the harder problem once again would be to explain why such conflicts ever arise in the first place. But if the spheres overlap (as they almost certainly do), then it is natural to suppose that conflicts, and hence questions of religious freedom, will arise within the area of overlap. And within that area, the dualist promise of a principled resolution cannot be fulfilled. Since both the spiritual and the temporal make a claim, any solution will necessarily reject one of those claims by giving primacy to the competing perspective.

And precisely because it recognizes that the spiritual and the temporal are *both* valuable, and that they are *independently* valuable (as opposed to one being derived from or a subset of the other), dualism cannot dictate which perspective should prevail. If the spiritual and the temporal are both real and autonomous, in other words, then there is no more encompassing principle to which they are both subordinate and which could be appealed to in resolving conflicts between them.

Any actual controversy involving religious freedom can serve to illustrate this controversy. Suppose that Native Americans assert a religious duty to use peyote in religious rituals, while a state insists on banning the use of harmful drugs, which in the state's view include peyote. The use of peyote in this context affects both a spiritual interest and a temporal interest. A dualist view would observe that both interests are independently valuable; neither is simply derivative of or reducible to the other. And the response to this dualist observation is, "Yes. That's exactly why we have a conflict." In this context the spiritual and temporal domains overlap, and in order to resolve the conflict, some authority—a court, a legislature—will have to treat either the spiritual or the temporal as primary and the other interest as subordinate.

This objection does not necessarily imply that the dualist view is wrong, I think, or that the dualist view cannot value religious freedom. The point is merely that dualism itself cannot provide any theory or principle defining the proper scope of religious freedom. On the contrary, the occurrence of actual controversies demonstrates that a point has been reached where the contribution of dualism is insufficient to produce peace. At that point a decision maker will be forced to give priority to either the spiritual or the temporal perspective, and we will once again be faced with the same problems that afflict the monistic positions.

THE INNUMERABLE CITIES

The moral of this story is that our concept of religious freedom gets its meaning within a dualist framework. But a dualist framework cannot honestly offer any useful principle, or support any theory, for adjudicating the problems we consider under the heading of religious freedom. So to the extent that religious freedom flourishes within a dualist system, it will necessarily reflect an accommodation or a modus vivendi among spiritual or temporal interests, not a deduction from theory or principle.

This conclusion should not be surprising. On a personal level, most of us are quite accustomed to negotiating between the spiritual and the temporal. True saints (if there are any) or true atheists (if there are any) may manage to achieve monistic peace. Meanwhile, most of us try to serve both masters, and so we live in tension, making choices that are at times arbitrary, intuitive, ad hoc, not regulated by any encompassing principle or theory. We might say that we "balance" the spiritual and the temporal, except that the metaphor of balancing suggests more precision than we really experience. It might be more accurate to say that we "juggle" the spiritual and the temporal, acknowledging that many of us are clumsy jugglers who are often forced to stoop and pick up the pieces. As we've been told, the "double-minded man is unstable in all his ways."[21]

On a more global level, the moral of the discussion is also a familiar one—famously presented in, for example, Augustine's *City of God.* Religious believers are citizens of two cities, Augustine explained—an earthly city and a heavenly one. Both cities seek "peace." This apparently common goal might make it seem that the cities are nicely harmonious; and indeed a limited harmony may be achievable.[22] But by "peace" the two cities in fact understand quite different things. "The earthly city, which does not live by faith, seeks an earthly peace, and the end it proposes . . . is the combination of men's wills to attain the things which are *helpful to this life*."[23] The heavenly city takes advantage of this peace, but it also understands that "the perfectly ordered and harmonious enjoyment of God and of one another in God" is what "alone can be truly called and esteemed the peace of reasonable creatures." These different conceptions and different ultimate attachments and aspirations sometimes come into conflict, and when that happens "the heavenly city has been compelled . . . to dissent, and to become obnoxious to those who think differently."[24]

In the final analysis, therefore, the heavenly city "lives like a captive and a stranger in the earthly city." The heavenly city can seek benign terms of captivity, or perhaps a sort of truce, from the earthly sovereign; it cannot hope for genuine understanding and union.

Augustine's analysis remains valid for our modern society, I think, except that our more developed pluralism—in the realms both of religion and of government—may make the description of two cities seem a little quaint. For us, it seems, there are not two but rather many cities—many conflicting faiths, worldviews, lifestyles, and cultural and political allegiances. This riotous pluralism merely underscores the conclusion suggested above: we may aspire to achieve a modus vivendi among these competing positions, but it is a mistake to suppose that there can be any encompassing theory or "neutral principle" to regulate their interaction.

PART II

WHAT SHALL WE DO?

(or How the Supreme Court Can Stop Making Things Worse)

IN THE MODERN discourse of religious freedom, the commitment to "religious equality" and the demand for a "theory" of religious freedom complement each other nicely. In a democracy, "equality" (along with its twin, neutrality) seems to be the most eligible value upon which to build a "theory," and that theory would in turn provide the standard for scrutinizing decisions and policies to ensure that different religions and religious claimants are treated "equally." Suppose, though, that the arguments in the preceding chapters are right: the commitment to equality is substantively empty, incapable of generating answers to particular controversies; and there can be no satisfactory theory of religious freedom. Do we have a problem? Can we get along without a "theory" of religious freedom?

To a lay person, the latter question might seem strange. After all, most of us go through life making decisions, large and small, without ever developing any "theory" of decision making either in general or for particular areas of life. You go into a restaurant, look over the menu, and order something. Suppose a friend asks, "What theory did you use in choosing the lasagna over the calzone?" The question will seem odd. Suppose you answer, "I don't have any theory," and your friend says, "Then how can you make a choice?" This question will seem even odder. Why on earth should you need a "theory" to make this sort of decision? Indeed, what sort of person would develop a theory for these matters?

Perhaps this example seems too trivial. So take something more important—marriage, perhaps. My own observation is that most people marry at some time in their lives, often more than once; and so far as I can tell most of these people do not act on any "theory of marriage," or "theory of partner selection." This does not mean that they act irrationally. They may—if we happen to be their parents we ardently hope they do—think through the pros and cons of particular marriage prospects. But the pros and cons are mostly quite uncertain and incommensurable; they do not reduce to anything that could be captured in a "theory." Indeed, we would again probably feel suspicious, and maybe even a little contemptuous, toward a person who thought he could make decisions of this kind in accordance with a "theory."

In most of the affairs of life, in short, we seem to get by without a "theory." And in the matters of religious freedom we have gotten by, for better or worse, without a satisfactory theory. Why then do the scholars of religious freedom seem to think it so imperative that decisions in this area be justified in theoretical terms?

Part of the answer is probably just that scholars—and to some degree lawyers and judges—are likely to be the sort of people who exhibit what we might call a "rationalist" mindset. Some of them might actually wonder whether it is possible to choose an entree from the menu without some at least implicit theory. (And if this sounds like an accusation, I should admit that it is also a confession.) In addition, lawyers and legal scholars are quite accustomed to claiming that law's special authority in our society derives from its rationality—its insistence that whatever is done be done in accordance with "reasons," and that these reasons need to form a coherent whole. This insistence on reasoning and coherence naturally generates the urgent demand for a theory, because a theory is precisely what ensures that reasons are being consistently applied. Conversely, the absence of a theory may seem tantamount to a confession that decisions suffer from qualities that the rationalist dreads—arbitrariness, or incoherence, or simply irrationality.

This need for theory is sharpened in the area of constitutional law because several generations of lawyers have been taught that constitutional decisions—always *prima facie* suspect because they tend to overrule the decisions of elected officials such as legislators—are "legitimate" only when they are "principled." And to be "principled" seems to mean something like reconcilable with other decisions in accordance with some satisfactory theory. In this perspective the absence of a theory threatens the very legitimacy of constitutional law and suggests that the Supreme Court is acting as, in Herbert Wechsler's memorable phrase, a "naked power organ."

So the strength of the demand for a theory of religious freedom, and for a theory that reflects our commitment to "equality," is easy enough to understand. The chapters in this section nonetheless seek to resist this demand. It is possible, I will argue, to deal prudently with the controversies that we regard as problems of religious freedom without any conscious theory of religious freedom, and without maintaining the pretense that our decisions are mandated by any principle of religious equality—or, for that matter, by any "principle" at all. The alternative, "unprincipled" approach, attuned to the virtue of tolerance over the "principle" of equality or neutrality, might support a less interventionist role for courts than the one they have assumed over the last few decades, but it would not foreclose judicial participation in our ongoing effort to maintain the condition that we are wont to call "religious freedom."

4

Unprincipled Religious Freedom

My deeper concern with the Court's current inclination to extract a few homespun absolutes from the complexities of a pluralistic tradition is derived from the conviction that in these matters the living practices of the American people bespeak our basic constitutional commitment more accurately than do the dogmatic pronouncements of the justices. . . . [T]he justices may waste the nation's inheritance if they constantly dip into principle.

—Mark DeWolfe Howe[1]

A CONFERENCE PROSPECTUS asked participants to set forth their theory of constitutional religious freedom and then to "explore in detail" how the more difficult religious freedom controversies should be resolved under that theory. This request probably seemed sensible enough to nearly everyone, but for me it amounted to a kind of trap. I had previously argued—at length, and more than once, along the lines of chapter 3—that there is not and cannot be any satisfactory theory or principle of religious freedom. How could I do what the letter demanded, then, without contradicting my own position?

But perhaps, I thought, there was a way around this dilemma. In this chapter, in any case, I want to explore the possibility that the *absence* of a satisfactory theory of religious freedom, and the accompanying skepticism about the viability of any principle of religious freedom, might themselves point us toward solutions to some church-state or free exercise controversies.

PRINCIPLE OR PRUDENCE?

Let us start by noticing a basic choice of strategies. In confronting political decisions or public policy questions, we sometimes suppose that it is possible and desirable to articulate relatively determinate principles or general propositions that can dictate answers in particular instances in an almost deductive fashion. For example, we say that laws that overtly discriminate on the basis of race are, except in unusual cases, illegitimate. Speech regulations that classify on the basis of content or viewpoint are presumptively unacceptable. When we encounter laws of this kind, we normally don't need to spend much time or effort considering the particular pros and cons; on general principles these laws are presumptively invalid.

In many other contexts, by contrast, we address questions case by case under a sort of ad hoc, all-relevant-factors approach. Most questions of war and peace, foreign aid, taxes, zoning and land use, operation of schools, health and safety regulation, and a host of other issues are routinely decided on the basis of heavily context-dependent and "prudential" considerations. To be sure, we may still refer to general criteria or values—or, if you want, "principles"—but the general factors do not dictate particular results in anything resembling a deductive fashion. "Do good and avoid evil" may be a universally applicable principle, but in concrete cases it leaves everything still to be decided.

The distinction between these approaches is rough—probably questions fall more on a continuum than into black and white categories—but it is nonetheless recognizable and, for some purposes, useful. So we might choose to treat issues involving religious freedom in either of these ways—as questions of "principle," or as largely prudential questions to be resolved on a case by case basis by considering various costs, benefits, and other practical, ethical, and political concerns.

For the last half-century, judges and legal scholars have supposed that religious freedom issues are matters of principle, and so they have proposed a variety of principles—principles of "strict separation," for example, or "neutrality," or noncoercion, or nonendorsement—under which these controversies might be resolved. It is natural that judges and legal scholars would favor the principled approach. The idea of principle enjoys high status in our culture; a person "of principle" is one having integrity, honor, moral courage, and commitment. In addition, at least since Herbert Wechsler's famous "Neutral Principles" essay,[2] a common assumption has been that *courts* act legitimately *only* when they act on the basis of principle. So it is hardly surprising that judges, as well as legal scholars who take it as their function to prescribe to judges, would seek to articulate a "principle" of religious freedom. But I want to argue that the received wisdom is misconceived in this context: we would be wiser, even more realistically honorable, to follow a more prudential course.

The Vices of Principle

The principled approach is objectionable in this context for two main reasons. First, there is no satisfactory theory supporting any definite principle of religious freedom. Second, the principled approach is undesirable on prudential grounds. Since we have already considered the first of these objections in chapter 3, let us go directly to the second objection.

We might start by noticing a conspicuous practical embarrassment of religion clause jurisprudence. Although judges and commentators have offered a variety of policy rationales for protecting religious freedom, perhaps the most influential and frequently invoked justification has been what is sometimes called the "civil peace" rationale: protecting religious freedom is necessary to avoid the strife associated with the wars of religion in early modern Europe and the English civil war. In recent years, this rationale has been fine-tuned into what might be called a "nonalienation" rationale. In this understanding, the point of protecting religious freedom is not merely to avoid active strife but to prevent citizens even from feeling alienated—or from feeling that they are "outsiders," or second-class citizens—on the basis of religion.

So we have become more delicate in defining the kind and degree of civic unity that the religion clauses are supposed to assure. And what have these efforts produced? The level of civil tension and alienation directly tied to religion seems at least as high in this country today as it has been at any time since the Supreme Court entered the field over a half-century ago. Suspicions and accusations separating groups like the ACLU and its supporters from groups like the Christian Coalition and *its* sympathizers are rampant.

What has gone wrong? The answer to that question is complex, no doubt, but it seems clear that an important part of the answer has to do with the aggressive conversion of religious freedom into a matter of constitutional principle enforceable by courts.[3] That transformation raises the stakes enormously, and thus aggravates the potential for acrimony and alienation, in at least two ways.

First, treating an issue as a matter of principle is a way of saying that it is a "moral" issue—or perhaps an issue of "character," or of fundamental community identity—that decent people ought to care about, and indeed to fight for, even if they personally are not much affected by the particular issue as a practical matter. On a mundane level, lawyers are familiar with clients who persist in litigation that is irrational in cost-benefit terms simply because of "the principle of it." The same motives surely help to explain the passion generated by issues of religious freedom where the material consequences seem almost nil.

For example, from a certain detached perspective it might seem that the issue of graduation prayer is quite trivial. Frederick Mark Gedicks has recently argued that "there is really not very much at stake in the constitutional controversy over this practice." The prayers are typically so innocuous, and so theologically empty, that "very little is lost when such prayers are . . . eliminated." Conversely, if graduation prayers are retained, "it ought not to be that large of an imposition to ask that nonbelievers sit quietly through thirty or forty seconds of vaguely religious platitudes." Gedicks concludes that the controversy generated by this issue reflects its symbolic, not its practical, significance: "While nothing very important seems to be at stake . . . , whether or not prayer is allowed in public schools has become a symbol of what has become known as the 'culture war.'"[4] And converting an issue into "a matter of principle" is precisely what makes it a natural battleground for cultural struggle.

But principles inflame not merely because of their symbolic significance. In a very down-to-earth way, the enlistment of constitutional principles in a controversy *does* vastly magnify the practical consequences of a particular decision. That is because in our legal system, constitutional principles are supposed to be enforceable against everyone throughout the country and on a whole range of (perhaps unforeseeable) issues that may be implicated by the principle; that is what it *means* to say that something is a constitutional principle. Robert Nagel explains that "[g]iven our assumptions about the Constitution as supreme law, constitutional prescriptions must apply uniformly across the nation and must subordinate all other interests. To the extent that an objective has authoritative constitutional status, judges are required to realize that objective everywhere and at all costs."[5] So everyone *does* have a significant practical stake in a controversy involving constitutional principles.

Suppose, for example, that a school board in Fundament, Louisiana, decides to teach creationism in its schools, and that a school board in Progress, Massachusetts, decides to *forbid* the teaching of creationism in *its* schools. Leave "constitutional principles" out of the picture, and the people in each locale might simply regard the decision of the other locale as one more manifestation of what they may already view, respectively, as the godless or backward culture of that alien place. They may be apathetic, or amused, or even angry, but they can afford to mind their own business. The other locale's decision does not directly govern *them*.

Now insert the notion that such decisions must be compatible with (or even an expression of) a constitutional principle, and suddenly everything changes. If the Louisiana decision is a correct application of principle, then that principle will bind Massachusetts as well, and vice versa—and not only in the matter of creationism versus evolution, but also in other matters. Perhaps no one in Louisiana or Massachusetts— or the Harvard Law School, or the Supreme Court—can foretell just what the implications of the "principle" will turn out to be. Some of those implications will probably be drawn, and enforced, by people who have not yet even entered law school, or who perhaps have not even been born. But one thing seems clear: "Live and let live" or "Mind our own business" no longer apply. Let principles enter the picture, and what happens in Louisiana or Massachusetts or anywhere else *is* everyone's business. *Everything* is now worth fighting about.

In short, although a laudable desire to promote civil peace or avoid alienation has motivated much of the case law and scholarship in this area, the conversion of religious freedom into a matter of principle is a course nicely calculated to frustrate these aims. Religion, as Sanford Levinson observes, becomes a principal battleground for "contemporary American 'public interest' litigation in which each side is represented by ideologically zealous organizations who view the actual clients as little more than pawns in larger struggles over control of American culture."[6]

The Virtues of Prudence

A prudential approach to religious freedom controversies would not try to find the "correct" solution to any particular controversy, but would instead seek to work out a relatively acceptable compromise or modus vivendi. By contrast to the "principled" approach, with its propensity to aggravate cultural conflict, a prudential approach lowers rather than raises the stakes of religious freedom controversies. Another significant virtue, I believe, is that the prudential approach should promote a healthier constitutional discourse because it allows for more honesty and realism in our discussions of religious freedom. More specifically, the prudential approach would permit us to acknowledge three facts that, if more widely appreciated, might enhance discussion on issues of religious freedom.

First, it would be beneficial to relinquish the pretense that there is an ideal or "correct" solution to most religious freedom controversies, and thus to admit that often the best we can hope to achieve is a good faith, minimally acceptable second- or third-best compromise. Most controversies involve a variety of people with sincerely held religious or secular beliefs and practices that *will* be adversely affected to different degrees by some resolutions, and perhaps by *any* particular resolution, of the controversy. In short, people *will* be injured. Consequently, the fact of injury is not in itself a sufficient reason for rejecting a policy or proposal that causes such injury.

Although this observation should perhaps be obvious, it is often suppressed in both public and academic debate. Typically, the parties to these controversies will maintain that there is a correct or "neutral" solution that is fair and nonprejudicial to everyone concerned, implying that conflicts arise only because some zealous faction gratuitously and perversely insists on imposing its own religious (or antireligious, or "secular humanist") views on the community. So long as this kind of characterization prevails, we can hardly expect any progress toward good faith compromises. The "principled" approach reinforces this kind of characterization, however, since each party to a controversy is virtually required to assert that the other side does not merely have different beliefs and interests but rather is acting in an "unprincipled" (and so, by implication, unlawful or immoral) fashion. The prudential approach, by contrast, makes this sort of pejorative characterization unnecessary.

Second, a prudential approach could admit that constitutional law—and thus judges, lawyers, and legal scholars—probably have no more than a modest contribution to make to the realization of religious freedom. A good deal of judicial and academic writing seems implicitly to presuppose that the religious freedom we enjoy is primarily a result of the correct understanding and vigilant enforcement of the Constitution by lawyers and judges. In turn, this presupposition tends both to make the institutions of the law more aggressive or more officious, and to belittle the importance of contributions of other sectors of society.

Without indulging in triumphalist nostalgia we can still usefully remind ourselves that all states terminated their official establishments of religion over a century before the Supreme Court thought of enforcing the religion clauses against them, that prosecutions for blasphemy, heresy, and witchcraft waned without compulsion by the Supreme Court, and that Arkansas's antievolution statute had been a dead letter for decades when the Supreme Court eagerly seized the opportunity to strike it down (and to issue gratuitous and inflammatory anti-Fundamentalist comments in the process).[7] It is also useful to remember that religious freedom has flourished, arguably about as well as it has here, in a country like Great Britain even without the institution of judicial review, and even with the presence of an official established church. We ought to find it reassuring, I think, that the fate of religious freedom does not hinge on the dubious ability of nine Justices (or of the motley assortment of lawyers and legal scholars who interest ourselves in religion clause controversies) to get things just right.

Consequently, the prudential approach suggests a more modest role in religious freedom controversies for courts (and legal scholars), who could not by this view simply arrive on the scene and decree that a potentially divisive or unpopular or expensive arrangement is what "the Constitution requires." Indeed, for those who believe that courts act legitimately *only* when they act to enforce legal principles, the rejection of the principled approach might imply that courts have *no* role to play in this area, and that judges should simply withdraw from the protection of religious freedom. Complicated jurisprudential questions lurk here which go well beyond the scope of this book. For present purposes I will merely say that although it does not seem to me to follow that courts have no role in this area (more on that presently), the rejection of a principled approach does suggest that the judicial role should be different, and in general more modest.

Third, a prudential approach might allow us to deal honestly with the fact that at least to some extent, as Justice Douglas said, "this is a religious nation whose institutions presuppose a Supreme Being."[8] Indeed, however offensive or regrettable the fact may be in some quarters, it is even true that in a complex and ambiguous sense this is a "Christian nation." Today as at many times in the past, an overwhelming majority of citizens identify themselves with some form of Christianity, and many of them at least *say* that this identification is very important to them.

Of course, this statement immediately calls for major qualifications. As a *constitutional* matter the United States is *not* a Christian nation in the sense that, say, England is an Anglican nation (even though as a *sociological* matter the United States may be *more* Christian than England is Anglican). Moreover, millions of citizens are *not* Christians, of course, and they are just as fully citizens as anyone else. And even the sociological question is complicated because people who claim the label can mean very different things by "Christianity." Their religious commitments, conscious or unconscious, vary tremendously: it gives one pause to read the occasional survey reporting on people (millions of them, evidently) who claim to be Christian and even to read the Bible regularly, but who cannot name any of the gospels or explain what Easter commemorates.

So I am not trying to draw any definite conclusion from the "Christian nation" claim. But I *do* think it is offensive to all concerned—and, more important, obfuscating and unhelpful—to engage in far-fetched, systematic denials of the nation's (admittedly very ambiguous) religious character, as in the now official view that practices such as legislative prayer or the national motto "In God We Trust" do not have religious content and significance. Our commitment to principled constitutional doctrine, coupled with the current vogue of construing the establishment clause to forbid any official statement or action that sends a message "endorsing" religion, has forced us into a situation where these sorts of disingenuous claims seem almost mandatory. After all, it *would* be a bit strange—wouldn't it?—to discover after all these years that not only the national motto and the Pledge of Allegiance ("one nation, under God") but also, if current nonendorsement principles were rigorously applied, other time-honored artifacts like Jefferson's famous Virginia Statute for Religious Freedom ("Almighty God hath created the mind free" so that infringements on freedom are "a departure from the plan of the holy author of our religion")[9] and the Declaration of Independence ("endowed by their Creator with certain unalienable rights"), not to mention the names of many major cities (Corpus Christi, Los Angeles)[10] all transgress the Constitution? How else to avoid such embarrassments but to insist, through clenched teeth, that these traditions and political landmarks have no real religious content or meaning?

A major virtue of the prudential approach, I suggest, is that it would spare us the necessity of indulging these sorts of insulting and offensive fictions. We might then make more progress toward understanding, and perhaps reconciling, some of our religious differences.

THE PRACTICAL APPLICATION OF PRUDENTIALISM

Thus far I have discussed two different general approaches to religious freedom controversies, but I have said little about what those approaches mean for particular controversies. Of course, if one favors the prudential approach that I have advocated, it becomes difficult to dictate solutions to particular controversies from afar. Prudentialism insists that solutions cannot be determined in the abstract; compromises must be worked out in particular contexts and on the basis of local information typically not available in a law school office, or conference hall, or marbled courtroom in the nation's capital. Nonetheless, prudentialism does have implications that might at least help to identify helpful and unhelpful ways of addressing particular controversies. We can reflect on those implications in connection with some familiar issues.

Most obviously, a prudential approach suggests (in a way that seems both platitudinous and yet strangely foreign to existing religion clause jurisprudence) that the resolutions of real world controversies ought to be influenced by a concern for enhancing actual religious freedom. Surveys show, after all, that nearly everyone in this country agrees that religious freedom is a value to be cherished.[11] One natural consequence of that consensus is that prudentially minded courts might be more inclined to intervene in disputes where there is significant impairment of religious freedom than in cases where there is not. This suggestion naturally prompts an examination of the different types of harm to religious freedom.

Such an examination leads, I think, to some conclusions quite at odds with current law. The discrepancy is not surprising. Given its primary concern with vindicating "principles," current law may studiously overlook severe harms that cannot be brought within the scope of an attractive or manageable principle; at other times the law converts questionable or negligible harms into serious ones in order to create a justiciable controversy in which courts can come to the aid of a beleaguered principle. A prudential approach, by contrast, is more concerned about harm in its own right, and thus permits a more realistic assessment of the severity of harm.

I will not attempt to give an exhaustive catalog of harms. Instead, I will discuss several harms that the current principled approach misclassifies in a way that greatly affects recurring religious freedom controversies. Then I will discuss a more complicated harm that has lately come to be important.

The Destruction of Religion

It would seem that the most severe harm to religious freedom occurs when government does not merely *prohibit* a religious belief or practice on pain of criminal sanctions—in that case, a believer can still choose to keep the faith and take the penalty, perhaps thereby gaining the blessedness of martyrdom—but when government actually *prevents* the exercise of religion, or *destroys* a necessary basis for the religion. Under current law, oddly enough, this most severe kind of harm goes unrecognized.

Thus, in *Lyng v. Northwest Cemetery Association*,[12] the Forest Service proposed to build a logging road on government land near a sacred site important to the practice of Native American religion. The Supreme Court majority conceded that the road could have "devastating effects" on Native American religion.[13] But because the Forest Service's action would merely *preclude* the practice of religion without actually *prohibiting* it, the Court found no constitutional objection to the proposed road, and indeed refused to consider the severe threat to religious practice against the government's debatable interest in building the road.

In *Lyng*, religious freedom was a casualty of the commitment to principle. The Court was evidently troubled by the very real difficulty of adopting a general principle that would require the government to justify, probably under some sort of "compelling interest" test, every decision about the use of public property that might implicate the practice of someone's religion. "Nothing *in the principle* for which [the Native American claimants] contend would distinguish this case," the Court fretted, from others in which the balance of interests was less clear.[14] So the Court avoided what it viewed as an unmanageable principle by adopting a different principle under which this sort of harm—the prevention or destruction of a religious practice—would not count at all.

From the more realistic perspective permitted by a prudential approach, this conclusion seems perverse. What could be a more serious harm to religion than an action that effectively prevents its practice by destroying the necessary means or place for religious activity? Thus, *Lyng* seems to present a situation where a prudential approach would indicate *more* protection for religious freedom—even more *judicial* protection—than the principled approach can provide.

Advancement of Religion

At the other end of the spectrum, a prudential approach would *not* regard as a harm per se a phenomenon that modern religion clause jurisprudence arguably has viewed as the quintessential evil to be avoided: advancement of religion by the state. Commentators and court decisions sometimes seem to treat religion the way they treat racism or pornography—that is, as an evil to which the state is in principle opposed but which it may be obligated to tolerate, at least in some contexts. But this attitude, though deeply entrenched in some neighborhoods of legal culture, is utterly at odds with our traditions. As Justice Douglas explained, "When the state encourages religious instruction . . . , it follows the best of our traditions. For then it respects the religious nature of our people and accommodates the public service to their spiritual needs."[15] To be sure, state support for religion may sometimes *cause* or *be accompanied by* harms to religious freedom. But in itself it is not a harm at all.

The notion that advancement of religion is a harm per se lies at the root of much of our establishment clause jurisprudence; consequently, discarding that notion would significantly alter our jurisprudence in what from a prudential perspective would seem a wholesome direction. For example, in the companion cases of *Grand Rapids School District v. Ball*[16] and *Aguilar v. Felton*,[17] the Supreme Court struck down state and federal programs designed to strengthen remedial education programs by, among other things, sending public school teachers into parochial schools for limited periods to teach subjects such as remedial reading and math. Although it was undisputed that the programs had "done so much good and little, if any, detectable harm,"[18] and although no one doubted that the purpose of the programs was permissible and indeed laudable, the Court concluded that there was a risk that the programs would have the effect of advancing religion.[19]

A central issue dividing the majority and dissenting Justices focused on whether public school teachers, despite promises to the contrary, might be influenced by the parochial school environment to support religion in their teaching. Justice O'Connor insisted that in nineteen years of experience with the federal program not a single instance of such religious teaching had been reported;[20] Justice Brennan replied that since students attend parochial schools precisely because they desire religious teaching, it could hardly be expected that they would complain even if such teaching did occur.[21] Brennan's reply seems plausible, but it raises a deeper question: If the students who might occasionally receive a smattering of religious teaching as part of their remedial reading or math courses do not object to that teaching, and indeed have chosen to attend parochial schools with the expectation of receiving religious instruction, then what exactly is the harm? How is religious freedom impaired?

Brennan's position evidently assumes that state advancement of religion, even though inadvertent and incident to a beneficial program, is an evil per se. Indeed, such advancement is, it seems, an especially egregious evil: the mere possibility that such advancement might occur justifies striking down a program that provides much needed remedial education to thousands of students. From a prudential perspective, by contrast, such thinking seems deeply obtuse and, as O'Connor observed, "tragic."[22]

Taxpayer Injury

One familiar response to the foregoing discussion suggests that the real injury to religious freedom in the remedial education cases was suffered not by parochial school students, who may indeed welcome religious instruction, but rather by objecting taxpayers who do not want their tax dollars used to support religion. As a general matter, the Supreme Court has refused to recognize payment of taxes as a cognizable injury; forced payment of taxes to be used in part for purposes that a taxpayer believes to be objectionable or even unconstitutional does not even give a person standing to sue. However, the Court's zeal for a nonestablishment principle has led it to create a special exception allowing objecting taxpayers to sue when government subsidizes religion.[23]

This exceptional treatment is difficult to justify on the basis of a realistic and prudential approach to religious freedom. It is true, of course, that payment of taxes to support causes one does not favor is in some sense a very real harm; the taxpayer is poorer, and she may be offended as well. But a taxpayer suffers *these* kinds of injuries whether the objectionable use of public money aids religion or not. So how is this sort of injury, normally not even cognizable, transformed into a violation of the taxpayer's *religious freedom*?

The lazy answer would simply define religious freedom to include a right not to contribute to any cause that may have the effect of aiding religion. But that answer is *too* easy; indeed, it is patently circular, attempting to settle the issue by definitional fiat.

A less question-begging, more realistic approach might start by distinguishing between a taxpayer's *religious objection*—an objection, that is, arising out of religious commitments or beliefs—to supporting a particular public project, on the one hand, and on the other hand a taxpayer's objection, however grounded, to the *religious use* of tax dollars, or to a use that benefits religion. The first kind of objection might plausibly be characterized as implicating the taxpayer's religious freedom insofar as she is being forced to act in contravention of, or at least to support something that is contrary to, her *religious* commitments. By contrast, the injury in the second situation, though real enough, seems more comparable to ordinary taxpayer injury. Thus, a Quaker who sincerely opposes the use of public money to support an undeclared war in Vietnam and an atheist who sincerely opposes the use of public money to support parochial schools both suffer real harm. But the atheist, unlike the Quaker, cannot as plausibly say that his harm consists in being forced to act contrary to his *religious* convictions (unless, that is, he tacitly imports an extremely loose definition of "religion" that for many other purposes he, and we, would probably be unable to embrace).

Ironically, however, in the kind of case where tax payment might plausibly be described as a violation of *religious* commitments, and hence perhaps of religious freedom, current law does *not* recognize the injury. Thus, the atheist's claim would likely be treated as presenting a religious freedom problem, while the Quaker's harm is probably not even a cognizable injury sufficient to confer standing to sue. Measured against a realistic appraisal of harm *to religious freedom,* current law seems topsy-turvy.

There are obvious difficulties, of course, in granting constitutional status to every religion-based objection to the use of public money. So my claim here is a modest one: I suggest only that if payment of taxes for what may be unconstitutional purposes is not normally a harm recognized by the law, then there is no reason why it should be given special status in this context merely because the nature of a particular taxpayer's objection is that the expenditure will have the effect of aiding religion.

This conclusion would have important consequences for what is probably the most persistent, and in a material sense most important, church-state controversy: aid to parochial schools (including many of the voucher programs that seem to enjoy growing political support). Once we recognize that advancement of religion is not an evil per se, and that there is no better reason to recognize taxpayer injury here than in other contexts, it follows that aid to parochial schools is no different from state aid to Chrysler Corporation, or the Shah of Iran, or the family farm, or the National Endowment for the Arts, or a host of other controversial causes and interests. Many people sincerely object—often on entirely plausible grounds of self-interest or political principle or moral scruples—to any of these grants of aid. But our working assumption has been that if government concludes that such aid will serve the public interest, the courts have no call to intervene. And there is no good reason to treat parochial schools differently.

Offense

A different sort of harm that we could call "offense" or "alienation" has been at the core of much recent litigation involving, for example, public religious symbols such as nativity scenes, crosses, and menorahs. Indeed, in view of the apparently growing appeal of "endorsement" thinking, it is arguable that the Supreme Court now treats this sort of injury as the *primary* harm, at least for establishment clause purposes. Conversely, commentators such as William Marshall have argued that "offense" should not count as a constitutional injury.[24] A prudential approach, I think, would be wary of both these contrary positions.

The difficulty arises, I think, because offense *is* a real harm—many people sincerely report that they suffer offense or psychic injury based on what they perceive as governmental endorsement or disapproval of religion—but it is also a complicated one. In the first place, felt offense differs significantly among different people—even among people whose basic religious or nonreligious views largely coincide. Several years ago, in a public high school that two of my children were attending, a controversy arose about the tradition of singing "Silent Night" at the choir holiday concert; views ranged from indignation about the inclusion of the song (expressed not only by non-Christians but by many Christians as well) to resentment (expressed by people identifying themselves both as Christians and Jews) of what they evidently regarded as Grinch-like opposition to a benign tradition. And there was no apparent reason to doubt the sincerity of any of these expressions.

Offense is also a polycentric problem. Eliminating a source of offense to some citizens is likely to offend other citizens. Leave the nativity scene in the traditional display (or "Silent Night" in the school's holiday concert), and some people will believe, sincerely, that the state is promoting Christianity. Take it out, and other citizens will think, sincerely, that the state is "taking Christ out of Christmas," and thereby disparaging Christianity.

The nativity scene example will probably provoke an objection that in fact points to a further complication: we do not regard all offense as equally legitimate, but our criteria for respecting some kinds of offense while discounting other kinds are murky and often question-begging. For example, we are likely to discount offense arising from simple misperceptions of the facts—when an uninformed complainant concludes that the city council's statements as partially reported in the newspapers were meant to endorse (or disparage) Christianity, perhaps, although informed persons who study the statement in context can easily see that this is not so. But the harder problems begin when we consider how to weigh offense based on *accurate* perceptions.

Suppose someone reports: "I deeply resent the fact that the senior senator from Massachusetts is Catholic. Catholics shouldn't serve in public office." A different citizen might be sincerely offended that atheists are allowed to serve in public office. These sentiments may be heartfelt, not to mention broadly consistent both with certain long-standing Anglo-American traditions and with the teachings of revered political thinkers like John Locke, and they are based on accurate perceptions of the world: Catholics and atheists *are* allowed to serve in public office. Nonetheless, today most of us would be inclined to discount *this* type of offense altogether, I expect, because we think it arises from views incompatible with religious freedom. Catholics and atheists have a right to serve in public office, we might say, so this kind of offense simply doesn't register in our calculus.

But if we discount the offense on these grounds, we end up with a circularity: religious freedom means among other things that government must not cause offense or alienation because of religion, but the only kind of offense or alienation that counts is the kind that arises from views consistent with the meaning of religious freedom. In this way, our talk about a seemingly empirical phenomenon—feelings of offense or alienation—becomes merely a deceptive way of importing our own notions of what religious freedom should mean without defending those notions directly.

Finally, offense is to some degree within our control, and we probably want and need citizens to learn to discipline or contain their feelings of offense. In a pluralistic society, in other words, citizens need to learn to be somewhat thick-skinned—even, or perhaps especially, in matters of religion. And we may be more likely to promote such containment by declining to reward feelings of offense, even though they are sincere.

These complications suggest, I think, that it will be very difficult to incorporate legitimate concerns about offense into any judicially manageable approach. Courts ought to be wary about intervening in political decisions on the basis of this harm; they are as likely to aggravate a situation as to improve it. For example, I would suggest that judges have no way of knowing whether their recent incursions into local controversies involving nativity scenes, crosses, menorahs, and slogans (such as the decision invalidating the Ohio motto, "In God, all things are possible")[25] have reduced levels of offense and alienation or have instead aggravated these harms. Perhaps in tacit recognition of this incapacity, judges do not for the most part even pretend to weigh the real harm— that is, actual offense or alienation felt by actual people—that supposedly motivates the judicial campaign against endorsement. Instead they engage in highly earnest (and agonizingly artificial) discussions about what sorts of hypothetical "reasonable observers" should be consulted and what these various hypothetical observers would observe.[26]

Consider, for instance, the debate in *Capitol Square Review Board v. Pinette* between Justice O'Connor, who advocated the use of "a hypothetical observer who is presumed to possess a certain level of information that all people might not share" and who "is similar to the 'reasonable person' in tort law," and Justice Stevens, who argued that O'Connor's observer "comes off as a well-schooled jurist, a being finer than the tort law model," who is "singularly out of place in the Establishment Clause context."[27] Like O'Connor, however, Stevens would not simply honor the actual perceptions of flesh and blood citizens, but would instead require that "an apprehension be objectively reasonable." For example, he opined that "[a] person who views an exotic cow at the zoo as a symbol of the Government's approval of the Hindu religion cannot survive this test."[28] Figuring out which among a variety of actual or possible perceptions is "objectively reasonable" is of course a highly subjective and standardless inquiry—and not a very dignified one. In one case, Justice Brennan discussed in apparent seriousness whether holiday displays including "a menorah next to a giant firecracker" and "a Latin cross next to an Easter bunny" would pass the endorsement test.[29] Reading such discussions, one is sometimes tempted to check back and verify that the volume in hand is *United States Reports,* not *Gulliver's Travels.*

Still, these multiple complications do not negate the fact that offense *is* a real harm. If the "reasonable observers" conjured up by the Justices are hypothetical, the citizens who feel offense at governmental endorsement or disapproval of religion are not. And because offense can be a harm, it is possible that it may in some instances warrant judicial relief.

Consider, for example, the occasionally reported instances in which a public school teacher repeatedly and gratuitously embarrasses a student because of her religious (or agnostic) beliefs—but without affecting the student's grades or imposing any kind of tangible punishment.[30] It seems to me that in an extreme case of this kind, a judicial remedy would be appropriate. So in the end I merely suggest that prudent courts should be very reluctant to intervene when the claimed harm is limited to "offense."

THE FORUM OF ANTIPRINCIPLE

The prudential consideration just discussed—severity of harm—seems obvious and commonsensical (even if it sometimes leads to conclusions at odds with current law). The factor to be discussed now departs more radically from the conventional wisdom of constitutional law.

As noted earlier, received wisdom holds that courts should exercise judicial review in accordance with constitutional principles. I have suggested that there are no satisfactory principles of religious freedom. If I am right, the most obvious consequence is that in this area courts cannot act on the basis of genuine principles. But there is another less obvious but perhaps more interesting consequence: *no one else*—not a legislature, not a school board—can act on the basis of genuine principles of religious freedom either.

It follows that when an institution of government takes some controversial action on the assumption that the action is required by a supposed constitutional principle of religious freedom, we can be confident that the action reflects a basic misconception. And much in the way that appellate courts sometimes remand cases not because a lower court acted contrary to the law but rather because the lower court acted under the misapprehension that the law allowed it no discretion in the matter, judicial intervention in religion controversies might be appropriate when public officials have acted on the mistaken assumption that they were *required* to make a particular decision by some "principle of religious freedom."

Consider the case of *Roberts v. Madigan*.[31] Kenneth Roberts, a fifth grade teacher in a Denver public school, kept a Bible on his desk; and although he never read aloud from it to the students, he did sometimes read the Bible silently during a fifteen-minute individual reading period. In addition, Roberts had a wall poster bearing the words "You have only to open your eyes to see the hand of God"; moreover, 2 of the 239 books in the classroom library (*The Bible in Pictures* and *The Story of Jesus*) had explicitly Christian content. The school principal, Kathleen Madigan, ordered Roberts to keep the Bible out of sight during classroom hours, to take down the poster, and to remove the two Bible books from the classroom library. She also removed a Bible from the main school library. Roberts thought these actions, together with the principal's lack of objection to books on Native American religion, Buddhism, and Greek gods and goddesses, evinced hostility to Christianity.

Together with several students and parents, Roberts filed suit against Madigan and the school district. A lower federal court sided with the principal. Roberts appealed, unsuccessfully.

One might have thought that under a "no endorsement" standard the case would be a hard one. After all, both the conflicting perceptions of the situation—that Roberts was endorsing Christianity, and that

Madigan was disapproving it—are at least understandable, and the record gave no reason to doubt that these conflicting perceptions were sincere. But Judge McKay's opinion for the federal Court of Appeals simply endorsed the principal's view in the most unilluminating and conclusory terms, making no attempt to consider how her actions, such as removing a Bible from the main school library, might also support a contrary perception.[32]

How might the discussion of this case differ under a more prudential approach? Initially, I would suggest that there is a strong prima facie case for leaving controversies of this kind for local resolution. What messages are sent by the teacher's or the principal's action, or what real injury (if any) has been incurred, or what compromises or remedial measures might alleviate concerns are all matters that might be worked out in good faith by the parties in an effort to achieve some sort of accommodation. In a given situation some students might object to Roberts's silent reading of the Bible during class (even if they do not formally complain); other students might be offended by a principal's decree that it is unsuitable to keep a book of Christian scripture on a teacher's desk during school hours even though books about other philosophies and religions are permitted. Competent officials might achieve a compromise; sensitive teachers and administrators might even find a way to use the occasion as an opportunity for teaching lessons about religious commitment, religious diversity, and tolerance.

So a prudential approach might seem to counsel judicial nonintervention, and thus to leave the principal's decisions intact. But there is a complication. It seems in this case that Madigan's ruling did not represent an effort to find a sensible compromise for a difficult practical problem. On the contrary, the evidence does not disclose any objection to Roberts's conduct by anyone except Madigan herself. Moreover, the principal's reasons for opposing Roberts's silent reading of the Bible are significant. Her opposition was apparently not based on any perception that students were silently offended by Roberts's practice; revealingly, no one seems to have inquired into that possibility, or to have regarded it as relevant. Neither was Madigan necessarily personally hostile to Christianity; Roberts and others inferred such hostility, but the inference is not compelled by the reported facts. It seems, rather, that the principal took action because she believed *the Constitution required* her to do what she did.

The majority opinion says simply that "[s]he explained to Mr. Roberts that 'separation of church and state' required that the books be removed.[33] A dissenting opinion explains that the lower court's findings that Roberts had taught and endorsed Christianity

> have no basis in *any* aggrieved testimony of fifth grade students or their parents, past or present. The only "live" complainant in this case was Principal Madigan, whose views on separation of church and state are absolute. She applied a "bright line" approach.[34]

In short, *Roberts v. Madigan* does not present a situation in which local citizens and officials tried in good faith to work out a modus vivendi for a difficult problem. Rather, the case reveals a local school administrator who determines that a situation is unacceptable on the basis of her own staunch commitment to a particular principle of religious freedom. The court then ratifies her action with the equivocal observation that, given her perception of the situation, it was her duty to act as she did.[35]

In a sense these events represent a triumph for the received wisdom of judicial review. The great hope of some constitutional theorists has been that by always proclaiming and acting on the basis of "principle," the judiciary—the "forum of principle"—might teach other officials and citizens to act from principle as well.[36] *Roberts* suggests that the strategy is working with a vengeance—and indeed that nonlawyers may be even more zealous in support of supposed constitutional principles than are the judges themselves.

From a different perspective, however, the case reflects the triumph of intolerance inspired by, or perhaps masquerading as, "principle." On the basis of her commitment to principle, the principal created a controversy where, for all we can tell, none previously existed. And far from promoting mutual respect and understanding, the principal's implacable and the court's more equivocal commitment to principle almost certainly left at least the teacher and the complaining students and parents with the conviction that the school (and perhaps, by inference, "the state") *were* hostile to Christianity. That conviction may or may not have been warranted, but it was surely not dispelled by anything in either the principal's conduct or Judge McKay's conclusory and feckless disclaimer.

More generally, by insisting on the sanctity of a "principle of religious freedom," the courts and constitutional scholars have undermined the ability of communities and institutions to work out acceptable accommodations for competing religious and secular concerns. Perhaps courts might undo some of the damage they have done by intervening on occasion to reverse and remand, for more mature and prudential consideration, decisions made on the basis of a misconceived commitment to "principle."

CONCLUSION

In the course of this chapter I've suggested positions regarding some of the recurring specific controversies that arise under the religion clauses. I've suggested, for instance, that the claims asserted by Native Americans in *Lyng* should have been accepted, but that the familiar objections to parochial school aid and related programs such as voucher plans should be viewed with skepticism.

My suggestions reflect, inevitably, *my* perspective—a perspective that is, again inevitably, severely limited. Sitting in my office, I cannot claim to have the information or experience that would be needed to dictate workable, appropriate resolutions for the tremendously varied problems that arise out of the practice of a multitude of different religions in a multitude of different communities. So people with other perspectives and experiences will doubtless find my specific suggestions unattractive, probably even obtuse.

As a sort of plea in the alternative, I ask readers with this reaction to consider this essay as a kind of backhanded performative demonstration of my larger thesis. There is no realistic expectation that the diverse array of problems and conflicts that we lump together and address under the heading of "religious freedom" can be wisely or sensibly resolved by a few people with training at elite law schools—people who from within the sanctity of their chambers, or their law school offices, ponder the meaning of religious freedom in the abstract and then seek to impose their conclusions across-the-board on the eclectic spectrum of American society. We would do better to follow a more modest, more prudential course—one that would leave room, as Mark Howe suggested, for the "living practices of the American people [to] bespeak our basic constitutional commitment."

5

The Unhappy Demise of the Doctrine of Tolerance

THE FREE EXERCISE clause, according to the Supreme Court, means that government cannot engage in religious persecution. Critics argue that the free exercise clause should mean much *more* than this. But surely we can all agree—can't we?—that the clause should mean at least this much. Would anyone doubt the wisdom of a constitutional prohibition on "religious persecution"?

The question turns out to be more complicated than one might think. I will argue that the reigning prohibition against persecution generates, inadvertently but perversely, a destructive discourse of religious freedom that sponsors demonizing inquiries and ad hominem argumentation. At least, I will argue this eventually—mostly in the next chapter. I cannot go directly to that claim because it is first necessary to consider two other topics: the role that "doctrine" plays in the legal approach to religious freedom, and the shift in religion clause doctrine from an emphasis on "tolerance" to a focus on "neutrality" (which, as noted earlier, is the twin of "equality"). Those topics, important and complicated in their own right, are also essential preliminaries to an account of how a nonpersecution principle—so appealing in the abstract—produces a discourse of demonization.

THE PARADOX OF CONSTITUTIONAL "DOCTRINE"

So let us begin this somewhat wide-ranging investigation by thinking about "doctrine." The essays in Part I focused on what the current discourse of religious freedom takes to be its basic values or commitments—equality and autonomy. In judicial decisions, though, abstract values like these are typically mediated through constitutional "doctrines"—rulelike formulas, often with three or four "prongs"—that purport to state the requirements or "tests" that challenged laws must meet in order to pass judicial scrutiny. In establishment clause controversies, for example, an obvious underlying value or commitment is "religious equality," or "religious neutrality"; but the doctrine the courts have fashioned in an effort to implement these and associated values holds that a law must satisfy three requirements: (1) the law must have a "secular purpose," (2) it must have a "principal or primary effect that neither advances nor inhibits religion," and (3) it must avoid "excessive entanglement" between government and religion. This doctrine is often called the "*Lemon* test" after the case in which it was first announced: *Lemon v. Kurtzman*.[1]

The idea that courts implement constitutional values by fashioning "doctrines" is by now so familiar as to seem inevitable. But current religion clause doctrines also present a conspicuous paradox. Critics often say that the doctrines are so nebulous and indeterminate that they are essentially meaningless. Harvard professor John Mansfield has observed that the Supreme Court's religion clause doctrines and decisions reflect "the incantation of verbal formulae devoid of explanatory value."[2] Douglas Laycock, a leading religion clause lawyer and scholar, once described establishment clause doctrine as "so elastic in its application that it means everything and nothing."[3] And yet even though the Court's doctrines are often said to be next to meaningless, they have not thereby lost their status as objects of intense interest and concern. On the contrary, Justices, lawyers, and scholars argue passionately over whether a particular doctrine should be retained, modified slightly, or replaced—and if so, replaced by what? For all their celebrated emptiness, it seems, religion clause doctrines still count, on some level, for a lot.

This paradox is manifest in the fierce public and scholarly reaction to the Supreme Court's decision, just over a decade ago, in *Employment Division v. Smith*—the peyote case.[4] We will consider the case in more detail later; for now, let us notice one puzzling phenomenon. Before *Smith*, commentators often observed that prevailing free exercise doctrine did not accurately describe the Court's actual cases, and that the doctrine was next to useless in explaining or predicting decisions.[5] Nonetheless, the Court's repudiation in *Smith* of what was widely regarded as settled doctrine produced an outpouring of indignant commentary from churches, libertarian groups, and scholars. (Much younger then, I joined in the chorus of criticism.)[6] Reacting to the near universal condemnation of the decision, Congress promptly and overwhelmingly voted to pass a statute, called the Religious Freedom Restoration Act, that sought to restore the pre-*Smith* doctrine—the same doctrine, yes, that had ostensibly been so ineffectual even when it was nominally in force. The Court then reasserted its role as magisterium over constitutional doctrine by striking down that statute.[7] Though one study has concluded that the change in doctrinal formulations has made little discernible difference in the outcomes of actual cases,[8] interest in the issue remains intense; and it is quite possible that by the time this book is published new legislation will have been adopted attempting to restore the old doctrine. So for all its apparent uselessness either for describing or for predicting actual decisions, the pre-*Smith* doctrine seems to have mattered a great deal to a great many people.

This paradox—the paradox, that is, of judges and lawyers and scholars contending earnestly and sometimes bitterly over doctrinal formulas that seem to make little difference in actual adjudication— might be ascribed to simple naivete: in reality doctrine makes no difference, but judges and scholars mistakenly think it does. This explanation may have some force; but it would be imprudent to dismiss so lightly a large group of judges and lawyers (who are, after all, active participants in the process of adjudication) and scholars (some of whom at least seem to be thoughtful and observant) on the ground that they simply fail to perceive the impotence of legal doctrine. Something more complicated seems to be at work.

Doctrine, perhaps, might be malleable and ineffectual in one sense or on one level, and yet have force or weight on a different level. If so, doctrine might be important and worth fighting about, even though it is also significantly indeterminate.

This is a nebulous suggestion: in order to make it clearer, we need to think more carefully about "doctrine." What role does legal doctrine play in constitutional adjudication? How does a legal doctrine actually work in the resolution of actual cases?

Formalism and Post Hoc Rationalization

One familiar account of the role played by legal doctrine in constitutional adjudication—and an account that though sometimes disparaged turns out to have perennial appeal—might be called the "formal" or "logical" view. In this view, a doctrine determines or dictates the proper resolution of particular controversies in a straightforward, logical way. In a given case, the legal doctrine provides the major premise, the facts of the case make up the minor premise, and the result in the case is deduced from these premises. The *doctrine* says, perhaps, that government cannot advance religion (major premise); the *facts* show that a particular aid program for private schools advances religion (minor premise); the *conclusion* is that the aid program is unconstitutional. Q.E.D.*

At the other, more skeptical extreme stands what might be called the "post hoc rationalization" account of legal doctrine. In this view, doctrine itself is, for practical purposes, manipulable and indeterminate; a judge can usually or always present a conclusion favoring either side in a case as if that conclusion were deduced from accepted doctrine. Since the doctrine itself is indeterminate, something else—politics, perhaps, or ideology, or the personal idiosyncrasies of the judge—must in reality be driving the decisions. But although this "something else" in fact determines the results in cases, the conventions of our legal culture forbid the judge to present her decision as the product of politics or personal idiosyncrasies. Hence, after the decision has been reached, the judge will use doctrine to construct a post hoc, legalistic rationalization for use in the public presentation of the decision.

For reasons already suggested, neither of these views seems wholly cogent with regard to religion clause doctrines. The renowned manipulability of those doctrines precludes a strongly formalistic or deductive account of the role served by doctrine in this area. But if the doctrines were nothing more than a highly manipulable source of post hoc rationalizations, it would seem odd to find judges and legal scholars contending with such fervor over conflicting but ultimately nondispositive formulations of doctrine.

---

* Of course, a proponent of this formalist account need not suppose that the actual *psychology* of judging constitutional cases is as clean-cut as this depiction suggests. He might make a distinction, for example, between the "discovery" and the "justification" of a decision, thereby suggesting that the judge forms opinions about the proper outcome in cases through some (perhaps subconscious) nondoctrinal means—perhaps through "politics," perhaps by relying on "hunches"—and then tests these opinions against authoritative doctrine to see whether they can be justified. Nonetheless, doctrine controls the results in cases by forcing judges to discard unjustified opinions or hunches, and it does so through the formal constraints of logic. See Richard A. Wasserstrom, The Judicial Decision: Toward a Theory of Legal Justification 12–38 (1961).

These objections to the more extreme positions might lead a judge or scholar to adopt a compromise between the formal and skeptical views. Legal determinacy, it might be argued, is a matter of degree. Sometimes legal doctrine dictates a particular conclusion in a case. Sometimes it does not, but even then it narrows the range of decisions a court can plausibly reach. It might be, for example, that establishment clause doctrine is indeterminate with respect to the question of school voucher programs, but that the doctrine plainly forbids outright grants of money to churches.

Most judges and scholars probably hold some version of this compromise, "partial determinacy" view—albeit with differing assessments of the *degree* of determinacy.[9] The compromise view might help to explain why judges and scholars take doctrinal questions seriously even when they also proclaim the indeterminacy of doctrine. If doctrine is *partially* determinate, then it seems likely that what we might call the "zone of determinacy" would differ from one doctrine to another. Under any doctrine, in other words, there will be "hard cases" and "easy cases," but the content of these categories will be different for different doctrines. The fact of "hard cases" reveals the indeterminacy of doctrine; the fact of "easy cases"—of *different* easy cases—makes doctrine meaningful and worth arguing about.

This compromise between the formal and skeptical accounts surely contains a measure of truth. Still, it does not fully capture what seems to be at stake in doctrinal disputes. The problem is that arguments about abstract constitutional doctrine and arguments about results in particular controversies seem to be, at least to some degree, independent of each other; and there does not appear to be any very close correlation between the positions a judge or scholar takes in one kind of dispute and the positions he or she takes in the other kind of dispute. With regard to establishment clause doctrine, for example, both Justice Scalia and Justice Kennedy have called for the repudiation of the *Lemon* test, and both have advocated the replacement of that test by a "no coercion" doctrine.[10] Yet Scalia accepts, while Kennedy rejects, the permissibility of prayer in public school graduation ceremonies.[11] On the specific issue of graduation prayer, Kennedy agrees with Justice O'Connor. Yet he has caustically assailed the "no endorsement" doctrine that O'Connor has consistently sponsored.[12] Justice Blackmun joined O'Connor in embracing the "no endorsement" test, but he and O'Connor decisively parted ways in school aid cases.[13] And these examples could easily be multiplied.

The point can be put more generally. Suppose it were possible to say that although all the possible doctrines are indeterminate in some contexts, cases A, B, and C are "easy cases" under the *Lemon* test while cases D, E, and F are easy under the "no coercion" doctrine, and the "no endorsement" test logically dictates particular results in cases X, Y, and Z. If this sort of description were plausible, then it might also be plausible to suppose that Justice Stevens likes the *Lemon* test because of the results it mandates in A, B, and C, that Justice Kennedy favors the "no coercion" doctrine because of its results in D, E, and F, and so forth. In reality, though, this sort of description seems inaccurate. On the contrary, with respect to the major controversial issues, such as school prayer, parochial school aid, or publicly sponsored religious displays, respectable arguments can nearly always be given for either outcome under any of the leading doctrinal formulations.

Of course, a Justice might believe that even though a particular doctrinal formulation does not compel or guarantee his preferred outcome on a particular issue, that formulation nonetheless has a *tendency* (and a stronger tendency than other formulations) to support this outcome. But just what would such a "tendency" consist of? If a doctrine does not logically dictate a particular result, what would it mean to say that the doctrine has a "tendency" to support that result?

A Third Alternative: The Discourse-Orienting Function of Doctrine

Consider this possibility: even when it does not dictate the results in particular cases, legal doctrine has the power to orient and direct the kind of discourse in which those cases are debated and decided. As an example, take free speech doctrine. Over the years, judges and commentators have proposed a variety of doctrinal approaches to the questions of censorship and speech regulation, including "balancing" approaches, "category" doctrines, and "content neutrality" requirements. In a given case—in a dispute, say, over whether demonstrators have the right to sleep in a public park—nonfrivolous arguments might be made from any of these doctrinal perspectives for either the park authorities or the demonstrators. It would not follow, though, that doctrinal differences are irrelevant to the controversy. On the contrary, although not dictating the conclusion in the case, a doctrinal formulation may powerfully influence the way in which the debate is framed.

If the court employs a balancing test, for example, debate will probably focus on the weight or importance of the interests served by park regulations as compared with the value of the demonstrators' expression (or, perhaps, of expression generally). This sort of debate would be consequentialist in its focus, and its vocabulary would be the diction of "weighing." A category doctrine, by contrast, might foster discussion not so much about the consequences of allowing or restricting this form of expression, but instead about the kind or class of expression at issue. How is "speech" to be distinguished from "conduct"? How should "political speech" be defined, and does this kind of demonstrative conduct fall into that category? A content neutrality doctrine would probably elicit a still different kind of debate—a debate not so much about the proper classification of the specific expression at issue, perhaps, as about the scope and purpose of the regulations on park use.

Acknowledging the "discourse-orienting" function of constitutional doctrine allows us to see merit in both the formal and the skeptical accounts. Like the formal account, the discourse-orienting view recognizes that doctrine matters. Doctrinal formulations may not logically dictate the results in particular cases. But they do mean that the arguments in cases will be carried on in one set of terms, not in some other set of terms, and will be centered on one set of issues or values rather than another set. Like the skeptical account, the discourse-orienting view concedes that insofar as judicial opinions purport simply to deduce a result from a particular doctrine, they usually cannot be accepted at face value. There is more behind a decision—much more—than the doctrinal analysis presented in the opinion.

If the discourse-orienting view accepts some aspects of the other accounts, however, it does so not in the sense of the compromise position described earlier. It does not just split the difference between claims of determinacy and indeterminacy by concluding that doctrine is "partially determinate," or that in some cases the doctrine is determinate and in some cases it is not (though of course these observations might also be correct). Instead, the discourse-orienting view describes a different function or power of legal doctrine—the power to influence the direction and the terms of the discourse in which legal issues are framed and resolved.

That power is important for at least two reasons. First, terms in which a debate is carried on seem likely to affect the outcomes of debate. A particular party or position may be likely to fare better in one kind of argument than in another. In this way, though not directly determining the outcome in particular cases, doctrine might indirectly influence those outcomes. It is in this sense that a judge or scholar might believe that a particular doctrine has a "tendency" to generate particular results, even if it does not logically entail those results.

Second, the terms of constitutional debate and the character of constitutional discourse may be important in their own right, quite apart from the specific results they generate. Scholars have often observed that constitutional discourse is constitutive; how we talk about fundamental legal and political issues helps to determine the kind of political community we are. In this way, the discursive quality of constitutional doctrine is arguably as important as the particular results it directly or indirectly produces.

Assessing Doctrine

Different views of the role played by constitutional doctrine suggest different ways of understanding, and of criticizing, doctrine. A formal view implies that understanding doctrine involves extracting a correct doctrinal statement or formula from the cases and then working out the logical consequences of that formula for concrete controversies. If doctrine is *understood* in terms of its logical consequences, moreover, it presumably should be *evaluated* in similar terms. This approach to doctrine roughly describes the bulk of conventional constitutional scholarship.

From a skeptical perspective, by contrast, this sort of doctrinal analysis seems misconceived. If doctrine is indeterminate, it has no logically entailed consequences; so an effort to understand or criticize it in terms of those consequences is futile. A skeptical scholar might therefore choose to pay no attention to doctrine (or to the "law on the books"), preferring instead to study the "law in action"—that is, the actual conduct of judges and government officials. Or she might believe that legal doctrine is misleading or aesthetically or politically pernicious, or that it serves to legitimate an oppressive legal regime. In that case, she might apply herself to subverting doctrine by showing it to be empty, or indeterminate, or internally contradictory.

From a discourse-orienting view, all these types of analysis may have their uses, but none gets to the heart of the matter. It may be illuminating both to work out the logical implications of doctrine and to show logical gaps or contradictions within doctrine. But the meaning and effect of a legal doctrine are not exhausted by its logical implications. Hence, neither the zealous formalist nor the strong skeptic has fully comprehended the object of his faith, or of her derision.

In understanding doctrine, rather, the scholar must consider its discursive qualities. What kind of debate does a particular doctrine promote? What kinds of issues and concerns does it make salient? Conversely, what kinds of issues and concerns does it exclude from view? What qualities of mind and character does a doctrine seek to call forth? A discourse-orienting approach suggests that in evaluating and criticizing doctrine, the commentator must concern herself not merely with particular results, but with the kind and quality of debate that a doctrine promotes—and with the qualities of character that it tries to elicit from participants in those debates.

This sort of doctrinal analysis is less familiar, in part no doubt because it is more difficult to do than either conventional doctrinal analysis or conventional debunking.[14] But we can use the Supreme Court's important and contrasting free exercise decisions in *Wisconsin v. Yoder* (the Amish school case) and *Employment Division v. Smith* (the peyote case) to explore this discourse-orienting function of legal doctrine.

FREE EXERCISE JURISPRUDENCE BEFORE *SMITH*: THE DISCOURSE OF TOLERANCE

There is a standard account of free exercise doctrine before the Supreme Court's 1990 decision in *Smith* that can be presented in two propositions. First, the Court's official doctrine under the free exercise clause purported to offer generous protection for the exercise of religion by means of a "compelling interest" balancing test. This doctrine was first announced in 1963 in the case of *Sherbert v. Verner*,[15] in which the Supreme Court ruled that a state could not classify a Seventh-Day Adventist as ineligible for unemployment compensation merely because she was unwilling to accept employment requiring her to work on Saturdays. The *Sherbert* doctrine, in the standard understanding, held that if a law burdened the exercise of a person's or group's religion, then the person or group should be excused from obeying the law—unless, that is, the state had a compelling interest in requiring compliance and had adopted the least restrictive means of achieving its objective.[16]

Second, the standard account holds that in actual practice the Court's application of this "compelling interest" doctrine was erratic and half-hearted. Although the doctrine promised strong protection for religion, in reality religious objectors almost never prevailed in their challenges to burdensome laws. Only in a handful of unemployment compensation cases practically indistinguishable on their facts from *Sherbert* and in *Wisconsin v. Yoder,*[17] where the Court sided with Amish parents who objected to sending their children to school beyond the eighth grade, did the Supreme Court actually require free exercise accommodation. In other cases, the Court denied relief, either by finding the state's interests sufficient or by devising excuses for not applying the compelling interest test at all. Writing shortly before the *Smith* decision, Mark Tushnet observed that "people are led to believe that there is a general doctrine of mandatory accommodation, a belief that the Court's decisions basically belie."[18]

Reevaluating the Standard Account

The standard depiction's emphasis on the ostensible "compelling interest" balancing component of pre-*Smith* doctrine deserves reassessment. To be sure, a number of free exercise decisions used the language of "balancing," and of "compelling interests." Given the almost paradigmatic status of a "balancing" conception of the judicial role during this period,[19] it was natural that the Court would sometimes use this kind of language—and that scholars anxious to glean a doctrinal formula from the decisions would seize upon such language to fashion, and ascribe to the Court, a "compelling interest" test. From a more detached perspective, however, it seems doubtful that the concepts of "balancing" and of "compelling interests" were as important—or were intended by the Court to be as important—as scholarly codifications have supposed.

In the first place, the Court did not in fact seriously engage in balancing in its free exercise decisions. Indeed, the standard account itself points out that the compelling interest formulation did not describe the Court's overall practice. Commentators may suppose that in a few cases—especially, perhaps, in *Wisconsin v. Yoder,* the Amish school case—the Court *did* balance the interest in religious liberty against a state's asserted interests. But upon closer inspection, this characterization seems dubious even in the *Yoder* case.

In *Yoder*, Amish parents successfully challenged a Wisconsin law that required them to send their children to school through age sixteen. The majority opinion in *Yoder*, it is true, *did* use some "balancing" language; we will return to this point in a moment. In the end, though, the opinion did not actually "balance" this religious interest against the state's asserted interest in having law-abiding, self-reliant citizens and then conclude that the religious interest was weightier or more important. Instead, the Court argued that the Amish way of life produced just the kind of citizen that the state desired, perhaps more effectively than the public school system did.[20] Hence, the state's interests were not so much overridden or "outweighed"; they were, rather, fully satisfied.

More generally, one can search the Court's free exercise opinions in vain for any sustained attempt to calculate or quantify the respective weight of the state and religious interests and then to balance them against each other in any serious and sensitive way. Not only did the Court fail to perform this kind of balancing; it could not have done so. As Alexander Aleinikoff has shown, the Court never developed any methodology for calculating and comparing diverse social interests, in this or any other area. Indeed, the Court never addressed, or made any serious effort to address, the basic conceptual questions—much less the intractable empirical questions—that a genuine commitment to balancing would have required it to resolve.[21]

A critic might respond that these observations merely underscore the Court's thoughtlessness or hypocrisy; the Court *said* it would use a balancing approach when in reality it could not have pursued this course, and may never have had any intention of doing so. But *did* the Court actually promise to apply a "compelling interest" balancing test? The answer is not as clear as commentators—and some Justices—have supposed. In reality, pre-*Smith* free exercise decisions constituted a motley assortment of rhetoric and rationales. Whether you find in that disparate mix a "compelling interest" balancing test depends largely on what you insist on seeing in the decisions. If you approach the materials from a formalist perspective and with the expectation that they will yield a formal doctrine, then you can easily—and, I admit, quite plausibly—conclude that they support a "compelling interest" test. But if you read the cases without these formalist presuppositions, that conclusion seems more tenuous.

Consider, once again, *Yoder*—arguably the most important free exercise case between *Sherbert* and *Smith*. *Yoder* did not use the term "compelling interest." To be sure, the majority opinion contained some vague balancing language.[22] This language is almost inconspicuous in a lengthy—and at times, perhaps, meandering—opinion mostly devoted to discussion of the concrete facts and claims and of an assortment of reasons that might bear in one way or another on the state's efforts to impose secular education on the Amish. A reader who came to the opinion without years of traditional legal training might barely notice the balancing language. Or, if she did notice it, she might easily regard this language as the sort of obligatory warm-up rhetoric, unilluminating and uninspired, that lawyers and judges (with their wearisome metaphors about the "scales of justice") might be expected to intone as they ready themselves for the real argumentative and analytical work. Conversely, a reader trained to suppose that every judicial decision must result from the logical application of something called a "rule" or "doctrine" to something else called "the facts" of the case will naturally seize upon *Yoder*'s balancing language, vague and scanty though it is, simply because it seems as close as anything the opinion offers to being a formal "doctrine." If this reader has studied other areas of constitutional law and so is already used to "compelling interest" tests as doctrinal frameworks, then he will likely infer that *Yoder* stands for just such a test—even though the decision carelessly neglects to use the canonical terminology.

For readers trained in conventional doctrinal analysis, this interpretation is natural and understandable. The *Yoder* opinion *does* contain language capable of supporting this reading. Nonetheless, from a detached perspective, the "compelling interest" doctrine may seem more the creation of the reader than of the Court. Presented with this doctrinal interpretation, the legally unsocialized reader might be puzzled. "Where did you find *that* in the opinion?" she might ask, or "Aren't you making a little too much out of a few random remarks in a lengthy essay?"

In its capacity to support these different readings (one formalist and doctrinal and the other more flexible and free style), *Yoder* is a microcosm of pre-*Smith* free exercise jurisprudence. Like *Yoder*, some decisions used vague balancing language that lacked the formulaic or ritualistic tone of legal prose designed to convey an official "doctrine" or "test." In *United States v. Lee*, for example, the Court said that "[t]he state may justify a limitation on religious liberty by showing that it is essential to accomplish an *overriding* interest"[23]—thereby suggesting, tautologically, that a state interest is weighty enough to prevail if and only if the state interest is weighty enough to prevail. Other decisions did use "compelling interest" language.[24] Still other decisions focused on the particular context of the dispute—the prison or military setting, for example—and made no attempt to state or apply any general balancing formula.[25] And as late as 1986 the Court seemed deeply confused—not just about what free exercise doctrine *should be* but, if one takes the various opinions in *Bowen v. Roy*[26] at face value, about what free exercise doctrine *was.*

If one approaches these disparate approaches with formalist expectations, one is likely to read them as adopting a "compelling interest" balancing test, with two kinds of qualifications. First, the Court was sometimes careless in its statement of this test; it sometimes neglected to recite the official doctrine or, as in *Yoder* and *Lee,* it recited the doctrine in different, murkier terms. Second, the Court carved out discrete exceptions, or areas in which the "compelling interest" test did not apply at all, such as in prison and military contexts. Conversely, from a less formalist perspective this codification will seem to be an imposition upon the cases. Balancing language will appear to be merely one feature in the Court's rhetorical repertoire, or one item in its capacious inventory of techniques.

Does this less formalist reading imply that the decisions, taken as a body, were incoherent? Not at all. Indeed, relaxing our fixation on the ostensible *Sherbert* formula allows us to perceive with less obstruction the consistent theme that runs through the decisions: this theme suggests simply that the state has a constitutional duty—not an absolute duty, to be sure, but a duty nonetheless—to *accommodate the practice of religion.*

A doctrinal formalist, of course, might cheerfully acknowledge this "duty to accommodate" theme and yet object that it cannot be taken as a satisfactory statement of *doctrine.* Saying that "the state has a nonabsolute duty to accommodate religion" seems almost like saying that "the state should *try,* or should make reasonable efforts, not to interfere with religious practices." This statement might be understood as an exhortation, or as the expression of an aspiration, but it cannot do what *doctrine,* from a formalist perspective, must do: it cannot be logically applied to decide specific cases. Doctrine must say what the state can and cannot do—not what it should "try to do," or what it must "think seriously about doing." For this reason, the formalist might naturally pass over the accommodationist theme as a candidate for doctrine (even though the decisions consistently support that theme) and seize instead upon the "compelling interest" formula (even though the decisions do *not* consistently support *that* theme).

Conversely, if one emphasizes the discursive quality of doctrine over its power to dictate results through sheer logic, this formalist objection to a doctrine framed in terms of accommodation loses much of its force. To be sure, doctrine imposing a nonabsolute duty of accommodation cannot logically determine the results in particular cases. But then, realistically, a "compelling interest" test cannot do that either: everyone knows this. What the accommodationist doctrine does is orient the debate about free exercise problems in terms of accommodation or, to use what I will argue is in this context a practically equivalent term, of *tolerance.*

My argument in this section, in short, is that pre-*Smith* free exercise jurisprudence can plausibly be understood as an effort to inculcate and practice the quality of tolerance, and that this essential aspect of the law has largely been overlooked, or at least marginalized, because of intellectual attachments to the paradigm of "balancing" and to a formalistic view of doctrine. In order to develop this account, I must first briefly discuss the meaning of tolerance. I will then try to show how free exercise jurisprudence before *Smith* worked to cultivate a discourse of tolerance.

The Ideal of Tolerance

The term "tolerance" denotes a complex quality—one with both behavioral and attitudinal aspects. In part, the term means permitting and respecting ideas or behavior with which one disagrees. Lee Bollinger observes that tolerance entails "self-restraint toward what we believe to be without social value."[27] In this respect, tolerance seems an accepting, inclusive characteristic—and one that is essential in a diverse community if people of differing views and values are to live peaceably together.

But tolerance also implies, on the level of behavior, two kinds of limits to the acceptance of difference. First, tolerance is not equivalent to acceptance in the strong sense of approval or endorsement. On the contrary, if an idea or practice is "tolerated," the connotation is that it is untrue or undesirable but that an individual, or the community, "puts up with" it nonetheless.[28] Second, the notion of tolerance implies that one need not or should not allow *all* objectionable ideas or behavior. Even a tolerant person or community will find some ideas or behavior "intolerable." "There are times," Bollinger observes, "when tolerance constitutes moral weakness and is itself properly to be condemned, just as there are times when responding 'intolerantly' is a sign of admirable moral strength."[29]

The idea of "putting up with" something expresses the *behavioral* aspect of tolerance; it describes what a tolerant person or government typically *does* with respect to disagreeable ideas, persons, or practices. However, "tolerance" also connotes a kind of *attitude* or mind-set. A person who "puts up with" others only because he has no choice, or who does so grudgingly and bitterly, would not typically be described as "tolerant." That is because tolerance also connotes a sympathetic, respectful attitude toward other people, or toward ideas and practices different from one's own. A tolerant person is one who tries to see what is good or true in the ideas and practices of others, and who assumes whenever possible that others are acting in good faith.

Closely related to this attitude of charity is a quality of humility, or an active recognition of one's own limitations and of the fallibility of one's own judgment. A person too certain of his own values and views may find it difficult to appreciate the possibility of goodness, truth, and good faith in positions that appear to clash with his own.[30]

However, on the level of attitude as on that of behavior, the notion of tolerance implies limits. A tolerant person *tries* to see the good in the ideas and practices of others, and in doing so she may come to embrace, at least in part, those previously alien ideas and practices. But the notion of tolerance does not require this to happen; a tolerant person, after trying to see another's view in the best possible light, might nonetheless reject that view, and conclude that her own initial view is more helpful or correct. Similarly, a tolerant person assumes where possible that others are acting in good faith; but she knows that this is not always the case, and that a contrary judgment will be indicated in some instances.[31]

In this respect, Charles Taylor's notion of a rebuttable presumption of value is instructive.[32] Taylor urges that in considering other major cultures one ought to presume that these cultures contain truth and value, and he explains the justification for this presumption:

[I]t is reasonable to suppose that cultures that have provided the horizon of meaning for large numbers of human beings, of diverse characters and temperaments, over a long period of time—that have, in other words, articulated their sense of the good, the holy, the admirable—are almost certain to have something that deserves our admiration and respect, even if it is accompanied by much that we have to abhor and reject.[33]

Indeed, "it would take a supreme arrogance to discount this possibility a priori."[34] Nonetheless, the presumption of value is rebuttable, and hence must be confirmed by what one learns in the process of understanding and assessing cultures. Thus, Taylor emphatically distinguishes the rebuttable presumption of value (which he heartily endorses) from a *demand* for recognition of *equal* value in all cultures (a demand which he argues is incoherent and ultimately disrespectful of all cultures).

Taylor's rebuttable presumption of value is at least closely akin to what I am here calling "tolerance." And the ideal of religious tolerance in turn correlates closely with a policy of religious accommodation. To "accommodate" another's religion is not to endorse that religion, or to accept it as one's own. To "accommodate" suggests, rather, treating a different religion with respect, and trying to find ways to avoid suppressing or infringing upon that religion, but without actually adopting it. Tolerance and accommodation are also similar in that both terms suggest limits, not specifiable in the abstract, in what one ought to respect and allow. Thus, a policy emphasizing religious accommodation amounts to the practice of religious tolerance.

Promoting Tolerance

The pre-*Smith* free exercise doctrine of accommodation fostered the practice and discourse of tolerance in several ways. That doctrine *permitted* government to adopt and implement a tolerant position toward unconventional religious practices. In addition, the doctrine *required* government to at least consider the possibilities of accommodating such practices. Finally, the doctrine encouraged the Court, in its better moments at least, to *exemplify* the characteristic of tolerance in its own discussions and decisions.

The first of these functions—that is, *permitting* tolerance—might seem trivial. If "to permit" meant nothing more than "not to forbid," then it would be true that free exercise doctrine permitted tolerance—

but just as true that Fifth Amendment doctrine, or Seventh Amendment doctrine, or Twenty-Fifth Amendment doctrine (if there is such a thing) permitted tolerance: none of these doctrines forbade government from practicing tolerance. Free exercise doctrine, however, permitted tolerance in a more affirmative way. Because of the construction the Court had given to the establishment clause, government was in fact not fully free to practice tolerance toward, or to accommodate, religious practices. Establishment clause decisions insisted that government must be "neutral" in matters of religion, and the *Lemon* doctrine purported to prohibit government from aiding or advancing religion. Since accommodation aids religion and in that sense departs from complete neutrality, accommodation is arguably inconsistent with establishment doctrine, as critics of accommodation have cogently maintained (and as the Court itself has sometimes held).[35] The free exercise doctrine of accommodation occasionally served to dilute or deflect this "no advancement" logic; in some cases the Court rejected nonestablishment-based attacks on legislatively adopted religious accommodations by invoking free exercise values.[36] In this way, free exercise doctrine functioned to preserve a zone within which the discourse and practice of tolerance could proceed.

More forcefully, free exercise doctrine appeared to require that government at least consider accommodating religious practices. Numerous decisions *said* that government must do this; and although the standard of judicial review was uncertain, decisions like *Sherbert* and *Yoder* indicated that there was at least a possibility that the courts might actually enforce this mandate in a particular case. In this way, free exercise doctrine served to make religious accommodation a subject of legislative attention and discussion; and in fact legislatures often did choose to grant religious accommodations.

The Court's decisions also served to express and exemplify the quality of tolerance. Critics might contend that most decisions performed this function badly. While reciting the doctrine of religious accommodation, the decisions may have reduced that doctrine to a kind of rote rhetoric devoid of sincerity or commitment. Michael McConnell expressed a common view when he observed that free exercise doctrine was "more talk than substance."[37] This critical assessment contains a measure of truth, but it needs to be qualified in several ways.

First, even in decisions rejecting free exercise claims, the value of religious tolerance was often expressed, with apparent conviction, in dissenting opinions. In *Goldman v. Weinberger,* for example, the Court upheld a military regulation that had the effect of preventing a Jewish service member from wearing a yarmulke; but a dissenting opinion by Justice O'Connor eloquently advocated the need for greater religious tolerance.[38]

Second, and perhaps more importantly, the fact that a decision ultimately declined to grant the relief claimed by a religious believer did not by itself prove that the Court was insincere in its expression of a commitment to tolerance. As discussed above, the notion of tolerance implies limits to what must be tolerated; it also entails the quality of humility in one's own judgments. So there would be a kind of hollowness—an internal instability, or perhaps a "performative contradiction," as philosophers say—in a doctrine under which courts regularly and self-confidently imposed their own notions of what is and is not tolerable on non-judicial institutions that from a closer vantage point had reached different conclusions in particular cases. Conversely, the best judicial method of promoting the discourse and practice of tolerance might well be for courts to urge a doctrine of tolerance and accommodation, while in most instances respecting the decisions of the various institutions of government about how that doctrine should be implemented.

Finally, in at least one decision the Court expounded and exemplified the ideal of tolerance with skill and conviction. That decision warrants closer scrutiny.

The Tolerance of *Yoder*

We have already referred to the Amish case, *Wisconsin v. Yoder.* The case involved a conflict between the state, which asserted interests in promoting an educated citizenry, and an Amish community, which argued that schooling beyond a certain stage would seriously undermine its religious tradition and way of life. The case thus presented a clash between what in some respects were radically different cultures. Amish culture was deeply religious, communal, and highly traditional. What might loosely be called "modern American culture" was more secular, individualistic, and, at least in aspiration, progressive. From the Amish perspective, the values inculcated in the state's high schools "emphasize[d] intellectual and scientific accomplishments, self-distinction, competitiveness, and social life with other students"[39]—qualities that the Amish faith sought to discourage.

Inevitably, the Supreme Court approached this conflict from the more secular or "worldly" side of the cultural divide. None of the Justices was Amish, of course, or anything close to it. None belonged to a religious community that had retreated from the world, shunning progress and technology. Quite the reverse: all the Justices had of necessity completed not only high school but also college and law school, and all were active participants in public life. In addition, the Court had recently ruled that the establishment clause imposes a regime of public secularism on government: this regime was manifest in the *Lemon* test's "secular purpose and effect" requirements.[40] And the Court had previously expressed its commitment to state-required and state-provided education, a commitment it reaffirmed in *Yoder*.[41]

Although speaking from a distinctly non-Amish perspective, however, the majority opinion by Chief Justice Burger evinced a conscientious effort to appreciate the value of the Amish way of life. The Court repeatedly noted that the Amish had a long history of nurturing the virtues of "reliability, self-reliance, and dedication to work."[42] The majority opinion sympathetically described the Amish philosophy of communal, agrarian life, and it noted that Amish people in many ways exemplified the very qualities the state purported to value, as well as the virtues admired by Jefferson.[43]

In appreciating these values, the Court surely did not *endorse* the Amish religion or culture, or prefer them over the more progressive alternative advocated by the state. On the contrary, the majority's ambivalence toward Amish culture—its mixture of admiration and reservation and, ultimately, its preference for secular, progressive culture— was discernible in its observation that Amish "religious beliefs and attitudes toward life, family, and home have remained constant—*perhaps some would say static*—in a period of *unparalleled progress in human knowledge* generally."[44]

But if this sentence disclosed approval for "unparalleled progress" over "static" tradition, the majority was also cautious in its judgments. In a pivotal paragraph, the Court made three related points that exhibit this humility. First, the Court noted that "in the Middle Ages important values of the civilization of the Western World were preserved by members of religious orders who isolated themselves from all worldly influences against great obstacles." The point was not elaborated, but the suggestion was that even if modern culture is on the whole more viable or attractive than the Amish way of life, the Amish might still be preserving genuine values that modern culture has neglected. Second, the Court observed that the mere fact that Amish views were rejected by a majority of people did not make those views wrong. Finally, the Court reiterated that although society might regard a particular way of life as "odd or even erratic," that way of life should not be condemned so long as it "interferes with no rights or interests of others."[45]

The generosity and modesty in this approach become conspicuous when the majority opinion is contrasted with the partially dissenting opinion of Justice Douglas. Douglas insisted that the majority's sympathetic characterizations of Amish life were "quite irrelevant." The state must be neutral toward religion, said Douglas: religion is religion is religion, whether or not the particular religion has a long history and whether or not its members are hardworking and law-abiding.[46] Though he criticized the majority for reciting the virtues of Amish religion, however, Douglas's own comparative assessments of modern and Amish cultures are readily discernable in his descriptions. And by contrast to Burger's ambivalence, Douglas's assessments reveal no nuance or hint of doubt. Modern American culture is described in unqualifiedly positive terms: it is "the new and amazing world of diversity that we have today." This world recognizes "the right of students to be masters of their own destiny"; a student is free to become "a pianist or an astronaut or an oceanographer."[47] By contrast, Douglas's depiction of Amish culture is undeniably dark: "If [a child] is *harnessed* to the Amish way of life by those in authority over him and if his education is *truncated*, his entire life may be *stunted* and *deformed*."[48] Although castigating the majority for reciting Amish virtues, Douglas was also moved to list some ostensible Amish vices: drinking, a preoccupation with filthy stories, rowdyism, and a suicide rate as high as that of the nation as a whole.[49]

In the end, Douglas did not side entirely with the state; he would allow Amish children to choose on their own to remain within their culture, and thus to forgo "entry into the new and amazing world of diversity that we have today." But this was purely a concession to individual autonomy. There was no hint of acknowledgment in Douglas's opinion that Amish religion or culture might embody important values that the larger culture had neglected.

The markedly divergent attitudes reflected in the majority opinion and in Justice Douglas's dissent nicely illustrate the analysis by Charles Taylor referred to earlier. Discussing the familiar attitude that smugly assumes the superiority of one's own culture and seeks to impose that culture on everyone, Taylor notes that so-called "liberal neutrality" is not immune to this defect. On the contrary, "Western liberal societies are thought to be supremely guilty" of adopting this position, which consequently produces the "marginalization of segments of their populations that stem from other cultures."[50] It is difficult not to discern such an attitude—and consequence—in Douglas's opinion.

Conversely, the majority opinion, in appreciating the Amish's long history of harmonious communal life, exemplifies Taylor's suggestion that a culture which has provided meaning for many people over a long period of time is "almost certain to have something that deserves our admiration and respect."[51] That opinion also exhibits the humility that must accompany Taylor's rebuttable presumption of value. As Taylor explains: "We only need a sense of our own limited part in the whole human story to accept the presumption. It is only arrogance, or some analogous moral failing, that can deprive us of this."[52]

FROM TOLERANCE TO NEUTRALITY

I have been arguing that pre-*Smith* free exercise jurisprudence and the *Yoder* opinion in particular reflected a commitment to tolerance. The Court's decision in *Smith,* the peyote case, signified a constitutional shift to the ideal of neutrality—already a long-standing ideal in establishment clause jurisprudence. Though its proponents see neutrality as an advance over tolerance, or as *more than* tolerance, I will argue that the shift to neutrality in reality reflects a backward step toward *intolerance.* The argument will require us to take a much closer look at the *Smith* doctrine and (in chapter 6) at the next major decision that solidified the new approach: the *Hialeah* "animal sacrifice" case.

Tolerance or Neutrality?

I have suggested above that the consistent doctrinal theme in pre-*Smith* free exercise jurisprudence was the government has a (nonabsolute) duty to accommodate the practice of religion. In *Smith,* the Court disavowed that doctrine. Rejecting the claims of Native Americans who had used peyote in religious ceremonies, the Court declared that exemptions are not constitutionally required so long as the law burdening religion is "generally applicable" and "neutral."[53] Although *Smith* indicated that legislatures may still choose to grant religious exemptions, the decision deprived the accommodation policy of its constitutional status and force. In effect, *Smith* substituted neutrality for tolerance as the constitutional commitment.

Whether or not one agrees with the decision, the underlying reasons for the change in doctrine are understandable. "Neutrality" in matters of religion promises attractive advantages for both the substance and process of constitutional law. So we will need to pay attention to both dimensions—the substantive and the process dimensions—of the neutrality approach.

In its substantive content (or, perhaps, its lack thereof), religious "neutrality" is a close corollary of, or even a virtual synonym for, the ideal of religious "equality" that I have discussed in chapter 1. The assumption is that by remaining scrupulously "neutral" in matters of religion, government will be treating all religions equally. This is an inviting prospect. By contrast, the notions of tolerance and accommodation may seem less appealing. Those notions arguably give religion both more and less than it deserves.

Accommodation arguably gives religion too much because in occasionally exempting religious objectors from generally applicable laws it confers a benefit that nonreligious objectors would not receive. For instance, while exempting the Amish from a compulsory schooling law, the Court in *Yoder* made it clear that a nonreligious objector—for some reason the Court chose Henry David Thoreau as its hypothetical example—would not be entitled to a similar exemption.[54] Critics argued that this kind of accommodation gave religion preferential status.

At the same time, "tolerance" may seem judgmental and condescending; it suggests that some person or position is in a superior position relative to others that are merely "tolerated." I earlier noted Thomas Paine's condemnation of tolerance as a deception and a mere "counterfeit" of intolerance. The ideal of "neutrality," by contrast, maintains that no position is preferred; all positions, whether religious or nonreligious, have equal value in the eyes of the law.

The difference between the ideals of tolerance and neutrality, and the relative appeal of neutrality, can be understood by comparing

Charles Taylor's rebuttable presumption of value with an alternative that he also considers: the *demand* for recognition of *equal* value. As I have mentioned, Taylor himself criticizes this demand, arguing that if everyone and every position is "respected" because of a conclusive presumption of equal value, then no one and no position is respected on their own merits—which is tantamount to saying that no one is truly respected at all.[55] Still, the appeal of the contrary position is readily understandable. After all, a person or government committed merely to a *defeasible presumption of value* might conclude, even after sympathetic examination, that a particular religious or nonreligious position has less value than some other positions—or even, perhaps, no value at all. Conversely, a person or government bound by a requirement or *conclusive presumption of equal value* would seem to be precluded from reaching these troublesome conclusions. This position of mandatory equality and neutrality resonates with the popular beliefs that government is obligated to treat all persons with "equal concern and respect," and that government is forbidden to act or speak in ways that will cause any citizen to feel like a lesser member of the community on religious grounds.[56]

In addition to its intrinsic substantive appeal, the ideal of neutrality is attractive for institutional or "process" reasons. We noted earlier the perennial attraction of a "formalist" approach to constitutional adjudication: in this conception the court simply applies "the law" to "the facts" and deduces the correct result. We also noted that modern religion clause jurisprudence falls far short of satisfying the formalist ideal. But perhaps, one might think, that is because religion clause doctrine has been badly formulated. As the earlier discussion revealed, tolerance is a complex quality: "tolerance" acknowledges that some things are "intolerable," and the line between what is and is not tolerable cannot be drawn in the abstract. Consequently, tolerance cannot plausibly be reduced to anything resembling a "rule" that a court might simply enforce according to its terms.[57] By contrast, the ideal of neutrality at least *seems* to be more susceptible to rulelike formulation and application. Indeed, establishment clause decisions sometimes describe "neutrality" in terms of a flat command: government is simply ordered to be "neutral," period.[58]

From a formalist perspective, therefore, neutrality may seem a more eligible candidate for adoption into constitutional doctrine. The apparent rule-susceptible quality of neutrality seems to have been especially important to Justice Scalia, author of the majority opinion in *Smith.* Scalia has not disguised his desire for a doctrine under which a court can simply look at a challenged law and determine whether it is valid, without becoming entangled in interest balancing, prudential judgments, questions of degree, and "totality of circumstances" assessments.[59] The *Smith* decision sought to achieve that goal. Henceforth, the majority said in essence, the Court will simply look at a law to see if it is "generally applicable" and "neutral." If it is, the Court's inquiry is over. Case closed.

The apparent formalist virtues of *Smith's* neutrality doctrine exert an appeal that is to some extent independent of the appeal inherent in the substantive content of a doctrine that resonates with our long-standing commitment to "equality." A closer examination of the doctrine's formalist promise is therefore in order, not only because that promise gives the doctrine much of its appeal, but also because this examination will prove illuminating when we return to consider the doctrine's substantive content as well—and its effects on the *discourse* of religious freedom.

"Neutrality" and the Promise of Formalism

If the *Smith* doctrine could actually work in the way that Justice Scalia contemplates, then perhaps the formalist ideal would be achievable after all. But can *Smith's* neutrality-oriented doctrine, with its focus on "general applicability" and "neutrality," actually achieve the formalist vision?

The short answer, which will need elaboration, is that neither of *Smith's* criteria—neither "general applicability" nor "neutrality"— can be applied in a merely formal or logical way. Instead, both criteria have the effect of forcing courts to determine constitutionality by considering (or, more accurately, *constructing*) legislative intent or motivation. Nor is there any merely formal method—or, for that matter, any generally accepted method at all—for making that construction. Consequently, the formalist aspirations of the *Smith* doctrine are doomed to frustration.

"General applicability." The criterion of "general applicability" may appear, at first glance, to be just the sort of test a formalist would want; it implies that a judge can simply check the text of a challenged law to see whether the law is generally applicable or not. This is an inviting

prospect, perhaps, but it also turns out to be an illusory one. That is because on a purely formal or logical level, *every law* is generally applicable in one sense, while in another sense *no law* is generally applicable. As a formal matter, therefore, the requirement of general applicability is simply useless in distinguishing valid from invalid laws.

A little reflection shows how this is so. Every law selects a defined class of persons (or legally cognizable entities, like corporations) and extends to that class some sort of legal treatment, such as a penalty, benefit, or duty. The class might include individuals with an annual income above a certain level, or persons who have committed murder or larceny, or out-of-state corporations doing business within a state; the legal treatment provided for these classes might be, respectively, a particular rate of taxation, or a jail term, or a registration requirement. Regardless of the particular class defined by the law and the particular legal consequence attached to membership in the class, however, the law is both "generally applicable" and *not* "generally applicable," depending on how the term is used. The law *is* generally applicable in the sense that it applies to every person within the jurisdiction: everyone is subject to the specified legal consequence *if* he, she, or it commits the defined act or otherwise possesses the characteristic of belonging to the defined class. The law is *not* generally applicable in the sense that the sanction or benefit or requirement it provides applies only to persons in the defined class, which will be a subset of the population generally.[60]

Consider, for example, a law providing that "any person who takes the property of another without the consent of the owner is guilty of a felony." Is this law "generally applicable"? In one sense it is; it covers everyone *if* he or she commits the defined crime. In another sense it is not; the penalty or status it imposes applies only to thieves. The same analysis can be applied to any law. Upon reflection, therefore, the answer to the question whether a law is "generally applicable" will always be "yes, in one sense; no, in another sense."

This conclusion may appear counterintuitive: some laws at least *seem* to be generally applicable in a way that others are not. The clearest case would be a law imposing a penalty or disability on only one person; and if we think about that kind of law, we can perhaps appreciate both the logical limitations and the rhetorical possibilities of the "general applicability" criterion. So let us suppose, for example, that Harold Stassen's social security number is 123-45-6789, and also that Congress, weary of Stassen's futile presidential campaigns but not wanting to single him out by name, enacts the following law: "Any person with the social security number 123-45-6789 shall be ineligible to run for public office." As a merely logical matter, the analysis given above still holds. In one sense, that is, the Stassen law applies only to Stassen. In another sense it applies to everyone; it prohibits all persons from running for office *if* they fall into the defined class (even though in fact this is a class of one). The law is in this sense "generally applicable," just as a law that prohibits threatening the life of the President would be "generally applicable" even if only one person were ever actually tempted to consider making such a threat. Of course, there are plenty of substantive reasons why the Stassen law is objectionable while the presidential protection law is not. But these reasons are independent of the quality of being "generally applicable" *in a formal sense.* In that formal respect, the laws do not differ.

Still, this analysis seems to neglect a critical commonsensical distinction. Challenged to articulate the distinction, someone might explain that although both laws define classes consisting of a single person, the Stassen law was *consciously intended* to apply only to one known person. In the case of the presidential protection law, by contrast, Congress presumably did not know that only one person would want to threaten the President; the class defined by the law happened to include only one person, but the law was not designed in that way. Or someone might say that the class in the Stassen law *could not have* included more than one person, while the class defined by the presidential protection law *could have* included more than one person—even though, as things turned out, it didn't.

Whether these explanations accurately capture the significant distinction is questionable. Suppose, for example, that Congress believes that only one person—Lady Fanny of Omaha, say—is willing and able to threaten the life of the President, and that Congress passes the presidential protection law to stop that one person. Would it follow that the presidential protection law is objectionable in the same way that the Stassen law is objectionable? Or would the Stassen law be less troublesome if the Social Security Administration on rare occasions randomly reissues numbers, so that it is just barely possible that someone besides Stassen may be included in the defined class? But we need not pursue these questions here. The critical point is this: whether or not the explanations just mentioned precisely capture the distinction in the laws that we intuitively sense, they do suggest that the relevant difference, if there is one, has something to do with what Congress had in mind, or with what Congress was trying to accomplish, by drafting the laws in the way that it did.

In short, the laws are distinguishable not because one is "generally applicable" *in any purely formal sense* while the other is not. They are different, rather, because the Stassen law seems to be the expression of an illegitimate or forbidden purpose (a purpose that would taint the law even if it happened that people besides Stassen were kept from running for President), while the presidential protection law seems to be based on an entirely legitimate purpose (even if it happens that only one person's behavior is altered, or punished).

That sort of difference in the legitimacy of the laws' respective purposes may be real and significant, and "general applicability" might be understood as an oblique and somewhat confusing way of referring to that difference. Still, general applicability is not something that inheres in the text of the law itself; it is a sort of catchword referring to something independent of the text, such as legislative motivation or purpose. And once general applicability is understood in this way—that is, as a shorthand or marker for some extratextual factor such as legislative motivation—then it becomes clear that general applicability cannot support the sort of formalistic adjudication in which the court simply applies constitutional doctrine to legislative text and deduces the proper conclusion.

This conclusion serves to negate a key virtue claimed for the *Smith* doctrine—but only in part. If "general applicability" turns out to be an oblique reference to legislative motivation or purpose, then it follows that a judge cannot just read *the text* of a challenged law and say whether it passes the "general applicability" test. Instead, the judge will have to inquire into (or at least make tacit assumptions about) *legislative motivation* or purpose. But suppose that legislative motivation or purpose is itself an ascertainable fact: if it is, then a rule requiring "general applicability" might be amenable to formal application, even though that application would require the court to discover a "fact" outside the text.

The problem is that legislative motivation or purpose is *not* a "fact" to be discovered. Before elaborating that problem, however, we should first consider what seems to be the more important criterion in the *Smith* doctrine: neutrality.

Neutrality. Smith held that laws burdening religion will be upheld if, in addition to being "generally applicable," they are also "neutral." The notion of religious neutrality comes in many versions, and it has been subjected to numerous critiques. For now, let us notice only one difficulty, which concerns what might be called the *locus* of neutrality. Where, or in what dimension or respect, must a law be "neutral"? Is it enough that a law be neutral in its *text*—that it avoid, in other words, explicitly naming religion for preferential or unfavorable treatment? Must the law also be neutral toward religion in its *effects* or *consequences?* Or is *motivation* or *purpose* the locus of neutrality, so that a law not actually animated by a purpose of helping or hurting religion might be approved even though it has such nonneutral consequences? The first version would place the locus of neutrality in the *text* of the law itself, the second would find it in the "output" of the law (its *effects* or *consequences*), and the third would locate it in the "input" that produced the law (its *motivation* or *purpose*).

If *textual* or facial neutrality were sufficient, then the Court might indeed achieve the formalist ideal—so long, that is, as it could develop a reliable lexicon of language that is religious or that names religion. (This is, in reality, a huge complication, but one that we need not pursue here.) This "textual neutrality" position would resemble the "formal neutrality" long advocated by Philip Kurland and a few other commentators.[61] Kurland argued that the religion clauses should be construed to mean that a law may not use religion as a criterion of classification, either to impose a burden or to confer a benefit. Kurland's proposal has generated ongoing interest—but also powerful objections. In this context, the principal objection to requiring neutrality only in a law's text, not in its consequences or purposes, is that this position allows for "religious gerrymanders."

As an illustration, suppose the County Commission, moved by hostility to the New Age Four Square Church, wants to preclude that church from running a day care center in its building located at 911 Main Street. If the Commission adopts an ordinance providing that "the New Age Four Square Church shall not operate a day care center," the law would violate a textual neutrality standard because it explicitly names religion for the purpose of imposing a legal burden or restriction. But the Commission can achieve its goal by being just slightly more adroit in its drafting. For example, the ordinance might forbid the operation of a day care center on the nine hundred block of Main Street. If the requirement of neutrality applies only to laws that explicitly name religion in their text, in short, government might readily achieve almost any objective of aiding or hindering different religions through the crafty drafting of laws.

Partly for this reason, most judges and commentators have not been satisfied with a merely facial or textual neutrality, and have instead urged a more substantial neutrality. In the abstract, this more substantial neutrality might be applicable to the output or effects of a law, or to its input or purpose, or to both. The *Lemon* establishment clause doctrine, for example, appears to require neutrality—it dubiously treats secularism as a kind of "neutrality"—in both the purposes and effects of laws. However, the *Smith* doctrine is self-consciously calculated *not* to require neutrality in the realm of consequences or effects. Under pre-*Smith* law, after all, an assertion of nonneutral effects was the core of a claim for free exercise accommodation. Free exercise objectors in essence contended: "This law [prohibiting the use of drugs including peyote, for example], although neutral toward religion on its face, has the effect of burdening the practice of our religion." *Smith* clearly ruled that this sort of claim would no longer be recognized under free exercise doctrine. So the more substantial neutrality required by *Smith* seems of necessity to be "input" neutrality—that is, neutrality in legislative motivation or purpose. *Smith* means, in essence, that a law violates the free exercise clause if either its text or *its motivation or purpose* is not "neutral" toward religion.

The application of *Smith*'s "neutrality" to motivation or purpose dispels the more grandiose formalist dream—the dream, that is, of a doctrine that can be logically applied without looking beyond the text of the challenged law. Once again, though, a more modest formalist ideal might still be realizable. If legislative motivation or purpose were a "fact" capable in principle of being discovered, then a doctrine of "input" neutrality might still allow for adjudication through the straightforward and logical application of doctrine to "the facts."

So the "neutrality" criterion under the *Smith* doctrine brings us around to the same question that the "general applicability" criterion left us with: Is legislative motivation or purpose an ascertainable "fact"? If it is, the *Smith* doctrine can plausibly promise something at least in the vicinity of the formalism that jurists like Scalia so ardently desire. The problem, it turns out, is that legislative motivation or purpose is just not that sort of thing.

The fiction of legislative motivation. Legislative motive tests have sometimes been criticized on the ground that this kind of collective motivation is difficult for courts to ascertain with any accuracy.[62] How can we be sure what motivated the legislators who voted for a challenged law, when most of them may never have explained their votes (and when in any case such explanations by legislators—that is, by politicians—are notoriously not to be taken at face value)? But insofar as this criticism suggests merely that courts are likely to make factual errors in discerning motivation, it understates the difficulty. The major obstacle to inquiries into legislative motivation is not evidentiary—although the relevant evidence may indeed be scanty and unreliable—but rather conceptual and even ontological. That is because the "intent of the legislature" is not something that exists at all in a way that would permit it to be treated as a discrete or elemental "fact" to be discovered.

Legislative motivation is, instead, a construct. And the fundamental problem is that there does not seem to be any persuasive or generally accepted account of how it should be constructed. For any law of even moderate complexity, in other words, legislators will probably have supported or opposed the law for a variety of reasons, some of which may be obscure even to the legislators themselves. A court will probably not have reliable evidence of the motivations of more than a few lawmakers; but even if it did, there is no accepted method of aggregating these diverse individual motivations into a single, controlling "intent of the legislature."[63] The absence of any accepted or uniform method becomes painfully apparent upon even a cursory examination of the multitude of diverse, creative, and often conflicting ways in which courts construct "legislative intent" from statutory text, committee reports, drafters' statements, sponsors' statements, postenactment statements or actions, and even from nothing at all—that is, from the failure of legislatures to do or say anything on an issue.[64]

Legislative motivation (or intent, or purpose), in short, is not a fact to be discovered—not even a very elusive or hidden fact; it is more in the nature of a fiction. As a consequence, for any law that is controversial a court will almost surely have a range of choices about how to construct this fiction.

To be sure, the range is not infinite. Even fiction, as opposed to "fantasy" or theater of the absurd, must maintain at least a loose connection to what is "real," or at least to what is possible. If a fiction about legislative motivation is to be plausible, readers must be able to believe that at least some legislators might have supported such a law for the reason assigned. Consequently, evidence is not irrelevant; in crafting a credible fiction it is helpful to point to facts or statements suggesting that at least some legislators *did* consciously hold the view that the court elevates into the "intent of the legislature." In the end, though, the fact remains that legislators, like other human beings, are diverse in their values and views; and, also like other human beings, they are typically neither inveterate devils nor consummate angels. Hence, for any law sane enough to get enacted but objectionable enough to provoke serious political and legal opposition, there will likely be evidence to support either a charitable or an uncharitable characterization of the legislative purpose or motive.

So a court engaging in motive analysis will have a choice. It can choose to be charitable, and thus in effect to defer to the legislature by fashioning a fiction in which the legislative motivation is respectable. Or the court can be ungenerous; it can highlight the unfavorable evidence, thus painting a picture of illicit motivation.

This conclusion—that is, that legislative motivation or purpose is necessarily a construct that can usually be constructed in quite different ways—deals a fatal blow to the hope that the *Smith* doctrine can achieve the formalist dream. The criteria of "general applicability" and "neutrality," it turns out, cannot simply be applied either to the "text" or to "the facts" to generate results in deductive fashion. Instead, both criteria mandate a consideration of legislative motivation or purpose—which turns out to be a factor that a court cannot deduce or find but instead must construct.

But how is a court to construct that dispositive element? The question brings us back to the substance of the neutrality doctrine, and to its troublesome implications for the discourse of religious freedom.

DISTORTION AND DEMONIZATION

We have seen that in *Smith* the Supreme Court repudiated the loose doctrinal approach exemplified in *Yoder*—an approach, I have argued, that supported a discourse oriented toward tolerance—and fashioned in its place a doctrine whose central tenets required of challenged laws only "general applicability" and "neutrality." Both these criteria, I have argued, have the effect of making the constitutionality of challenged laws depend on the fictional or constructed entity of legislative motivation. And we can now begin to see how, in doing this, the *Smith* doctrine inadvertently promotes a free exercise discourse of distortion and demonization.

The term "distortion" is simply another way of saying that the legislative motive that is constructed and ascribed to a legislature will not, and typically could not, accurately and fully describe the actual motives of the various legislators. In theory, this sort of distortion need not be ungenerous or unwelcome. Suppose a court sifts through the variety of possible motives that might plausibly have generated a controversial law and constructs a wise and benevolent purpose, which the court then attributes to the legislators. This characterization would presumably be gratifying to the legislature, but it would still be a charitable distortion. Or, if "distortion" sounds inescapably pejorative, it would be a benign "oversimplification."

Although the distortion that occurs in the construction of legislative motivation *can* be charitable, however, the dynamics of adversarial discourse under a motive-oriented doctrine virtually ensure that it will often be less generous. If the invalidation of a law turns on a finding of illicit motivation, that is, then parties challenging a law will have every incentive to present their opponents' motivation not in the worst *possible* light, perhaps, but in the worst *plausible* light. Ad hominem argumentation is commonly deplored as an unfortunate and demeaning feature of political campaigns and debates. A motive approach to constitutional adjudication, however, not only permits such argumentation; the approach in essence *demands* that legal debate be carried on in these terms, and ensures that the outcome of constitutional issues will turn on the effectiveness of this kind of pejorative characterization. In short, the motive approach promotes a constitutional discourse in which advocates dedicate their efforts to demonizing their opponents.

Of course, a court is not obligated to accept demonizing characterizations. Courts often adopt deferential constructions of legislative purpose. A court can, in other words, embrace the notion of charity in interpretation and follow the familiar counsel to interpret an object—in this case, the legislative purpose—so as to make it "the best it can be." If this deferential course were uniformly followed, however, it would effectively end the practice of judicial review under the free exercise clause (except, perhaps, when a legislature is so clumsy as to commit religious discrimination on the face of the text). Conversely, if a court wishes to invalidate a law, the motive approach will lead it to eschew charity, and to adopt the "worst plausible construction" of legislative intent. Indeed, if your goal is to invalidate a law, then paradoxically you make the law's purpose "the *best* it can be"—the best, that is, for achieving your goal of invalidation—precisely by making it the *worst* it can plausibly be.

Consequently, a neutrality-oriented doctrine focusing on legislative purpose or motivation is not merely *different from* a doctrine focusing on tolerance; a neutrality doctrine is in a sense the *opposite of* a doctrine of tolerance, at least in the discursive tendencies it promotes. A doctrine of tolerance calls for an effort to see the goodness, truth, and good faith in positions different from one's own. A doctrine of neutrality, by contrast, has the effect of encouraging efforts to see and depict other positions in the worst plausible light.

To this point, my argument that a neutrality-oriented doctrine will lead to a discourse of demonization has been abstract. I have been trying to identify, that is, an internal dynamic or logic in a "neutrality" doctrine that naturally generates this sort of demonizing discourse. But is this abstract analysis purely "academic" in the pejorative sense of that term? Or does the logic I have described actually manifest itself in real decisions? The next chapter addresses that question.

6

Demons in the Discourse

THE PRECEDING CHAPTER described an internal logic, or doctrinal dynamic, that leads ineluctably to a discourse of demonization. That logic or dynamic might be summarized as follows. A commitment to religious "equality" leads naturally to constitutional doctrines that impose a requirement of "religious neutrality" on government: government treats religions "equally," we think, by being "neutral" toward them. But then it seems miserly—almost pointless—to limit that requirement of neutrality to the *text* of laws adopted by the state, and thus to forbid only overt and explicit religious discrimination. A more substantial neutrality seems to be demanded. What form should that more substantial neutrality take? Since religions differ greatly in their interests, activities, and beliefs, it seems impractical and probably impossible to demand that laws and government actions be neutral in their "output" or *consequences,* or that they burden or benefit all religions equally: the consequences of any law will inevitably be more favorable toward the beliefs and interests of some religions than others. So the demand for a more substantial neutrality evolves naturally into a requirement that focuses on "input"—government must be religiously neutral in its *motives or purposes*—and hence into a prohibition on laws or actions that are motivated by a desire to discriminate against or to persecute any religion.

But this sort of doctrine—a doctrine, that is, that makes "motive" or "purpose" dispositive of constitutionality—inevitably encourages opponents of a particular law to try to show that the law was animated by religious hostility or bigotry. A neutrality doctrine thus sponsors a constitutional discourse in which adversaries try to demonize each other, or to portray each other in the worst plausible light.

That is the pernicious dynamic that the preceding chapter described, though in abstract terms. This chapter examines the working of that dynamic in concrete cases. I look first, and somewhat summarily, at two major establishment clause cases. I will then consider in greater detail the decision (the animal sacrifice case) that is the leading example of the Supreme Court's current free exercise doctrine.

DEMONIZATION IN ESTABLISHMENT CLAUSE DISCOURSE

As noted earlier, the first requirement in the three-pronged establishment clause doctrine, or the so-called *Lemon* test, requires that a law have a "secular purpose." The doctrine thereby invalidates laws primarily devoted to "religious" purposes or objectives. As it happens, only a few of the Supreme Court's decisions have turned on this requirement; more often the decisions have been made on the basis of the other two requirements focusing on "effects" and "entanglement." However, the few decisions that have turned on "purpose" serve to illustrate the demonizing dynamic that I have described above.

A good example is *Epperson v. Arkansas*,[1] in which the Court struck down an Arkansas law, adopted by state initiative in the 1920s, prohibiting the teaching of evolution in the public schools. The Court held that the law had been adopted for the purpose of protecting, and thus aiding, fundamentalist Christianity.

How did the Court know that the law had been enacted for this purpose? One possibility might be that no other plausible purpose could even be imagined; so even without any supporting evidence the Court's construction would be persuasive. And indeed, for many educated people in this country, this conclusion may seem self-evident. Is an antievolution measure the work of "fundamentalists"? Is the pope Catholic?

In fact, though, there were other possibilities. Though he voted to strike down the law on other grounds, for example, Justice Black argued that the majority's ascription to the state of an impermissible purpose of helping fundamentalist religion was unpersuasive: the state might simply have wanted to avoid inserting into the curriculum a subject that was unduly controversial and divisive.[2] One can also imagine that some citizens may have believed—whether reflectively or carelessly, and whether on religious or scientific or mixed grounds—that the theory of evolution was simply *false*: even today it remains true, to the chagrin of the more scientifically orthodox, that not every educated person who studies the matter finds the prevailing accounts of evolution persuasive.[3] Other voters might have opposed teaching evolution because they favored a practical, skills-oriented program and saw no need to distract students with speculative questions about remote biological origins. Among the thousands of Arkansas citizens who voted on the measure, it is plausible to suppose that some citizens were influenced by any or all of these grounds—and perhaps by other considerations that might seem surprising or far-fetched but that nonetheless were not equivalent to a desire to advance fundamentalist religion.

Without deigning to notice the array of possible purposes, however, the majority opinion by Justice Fortas—a man prodigiously blessed with self-esteem[4]—declared peremptorily that "there can be no doubt"[5] that the state's motivation had been illicit. For direct evidence, the Court cited a newspaper advertisement and four letters to the editor.[6] In addition, the Court quoted a law review article by the Dean of the University of Arkansas School of Law (written almost three decades after the law had been passed), and several secondary sources (mostly general histories also written long after the enactment of the law).[7]

The Court also inferred that the Arkansas law must have had the same religious purpose as the Tennessee antievolution law of Scopes trial fame[8] (and remembered by most of us in connection with the movie *Inherit the Wind*—which itself deviated dramatically from the historical facts).[9] The Arkansas and Tennessee laws were not identical: whereas the Tennessee law had expressly stated a religious purpose, the Arkansas statute (enacted after the Tennessee law and, significantly, after the Tennessee law had been upheld in the courts) contained no similar religious language. If the Arkansas law was modeled after the Tennessee law, as the Court supposed, this difference might seem to have reflected a conscious decision not to embrace a religious purpose. Moreover, given the moribund condition of religion clause jurisprudence in the 1920s and the recent judicial validation of the Tennessee law, it seems unlikely that Arkansas's decision not to include religious language was taken to avoid invalidation of the law (though of course it might have reflected a desire to avoid public criticism). So the deletion might have supported an inference that Arkansas had differed from Tennessee with respect to statutory purpose. Fortas drew the opposite inference, however, declaring with characteristic unwavering confidence that "there is no doubt that the motivation for the law was the same" as in Tennessee.[10]

The important point here is not that the Court was wrong in a factual sense in its characterization of Arkansas's motivation. As discussed in chapter 5, the notion of a collective motivation is a fiction in any event—hardly capable of being simply "true" or "false." It seems likely, moreover, that many Arkansas voters *were* in fact influenced by something like the religious motive seized upon by the Court, and it is at least possible that most voters acted on this kind of motivation. *Possible,* but hardly *proven*: the evidence cited by the Court certainly does not establish this conclusion. Indeed, if the question of motivation were actually a live or open one to begin with, the evidence mustered by the Court would seem almost pathetically thin. Conversely, that evidence is more than ample for an interpreter already certain of, or at least bent on finding, illicit motivation.

When the decision is regarded in this light, the Court's curious, out-of-place footnotes making light of religious fundamentalism become more understandable.[11] Noting that the antievolution law seemed to be pretty much a dead letter in Arkansas, the majority opinion stated: "It is possible that the statute is presently more of a curiosity than a vital fact of life in these States." To this textual sentence the following enigmatic footnote was attached:

> Clarence Darrow, who was counsel for the defense in the Scopes trial, in his biography published in 1932, somewhat sardonically pointed out that States with anti-evolution laws did not insist upon the fundamentalist theory in all respects. He said: "I understand that the States of Tennessee and Mississippi both continue to teach that the earth is round and that the revolution on its axis brings the day and night, in spite of all opposition." The Story of My Life 247 (1932).

Later, in describing the proceedings below, the majority opinion said of the decision by the Arkansas Supreme Court: "That court, perhaps reflecting the discomfort which the statute's quixotic prohibition necessarily engenders in the modern mind, states that it 'expresses no opinion' as to whether the Act prohibits 'explanation' of the theory of evolution or merely forbids 'teaching that the theory is true.'" The footnote to this sentence read:

> R. Hofstadter & W. Metzger, in The Development of Academic Freedom in the United States 324 (1955), refer to some of Darwin's opponents as "exhibiting a kind of phylogenetic snobbery [which led them]

to think that Darwin had libeled the [human] race by discovering simian rather than seraphic ancestors."

At first reading, those footnotes seem to be gratuitous ridicule. The footnotes have no apparent relevance to the factual or legal issues in the case; indeed, it is difficult to see how they are even connected to the textual statements to which they are attached. The derisive footnotes seem the work of someone who is determined to tell a (demeaning) joke he has heard—whether the joke relates to anything in the conversation or not.

Upon reflection, though, it becomes apparent that it is precisely the condescending and contemptuous attitude expressed in—and elicited by—the footnotes that does the real work in the opinion. The contemptuous attitude creates the psychological conditions for the demonizing construction of the Arkansas electorate that is essential to the Court's conclusion. In short, the *Epperson* Court invalidated the law by declining to adopt a charitable construction of its purpose, instead impugning the motives and the mentality of the kind of citizens that the Court thought would vote for such a law.

Nor is *Epperson* anomalous. A similar orientation is discernible in the more recent case of *Wallace v. Jaffree*,[12] in which the Court struck down an Alabama "moment of silence" law on the ground that its real purpose was to promote prayer. In support of this conclusion, the Court relied primarily on two items of evidence. First, the Court cited direct evidence of motivation—in particular the testimony of the sponsor of the law, State Senator Donald Holmes, who stated that the bill was "an effort to return voluntary prayer" to public schools and that he "did not have no other purpose in mind."[13] Second, before enacting the law in question, Alabama had already passed a more limited law, applicable to public school students in grades one through six, allowing a moment of silence for "meditation." Meditation already included prayer, the Court opined, so the addition of express language authorizing silent prayer ("meditation *or voluntary prayer*") was unnecessary and must have been intended to send a message endorsing prayer.[14]

Although this evidence was compatible with the Court's construction, it was also easily consistent with a more benign characterization of the legislature's motivation. Imagine the following scenario: The prior law authorizing "meditation" has proven in practice to be largely satisfactory, but it also exhibits one major and one smaller shortcoming. The major limitation is that the law does not apply at all to grades seven through twelve. The smaller defect is that the law is not entirely clear about whether "meditation" includes "prayer"; the better reading holds that it does, perhaps, but not all administrators and teachers have been sure about this, and indeed the Supreme Court's earlier school prayer decisions have inadvertently created (as Senator Holmes explained) "a widespread misunderstanding that a school-child is legally *prohibited* from engaging in silent, individual prayer once he steps inside a public school."[15]

So the legislature enacts a new law. Its principal objective is simply to extend the existing policy to all grades. But since the law is being revised anyway, the legislature takes the opportunity to clarify that voluntary silent "prayer" is authorized along with silent "meditation." With respect to this aspect of the new law, Senator Holmes explains in essence that the bill is intended to ensure that students who wish to use the moment of silence to pray—to engage in *"voluntary* prayer"—will be permitted to do so. Holmes's language may be somewhat ill-chosen; his grammatical difficulties, which Justice Stevens's majority opinion dutifully exposed, suggest that he is not an accomplished craftsman in English usage. His point might have been slightly more clear if instead of talking about returning "voluntary prayer" to the schools, he had spoken of restoring or affirming a student's "right to pray silently" during the moment of silence. But Holmes's more complete explanation (studiously ignored in the majority opinion) that the bill was intended to dispel the confusion on this point makes his meaning clear enough. To an observer inclined to exercise even a modicum of charity, this account of the Alabama law should seem at least possible, perhaps even likely.

But the majority opinion reflects a determination to fend off this sort of charitable construction. Indeed, so intent was Justice Stevens on demonizing the Alabama legislature that he failed to notice an embarrassing logical gaffe in his own reasoning. With regard to the contention that the new law had been enacted mainly for the purpose of extending the previously recognized "moment of silence" to grades seven through twelve, Stevens asserted that this point was "of no relevance" *because the three juvenile plaintiffs were not in those grades.*[16] Surely, though, Alabama had *some* schoolchildren in grades seven through twelve. And the legislature presumably did not enact the "moment of silence" law for the exclusive benefit of the three Jaffree children involved in the case; probably the legislators were not even aware of those particular children's existence. Hence, what was palpably "of no relevance" was Stevens's assertion dismissing a plausible and legitimate legislative purpose.

Once again, however, the point is not that the Court was factually wrong in its description of the legislature's intent. The Court was free to construct a generous or an ungenerous characterization of that (ultimately fictional) group intent. Either characterization could claim some plausible connection to "the facts." With some effort the Court managed to choose the ungenerous characterization. Its decision may have violated the notion of charity in interpretation, but under a motive approach the decision was necessary if the Court was not simply to defer to the state. The Court's uncharitable course thus reflected the natural discursive tendency of a doctrine that frames constitutional debate as a search for illicit motivation.[17]

ANIMAL SACRIFICE AND THE QUEST FOR PERSECUTION

As the preceding chapter explained, the free exercise doctrine adopted by the Supreme Court in *Employment Division v. Smith* (the peyote case), though phrased in terms of criteria of "general applicability" and "neutrality," leads naturally to a focus on persecutory motivation as the test of constitutionality. In this respect, free exercise doctrine now parallels the purpose component of establishment clause doctrine, and one might therefore expect it to elicit the same kind of ad hominem argumentation that is reflected in "purpose" cases under the establishment clause, such as *Epperson* and *Jaffree*. The majority opinion in *Church of the Lukumi Babalu Aye v. Hialeah,* the major free exercise decision applying the *Smith* doctrine, amply fulfills this gloomy expectation.

The Animal Sacrifice Controversy

The *Hialeah* case[18] involved a free exercise challenge to several ordinances adopted by the Florida city of Hialeah, a neighbor to Miami and home of about two hundred thousand people, in an effort to eliminate animal sacrifice as practiced by the devotees of Santeria. Santeria is a religion that developed from the mixture of Catholicism with the Yoruba religion carried by African slaves to Cuba. Brought to this country by Cuban exiles, the religion claimed at the time of the case an estimated fifty thousand followers in South Florida.

Santeria practitioners raise and sacrifice a variety of animals, including birds, sheep, goats, and turtles, as a way of worshiping or seeking the aid of *orishas* or spirits. Santeria priests perform the ritual by thrusting a knife into the neck of the sacrificial animal and collecting the blood in clay pots; the pots of blood are then placed before Santeria deities. The carcasses of sacrificed animals are often left in public places—most often near rivers and canals, by four-way stop signs, and sometimes in yards and doorways.

Because of the hostile conditions in which it developed, Santeria has traditionally been practiced in secret. In the spring of 1987, however, Ernesto Pichardo, a Santeria Italero or priest, announced plans to establish a church, school, and museum in Hialeah on property leased by his church, the Church of the Lukumi Babalu Aye. This announcement generated opposition among city residents, and on June 9, 1987, a city council meeting was held to discuss the issue. At this meeting, the council adopted a resolution expressing "concern . . . that certain religions may propose to engage in practices which are inconsistent with public morals, peace, and safety." The council also adopted an ordinance generally incorporating Florida's animal cruelty statute.

Later, in September, the city council adopted three additional ordinances that in essence prohibited, with various exceptions and limitations, the ritual killing of animals and the ownership or possession of animals for such purposes. These laws were not expressly limited to the killing of animals by Santeria followers, and indeed did not explicitly refer to Santeria. But they were crafted so that, as the Supreme Court later argued at length, "almost the only conduct subject to [the ordinances was] the religious exercise of Santeria church members."[19]

Pichardo and the church then filed suit in federal court, challenging the ordinances on free exercise grounds. After a nine-day trial, the district court rejected this challenge. Judge Spellman's opinion sympathetically described Santeria, with its origins in slavery and persecution, and treated it as a sincere and genuine religion. However, the judge ruled that the ordinances were justified by governmental interests in preventing the killing and suffering of animals, controlling the sanitation problems that resulted from the public dumping of animal carcasses, and preventing psychological harm to children who witnessed the ritual killing of animals. The court also ruled that the City's objectives could not be attained by means less restrictive of Santeria religious practice.

The Court of Appeals affirmed without a published opinion,[20] and the church then appealed to the Supreme Court, which unanimously reversed. Although their rationales differed somewhat—Justices Souter, Blackmun, and O'Connor, for example, urged reconsideration of *Smith*, while Justice Scalia argued that the majority had partially misinterpreted *Smith*—all the Justices accepted the primary contention of the majority opinion written by Justice Kennedy: the Hialeah ordinances amounted to persecution of Santeria. Hence, the ordinances failed the test of neutrality.

The Nonpersecution Principle

The preceding chapter argued that although *Smith*'s doctrinal requirements of "general applicability" and "neutrality" might aspire to purely formal application, these requirements would of necessity lead courts to focus upon an extratextual factor—legislative motivation or purpose. The majority opinion in *Hialeah* confirms this analysis. Both criteria were understood to require an inquiry into the motive or purpose of the ordinance. With regard to "neutrality," the Court acted out the logic described above: declaring that "[f]acial neutrality is not determinative," the Court focused instead on purpose or motivation. "[I]f the object of a law is to infringe upon or restrict practices because of their religious motivation, the law is not neutral."[21] Consequently, most of the majority opinion was devoted to showing that "[t]he ordinances had as their object the suppression of religion,"[22] or that they "targeted" the Santeria religion.[23]

The Court assigned a separate section of its opinion to the requirement of "general applicability," but it did not explain how this component differed from a requirement of "neutrality." In fact, the Court expressly declined to provide any definition of "general applicability,"[24] and Justice Souter innocently opined that "general applicability is, for the most part, self-explanatory."[25] However, the analysis in this section of the majority opinion is difficult to distinguish from the analysis in the neutrality section. Both discussions seek to show that the City had singled out for prohibition the kind of animal sacrifice performed in Santeria worship while leaving other kinds of killing of animals unregulated. Thus, the "neutrality" and "general applicability" requirements appeared to converge, at least in their practical meaning. And indeed, the Court acknowledged that "[n]eutrality and general applicability are interrelated" and that "failure to satisfy one requirement is a likely indication that the other has not been satisfied."[26]

In sum, the *Smith* doctrine as interpreted in the *Hialeah* majority opinion amounts to what the Court called a "nonpersecution principle."[27] A law is not unconstitutional merely because it *burdens* religion, but it is unconstitutional if it represents the *persecution* of religion. The critical question is what the law was intended to do or, in other words, what its objective or purpose was.

Constructing Persecution

I argued earlier that legislative purpose or motivation is a construct or fiction, not a discoverable fact, and that for any controversial law a court is likely to have a range of plausible alternative constructions, some generous and some ungenerous, regarding the motive or purpose of the law. *Hialeah* may seem to belie this contention, or at least to constitute a counterexample. Despite differences in their analyses, the Justices largely agreed that the purpose of the ordinances was to persecute Santeria. If this was indeed the only plausible construction, then the claim of indeterminacy, and of judicial choice, would seem to be invalid, at least in this case.

Purposes besides persecution? A quick and helpful rejoinder, although ultimately not a conclusive one, is that the possibility of a different and more charitable construction is evident from the fact that the district court not only imagined but actually endorsed such a construction. As Judge Spellman saw the matter (again, after a lengthy trial), the Hialeah ordinances were based not on animosity to Santeria per se, but rather on several respectable and even powerful secular rationales. First, Santeria's treatment of animals was cruel: beyond the obvious fact that Santeria rituals resulted in the deaths of animals, the method of execution did not ensure that animals died quickly and with as little pain as possible. Second, testimony indicated that the carcasses of animals sacrificed in Santeria rituals were often left on the streets or even in yards and doorways, and these spoiling carcasses might be a source of disease or a breeding ground for flies and rodents. Third, expert testimony indicated that children who watched the ritual killing of animals might suffer psychological damage that could incline them to violent behavior toward human beings.[28]

These proffered rationales for the ban on animal sacrifice seem respectable and at least plausible, and they were supported by considerable evidence at trial. Thus, the district court concluded:

> The Church . . . alleges that the ordinances were passed because of the council members' intent to discriminate against the Church and to keep the Church from establishing a physical presence in the City. There was no evidence to support this contention. All the evidence established was that the council members' intent was to stop the practice of animal sacrifice in the City. Although this concern was prompted by the Church's public announcement that it intended to come out into the open and practice its religious rituals, including animal sacrifice, the council's intent was to stop animal sacrifice whatever individual, religion or cult it was practiced by.[29]

The district court opinion shows that a different, more generous construction of legislative purpose was at least *possible*. That observation, however, might not be sufficient to show that the Supreme Court gratuitously adopted a more negative characterization. Upon closer examination, the picture drawn by the district court might prove implausible as an interpretation of what motivated the Hialeah ordinances; it might deviate too far from the facts to be even a credible fiction or a viable oversimplification. This is just what Justice Kennedy, writing for the majority, contended.

The majority opinion argued from the structure or design of the ordinances that they could be plausibly explained only as a product of persecution. First, the majority argued at length that the Hialeah ordinances, when taken in combination, applied only to animal sacrifice as practiced in Santeria. The ordinances did not forbid the killing of animals, for example, for purposes of hunting, rodent control, euthanasia, scientific research, consumption, or kosher slaughter.[30] Second, the Court argued that the City could have achieved its legitimate objectives through means less restrictive of Santeria religious practice, such as regulations governing the disposal of animal carcasses,[31] and the scope of the ordinances could therefore not be explained simply by reference to the City's stated objectives. The only plausible conclusion, therefore, was that the ordinances were calculated to "target" or "persecute" or "suppress" Santeria.

So were the Hialeah ordinances calculated (as Judge Spellman thought) to prevent cruelty to animals, protect public health, and spare children from the harmful effects of watching the slaughter of animals? Or were the ordinances intended (as Justice Kennedy maintained) to suppress the Santeria form of worship? But when the controversy is framed in this way, it immediately becomes apparent that the answer to *both* questions might well be "yes." Judge Spellman did not deny, after all, that the ordinances were aimed at Santeria, or even that they reflected opposition to Santeria; he merely found that the ordinances were not animated by *religious* hostility, or by a desire to *persecute*. So the case involved much more than an evidentiary dispute; it involved a delicate conceptual question about the meaning of religious persecution. Only after considering that question can we assess the force of the majority's accusations.

What is "persecution"? So what exactly *does* "religious persecution" mean? Here we need to take seriously a distinction that is implicit in the idea of "persecution," and that the majority itself repeatedly tried to articulate. The distinction is between measures that "target" a religion *on religious grounds* and because it is objectionable *as a religion* and, on the other hand, measures that "target" a religion only in the sense that they prohibit a practice of the religion because the practice is objectionable *on independent or nonreligious grounds.*

To illustrate the first of these possibilities, suppose that the New Age Four Square Church teaches doctrines about the nature of deity that most members of a particular community find deeply offensive, even threatening, on theological grounds. The church also enjoins its adherents to wear orange and black striped socks (which no one else in the community wears). If the community adopts an ordinance prohibiting the possession or use of orange and black striped socks, the natural conclusion is that the community has targeted the New Age Four Square Church because the church is objectionable *on religious grounds* and *as a religion.* Of course, orange and black striped socks may be unfashionable. But the community does not normally regulate fashion through law, so it seems more likely that the sock law is a thinly disguised attempt to persecute or suppress the church because of its offensive theology.

Conversely, imagine that the newly formed Church of the Sacred Canine teaches theological ideas that most people in the community regard as bizarre; and the church also imposes a religious duty on its members to urinate on every fire hydrant they pass. This is a practice, let us imagine, that no one else in the community follows, and that accordingly had not previously been regulated by law. If the community now passes a law prohibiting urinating on fire hydrants,* it has in one sense "targeted" the Church of the Sacred Canine. Although applicable by its terms to everyone, that is, the law prohibits a practice that almost no one except members of that church wishes to engage in; moreover, the circumstances of the law's enactment plainly show that it was adopted with that church and its practice in mind. Nonetheless, it seems plausible to conclude that the law "targets" the church *not* because it is objectionable on religious grounds or *as a religion,* but rather because it engages in a practice that many people sincerely find objectionable wholly apart from religious considerations. That is, citizens and officials might with good reason believe that urinating on fire hydrants is unseemly and unsanitary. And although members of the community may also regard the church's beliefs as bizarre, if this is like most large and diverse American communities, its residents have probably become accustomed to putting up with, and even welcoming, people holding all sorts of beliefs that most citizens would regard as peculiar. Hence, it is perfectly plausible to suppose that the "no urination" law was motivated by the intelligible and nonreligious reasons that the community offers in the law's defense.

If a law "targets" a religion only because and only to the extent that the religion engages in a practice objectionable on nonreligious grounds, it seems misleading to say that the law is animated by hostility to the religion, or that it constitutes *religious* "persecution." The *Hialeah* majority opinion acknowledged as much: it explained that a law manifests impermissible persecution only if it "regulates or prohibits conduct *because it is undertaken for religion reasons*" or if its object is to "restrict practices *because of their religious motivation.*" Justice Kennedy as-

---

* Why would the community pass this kind of law, one might ask, instead of simply enacting a more general law prohibiting public urination altogether? But a community might have plausible reasons not grounded in religious hostility for enacting a narrower law. Perhaps not all public urination *should* be prohibited. Sometimes the action may be a necessity, and if discretely executed it can be quite harmless. Faced with the difficult challenge of defining just when urination is and is not permissible, and just what would count as "public" urination, a governmental body might understandably choose to avoid that quagmire by simply focusing on the only practice that in fact is controversial and deciding whether that specific practice does or does not offend secular interests. The point is important because the regulation of animal sacrifice implicates similar issues.

serted that a law is invalid if it is enacted "because of" and not merely "in spite of" its suppression of a religious practice.[32]

So one must ask whether the Hialeah ordinances themselves were motivated by hostility based on *religious* objections to Santeria, or whether they "targeted" Santeria only because and to the extent that it engaged in a practice objectionable on nonreligious grounds.

Reexamining *Hialeah*

If the question is asked in this way, the Supreme Court's characterization of the motivation behind the ordinances seems problematic. Judge Spellman found, once again, that the City had acted to promote secular objectives; and those objectives—preventing cruelty to animals, curtailing the health hazards that attend dumping animal carcasses in public places, and avoiding psychological injury to children who would witness animal slaughter—do not on their face seem especially suspect or spurious. Is it implausible to suppose, for example, that city residents would be offended and concerned (quite apart from any religious commitments) to find the carcasses of butchered goats, sheep, or turtles dumped in yards, intersections, and doorways?

The "only Santeria" argument. Against Hialeah's stated justifications, the Court emphasized that the City had pursued its ostensible objectives only with respect to Santeria practices. If the City had genuinely cared about animal suffering, public health, and the psychological welfare of children, the Court asked, why did it prohibit only the ritual killing of animals while continuing to permit the killing of animals in hunting, pest control, scientific research, kosher slaughter, and so forth?

There is little reason to doubt the Court's contention that although the ordinances did not explicitly name Santeria, their "burden . . . in practical terms, [fell] on Santeria adherents but almost no others."[33] It is also manifest that the city council was aware of this fact: the ordinances were consciously designed to deal with animal sacrifice as practiced by Santeria, and to steer clear of other modes of animal slaughter. Upon reflection, though, this point seems less potent than the Court imagined. On the contrary, it is wholly plausible to suppose that the City might consciously act to regulate only Santeria, but might nonetheless do so in good faith and for the secular reasons the City articulated.

After all, social attitudes toward the killing of animals are complex, conflicting, and far from static. The complexity is not limited to the diversity of attitudes among different people about animal rights, vegetarianism, hunting, the use of animals in laboratories, and related issues. Even an individual may find that his views on these questions are uncertain and difficult to reduce to any general principle or consistent theory. Opinions and intuitions may vary depending on factors like the *kind of animal* (Do dogs deserve better treatment than birds? Than squirrels? Cockroaches? Why?), the *purpose* for which an animal is killed (Hunting? Food? Fur coats? Testing medical or pharmaceutical products? Other, more theoretical scientific research?), the *method of killing*, and the *familiarity of the practice*. It seems unlikely that most individuals, much less a community of any size, could reconcile these conflicting views and feelings or distill them into any coherent theory of appropriate animal treatment. And given the confused and fluctuating condition of opinion on these questions, it may be entirely sensible for government to deal with problems involving the treatment of animals on an issue-by-issue basis. Indeed, a relatively ad hoc approach to such problems may be the only alternative realistically available to government.

In short, the Santeria controversy presented Hialeah officials with a specific practice of animal killing that implicated legitimate secular interests. The city council considered the issue and decided that ritual animal sacrifice should be prohibited; it made no effort to articulate any general theory of proper animal treatment or to extrapolate the logical consequences of its immediate decision for a host of other practices that would also touch on some of these same interests or values, but in different ways and to different degrees. In short, the council did what governments usually do: it dealt with the matter at hand. The council's conclusion might be criticized on various grounds; it might be criticized, for example, for being insensitive and intolerant toward a minority religion. But it is not plausible to conclude merely from the fact that the council acted only with respect to one discrete and very live controversy that the council must have been motivated by *religious* hostility to Santeria, or that it was "persecuting" Santeria.

"Less restrictive means"? The Supreme Court's "less restrictive means" analysis was likewise tenuous at best. The majority opinion argued that the City could have secured its legitimate interests by, for instance, regulating the disposal of carcasses without actually prohibiting ritual sacrifice. Even if feasible, this ostensibly "less restrictive" approach might not have avoided interference with religious practices. Though the Supreme Court omitted to notice the fact, Pichardo had tes-

tified that some Santeria priests believe the religion *requires* carcasses to be left in public places (although he himself did not share this view).[34] But in any case, the Court's "less restrictive means" argument is subject to cogent objections.

First, the district court had concluded that a less restrictive regulation would be impossible to police effectively. Justice Kennedy peremptorily rejected this conclusion, treating it as obvious that a regulation of "public" behavior—that is, the disposal of animal carcasses—would be easier to enforce than a regulation of "private" sacrifice rituals.[35] But Kennedy's argument simply reflected a sloppy use of terms. The district court had found that Santeria rituals, although conducted in "private" residences, were not merely detectable but indeed were often disturbing to neighbors because they were a scene of constant traffic in and out of the house.[36] Conversely, the dumping of carcasses, though a "public" act, might occur at night and anywhere in the City; and once dumped a carcass might be impossible to trace to any specific Santeria practitioner.[37] So the district court's conclusion that it would be feasible to ban the rituals themselves but not to police effectively the dumping of carcasses seems eminently plausible; and Justice Kennedy's facile invocation of the terms "public" and "private" simply failed to address the real issue.

Even if the Court's point about less restrictive regulation were correct with respect to an ordinance regulating disposal of carcasses, however, it would be implausible to make a similar suggestion regarding the City's asserted interest in preventing cruelty to animals. A flat prohibition on ritual killing might be enforceable; but it would be difficult or impossible (not to mention highly objectionable on establishment clause grounds of religious "entanglement") to have public officials present at rituals to ensure that animals were killed in some prescribed and less brutal fashion. Hence, in suggesting that the City might regulate the method of slaughter instead of actually prohibiting ritual sacrifice,[38] the Court conspicuously omitted to address the question of enforceability.

And of course, even if regulations dealing with carcass disposal and method of slaughter could be enforced, such regulations would do nothing to alleviate concerns about the psychological effect of ritual animal killing on children who watched the sacrifices, or about what residents and officials regarded as the unjustified *killing* of animals. Those concerns could be satisfied only by a prohibition on animal sacrifice.

The "statement" evidence. Thus, the Court's efforts to show that the structure of the Hialeah ordinances compelled an inference of persecution—of hositility to Santeria on *religious grounds*—were patently unpersuasive. In an effort to shore up his condemnatory construction of the ordinances' purpose, Justice Kennedy also cited statements made by city officials and residents of their reasons for supporting the ordinances (although only Justice Stevens joined in this section of his opinion). Kennedy relied on the fact that at the first city council meeting at which the opening of the Santeria church was discussed, there was "significant hostility exhibited by residents, members of the city council, and other city officials toward the Santeria religion and its practice of animal sacrifice."[39] Though the evidence supported this assertion, that evidence for the most part did not address the crucial distinction noted earlier: it did not indicate whether residents and officials were hostile to Santeria *as a religion* and *on religious grounds* or, conversely, whether they opposed Santeria because and insofar as it engaged in practices (such as dumping animal carcasses in streets, yards, and doorways) that residents and officials found objectionable quite apart from religion.

Admittedly, one statement quoted by Kennedy plainly expressed religious opposition to Santeria. A police chaplain asserted, "We need to be helping people and sharing with them the truth that is found in Jesus Christ." Based on this standard, the chaplain urged that the City should "not . . . permit this Church to exist" because it was "an abomination to the Lord" and engaged in demon worship.[40] It is not surprising—indeed, in a city of almost two hundred thousand people it is probably inevitable—that some residents and even some officials (in particular a chaplain) would hold this view. At the same time, there is no reason to suppose that the chaplain's statements reflected a dominant or majority position, or that the City generally accepted his pro-Christian view of appropriate public policy. Indeed, the fact that the ordinances exempted kosher slaughter suggests the contrary. And the other statements quoted by Kennedy are easily amenable to the interpretation that residents and officials objected to Santeria not on religious grounds per se, but simply because it engaged in a highly objectionable practice.

The resolution adopted at the city council meeting supports this construction. That resolution expressed "concern . . . that certain religions may propose to engage in *practices which are inconsistent with public morals, peace or safety,*" and it stated a commitment to prohibit "any and all acts of *any and all religious groups* which are *inconsistent with public morals, peace, or safety.*"[41]

To be sure, the distinction between opposing a religion as a religion on religious grounds and opposing a religion on nonreligious grounds because of a practice it engages in is an elusive one. The distinction is difficult to articulate clearly, and even more difficult to apply in practice. Freewheeling public debate on controversial issues is normally not conducive to subtle analytical distinctions. Indeed, most citizens might not understand or accept the distinction even if they could contemplate it at leisure. Suppose that in a quiet moment a typical resident of Hialeah were asked: "Do you oppose Santeria because it is a bad religion or, on the other hand, because it sacrifices animals and leaves their carcasses on the streets?" The resident might naturally reply, "I don't understand the question" or, more simply, "Yes." Given these complexities, it is hardly surprising that the statements quoted by Justice Kennedy do not for the most part fall easily onto either side of the "persecution" distinction. But this difficulty is simply inherent in a doctrinal test which holds that a law is not invalid if it merely "burdens" religion, but that the law is invalid if it "persecutes" religion.*

---

* In one important sense, *any* governmental decision declining to accommodate religious practice implicitly rejects the claimants' religious beliefs. On the basis of their religious faith, in other words, Santeria practitioners believe that their ritual sacrifice of animals is justified: if Hialeah officials had shared this faith, or had treated it with complete respect, the City would presumably have reached the same conclusion—that is, that ritual sacrifice should not be prohibited. In the same way, if Oregon officials had accepted, or sufficiently respected, the Native American belief that the use of peyote in religious ceremonies is a sacred duty, they would not have prohibited the use of peyote for religious purposes; and if federal welfare officials had shared or fully respected the religious belief that governmental use of social security numbers robs a recipient of her spirit they presumably would not use social security numbers. See Bowen v. Roy, 476 U.S. 693 (1986). In each instance, governmental officials in effect rejected (by not accepting) a claimant's religious beliefs. And they may well have rejected those beliefs, at least in part, on the basis of their own contrary religious beliefs. (In Hialeah, for instance, one city councilman rejected the religious necessity of animal sacrifice based on his own interpretation of the Bible.) But it hardly follows that in rejecting a claimant's religious belief—a belief that if accepted would have entailed a different law—government officials were seeking to *persecute* the claimant because of that belief. Rejection of another's religious belief is not equivalent to "persecution," even if the rejection is based on one's own contrary religious belief (as it typically is). In short, a citizen or official might well reject the religious argument for *exemption* from a regulation (and might do so on the basis of his own contrary religious beliefs), but still support the regulation itself for nonreligious reasons.

Moreover, the elusiveness of the distinction merely augments the possibilities for distortion and demonization in the way a court chooses to characterize legislative motivation. It will virtually always be possible, and plausible, to do what the district court did in *Hialeah*—that is, to emphasize the secular reasons that led government to regulate, or refuse to exempt, a religious practice. Conversely, there will nearly always be evidence that some people did not accept or agree with a particular religion. After all, in a highly diverse society where no particular religion comes close to commanding majority support, most people inevitably *will* disagree with any specific religion: and during moments of controversy and passion these disagreements will sometimes be expressed. Consequently, it will be possible to find and use such expressions to characterize the governmental decision as a form of persecution. That is just what Justice Kennedy did.

The point of this discussion, to reiterate, is not that the Court's conclusion, or its construction of legislative motivation, was simply wrong as a factual matter. The point, rather, is that an alternative, validating construction of the City's motivation was available, and Justice Kennedy's analysis fell well short of showing that construction to be untenable. The evidence hardly compelled a demonizing construction of Hialeah's actions. But the nature of current free exercise doctrine invited such a construction, and the Court could not resist the invitation.

The Frustrations of Justice Scalia

More than other members of the Court, Justice Scalia appears to have perceived the peril of the Court's new course. He acknowledged the fragility of the majority's characterization of Hialeah's motivation; for all the record showed, he observed, the ordinances might have been passed "with no motive on the part of any councilman except the ardent desire to prevent cruelty to animals."[42] More importantly, Scalia comprehended the broader consequence of the course chosen by the majority. That approach, he suggested, will "put [the Court] in the business of invalidating laws by reason of the evil motives of their authors."[43]

Indeed, Scalia must have wondered whether he had created a monster. Just three years earlier, in *Smith,* he had prevailed upon the Court to depart from earlier free exercise jurisprudence and to embrace a new "neutrality"-oriented doctrine more to his liking. Yet *Hialeah* reveals that the new free exercise doctrine turns out to be similar in important respects to prevailing establishment clause doctrine, which Scalia deplores.[44] Free exercise doctrine is now like establishment clause doctrine not only in its embrace of the ideal of neutrality, but also in its adoption of that part of the *Lemon* test—analysis of legislative motivation or purpose—that Scalia has most scathingly and persuasively criticized.[45]

Joined by Chief Justice Rehnquist, Scalia concurred separately in *Hialeah* to protest against the Court's new course. But although his aversion to judicial excursions in search of "evil motives" is well warranted, Scalia could not articulate a feasible alternative to the direction in which the majority took the doctrine he had devised in *Smith*. He offered two suggestions. First, Scalia proposed that courts should "focus on the object of the *laws* at issue" instead of concerning themselves with "the subjective motivation of the *lawmakers.*" Scalia also suggested that the constitutionality of a law should be determined by examining the law's *effects*, not the *motivations* that generated it.[46] But upon examination, neither of these suggestions appears to be viable.

Can "laws" have objectives? Consider first Scalia's proposal to focus on the objectives of "the law" rather than the motivation of the lawmakers. An obvious but perhaps too simple objection is that this proposal commits a basic category mistake. "Purposes" or "objectives" are qualities or properties of "subjects"—of human beings, or at least of mindful, purposive agents—not of objects, or of dead marks on a dry page. Thus, it might be argued that when a judge or scholar talks about the objective of a law, he commits a category mistake by attributing to the bare "law" a property that things in its class do not possess.

When presented in this blunt form, this objection may seem a bit obtuse. After all, we often talk about objects as having purposes in a metaphorical or elliptical sense, as when we describe the purpose for which persons use an object or tool. When we say "the purpose of a hammer is to pound nails," we do not commit a category mistake because our fuller and understood meaning is that *people* make and use hammers to pound nails. We might talk about the purpose or objective of a "law" in a similar way.

While salvaging familiar talk about the purpose of "the law," however, this explanation does nothing to rescue Scalia's specific suggestion. By this account, rather, Scalia's proposal is intelligible only if references to the object of "the law" are understood as elliptically referring to *some person or group of persons that makes or uses a law* to achieve an objective. So who is that person or group of persons? Scalia doesn't say, but the most obvious answer seems to be . . . the lawmakers, or the legislators. So by this view, Scalia has engaged in a kind of verbal subterfuge; he has not offered an alternative to the majority's focus on legislative motivation, but has merely tried to conceal that focus by using "the law's purpose" as an obfuscating euphemism for "the lawmakers' purpose."

Euphemisms have their place, no doubt. By excluding statements of subjective motivation, Scalia might keep judicial discourse from being as directly and personally insulting to government officials as it was in the legislative history section of Justice Kennedy's opinion. Under Scalia's approach, that is, accusations of religious hostility and persecution would be directed not against government officials—not explicitly, at least—but instead, more evasively, against "the law" they supported and enacted to serve their purposes. It seems unlikely, though, that Scalia wrote a separate, critical opinion out of a concern for judicial etiquette or tact: polite diplomacy is hardly his forte. And in any case, however veiled the accusations (and in this case the veil is almost transparent), the focus would still be on legislative motivation.

Alternatively, Scalia's implicit reference conceivably might be to some person or group *other than* the legislators—to the general society, perhaps, or the police department, or the judiciary, or even some fictitious or constructed author or user of the law. To put the point differently, it is arguable that a judge who insists on talking about the purpose of the *law*, as opposed to the motives of the *legislators*, in effect "personifies" the law itself; he endows it with the character of a person or subject capable of having intentions, pursuing objectives, and so forth. Like Pinocchio, the law is elevated from an artifact to a "person"—a "person" who is clearly fictional.

But a reference to a person or group other than the actual legislators hardly makes Scalia's position more attractive. It is hard to explain why a law should be declared invalid because of improper motives or purposes on the part of someone who did not even enact the law, and who may be merely fictional. And even if this explanation could be supplied, a reference to the objectives or purposes of some group other than the legislators does nothing to dispel the difficulties (including the incentives for demonization) that attend motive inquiries; it merely shifts those difficulties to a new set of persons.

The "effects" inquiry. Scalia's other proposal—his proposal, that is, to focus on the "effects" of a law, not on its motivations—also proves empty. In the first place, just what "effects" would render a law invalid? Scalia was unclear on the point. He surely did not mean that a law is invalid if it has the effect of *burdening* religious practice; after all, that was precisely the position he had repudiated in *Smith*. Instead, he seemed to be suggesting that a law is unconstitutional, regardless of motivation, if it has the effect of regulating or prohibiting behavior that is practiced *only for religious reasons,* or perhaps if it is practiced *only by one religion.* Thus, a law is unconstitutional if it "in fact singles out a religious practice for special burdens" even if the motives of the enacting legislators were entirely "pure-hearted."[47]

Scalia seemed to say this. More bluntly, he *did* say this, but it is hard to suppose that he seriously meant it. For example, change the issue from *animal* sacrifice to *child* sacrifice: suppose that only one religious group in the country—call it the religion of Moloch—performs a religious ritual in which children are sacrificed by fire to the god Moloch. Suppose further that a legislature enacts a law specifically prohibiting ritual child sacrifice. The law does not expressly refer to the Moloch religion; formally, or on its face, the law covers everyone (just as the Hialeah ordinances covered everyone, and did not explicitly mention Santeria). But in fact Moloch worshipers are the only ones that practice this ritual. So the law for practical purposes "singles out" Moloch worship in the same way that the Hialeah ordinances "singled out" Santeria. Scalia's statements suggest that the child sacrifice law is unconstitutional. But it is hard to believe that he means this. *Why* should child sacrifice be immune just because the Moloch religion is the only group to practice it?

Or perhaps Scalia would say that the child sacrifice law is unconstitutional because it affects only Moloch-worshipers, but that the Moloch practice can still be curbed under general homicide and child protection laws. This position would mean, in essence, that the state can suppress a vicious practice by a religious group so long as the practice is similar enough to other evil practices that it can be swept under more general laws; but if the religious practice represents a distinct evil not covered by other more general laws, the state is powerless to respond. It is hard to see what this position has to recommend it. In any event, if this were Scalia's position then while voting to invalidate those Hialeah ordinances that were tailored specifically to Santeria, he should have voted to uphold the ordinance that merely incorporated Florida's general "animal cruelty" statute. The majority struck down even that generic ordinance on the assumption that, like the ordinances more specifically tailored to Santeria, it was also motivated by hostility to Santeria. But for Scalia motive was ostensibly irrelevant, and the general animal cruelty ordinance plainly did not "single out" Santeria rituals; it was broadly applicable, as even the majority conceded. Nonetheless, Scalia voted to invalidate all the ordinances.

In the end, although Scalia protested against the course taken by the majority, he had nothing better to suggest. Indeed, his opinion at least seemed the expression of a man who was seriously, if staunchly, confused. And perhaps Scalia *was* confused. But there is another possibility: Scalia may have perceived the predicament created by the *Smith* approach, and he may have been trying—through that familiar judicial tactic, obfuscation—to make the best of a bad situation for which he himself, as the author of *Smith,* was partly responsible. Either way, in acknowledging that the *Smith* doctrine makes legislative motivation dispositive and thus prompts an effort to find (or construct) "evil motives," the majority was being more candid and more faithful to the doctrine Scalia had devised than Scalia himself was able or willing to be.

THE DISCOURSE OF DISRESPECT

In *Smith,* the Court started down a doctrinal path that leads to a constitutional discourse in which contending parties accuse each other of hostility, persecution, and bad faith. *Smith* chose—perhaps inadvertently, and under the benign heading of "neutrality"—to promote a discourse that turns out to be the opposite of tolerance. *Hialeah* represented the first, bitter fruits of that choice.

The degeneration of free exercise jurisprudence has precedents in other areas of constitutional law. As discussed earlier in this chapter, establishment clause decisions exhibit similar tendencies; only the fact that establishment cases are usually not decided under the *Lemon* test's "purpose" prong saves that jurisprudence from collapsing into a rampantly ad hominem discourse. More generally, the dynamic that produces this kind of discourse would seem to be present in any constitutional doctrine that makes illicit legislative purpose—or, more bluntly, "evil motives"—the basis for invalidating laws.

Not surprisingly, therefore, parallel developments are visible in equal protection analysis (which Justice Kennedy expressly invoked as a source of guidance in *Hialeah*). "Equality," as noted, is a close cousin to or even an *alter ego* of "neutrality"; and it naturally generates a similar focus on legislative motivation. The basic dynamic is familiar and straightforward: it is not enough to require that laws be "facially" nondiscriminatory, but in many contexts it may also be impractical to invalidate laws merely because they have a "disparate impact." So a focus on discriminatory legislative motivation seems the only viable alternative.[48] In equal protection cases, consequently, success in challenging a law may depend upon characterizing the motivation of legislators, voters, or government officials as racist, sexist, or homophobic. The recent case of *Romer v. Evans*, in which the Court struck down Colorado's "Amendment 2" denying "special rights" to gays and lesbians, is exemplary. Perhaps the most accessible claim in an opinion (written, as was *Hialeah*, by Justice Kennedy) that supporters and opponents alike have found largely impenetrable is the accusation that Colorado voters acted from homophobic prejudice.[49]

Debate framed in these terms may be simplistic and unfair. It may also be divisive and unproductive of mutual respect and understanding. But this sort of demonizing debate is precisely what a doctrinal emphasis on "persecution"—or, more generally, on bad motives—as a dispositive factor is calculated to elicit. Thus, citing "a substantial number of Supreme Court decisions, involving a range of legal subjects, that condemn public enactments as being expressions of prejudice or irrationality or invidiousness," Robert Nagel observes that "to a remarkable extent our courts have become places where the name-calling and exaggeration that mark the lower depths of our political debate are simply given a more acceptable, authoritative form."[50] In short, the imputations of evil motives advanced in *Hialeah* are an example in miniature of a larger, mean-spirited tendency in constitutional discourse.

Although *Hialeah* was hailed by some as a victory for religious freedom, there is little to celebrate in the discursive tendency it reflects. And if one is searching for alternatives, then pre-*Smith* free exercise jurisprudence—not so much the "compelling interest" balancing test that can perhaps be formally restored by statute, but rather the discourse of humility and tolerance exemplified in *Yoder*—deserves renewed consideration.

PART III

CAN FAITH TOLERATE?

"TOLERANCE ENDS," LEARNED Hand once observed, "where faith begins."[1] Was Hand right? And if so, how do we account for the American achievement in religious freedom?

The questions are urgent for the overall argument of this book. If there has been a single overall normative theme running through the book, it is that our professions of commitment to religious equality or its twin, religious neutrality, are misconceived and empty (though perhaps diplomatically useful in some contexts) and that instead we ought to cultivate the virtue of tolerance. But according to Hand's view—and he was hardly alone in holding it—the price of tolerance would be the relinquishing of faith. To be sure, many would willingly, even joyously, pay this price: in this vein theorists like Stephen Macedo argue that we should affirmatively cultivate a "wishy-washy" or "watered-down religiosity."[2] But by now the evidence seems to show that this is not a realistic option: contrary to the fond hopes of secularists and the prophecies of generations of social scientists, Americans seem determined to hold onto their religious faiths in all their pluralistic splendor. Moreover, even if a loss of faith were necessary to achieve tolerance, devout believers might consider the sacrifice to be too great. "What doth it profit a man . . . ?"

So an urgent question presents itself: Is religious tolerance possible in a nation that is deeply, but diversely, religious? And if so, how?

For many, these questions may seem obtuse. Though we vaguely remember that religious intolerance was once the dominant pattern, and though we perceive outbreaks of intolerance even today and even in our own nation, still it may seem that our national experience over the last two centuries proves that religious tolerance is . . . well, just the only sensible stance for a person to take, whether she is religious or not, and whether she is thinking about practical or religious matters. Michael Walzer describes (and, in the course of his book on the subject, largely manifests) the prevailing attitude:

Most people in the United States, in the West generally, believe that religious toleration is easy. They read about religious wars near to home (in Ireland and Bosnia) or far away (in the Middle East or Southeast Asia) with incomprehension. Religion in those places must be contaminated by ethnicity or nationalism, or it must take some extreme, fanatical, and therefore (as we understand things) unusual form. For haven't we proved that freedom of worship, voluntary association, and political neutrality work together to reduce the stakes of religious difference? Don't these tenets of American pluralism encourage mutual forbearance and make for a happy coexistence? We allow individuals to believe what they want to believe, to join freely with fellow believers, to attend the church of their choice—or to disbelieve what they want to disbelieve, to stay away from the church of their choice, and so on. What more could anyone want?[3]

Countering this complacent view, Stanley Fish asserts peremptorily that "[t]he incoherence of toleration, both as an ideal and as a basis for a politics, seems obvious even on a moment's reflection."[4] Fish's is a minority viewpoint, probably, but by no means an idiosyncratic one: he is preceded, in important respects, by eminent and diverse thinkers from Montaigne to Hobbes to Maistre to Holmes; and his avowedly "antiliberal" claims are joined in essential points by impeccably "liberal" theorists like Macedo. The common strand uniting these thinkers is a deep-seated suspicion that people who embrace incompatible creeds—who truly believe in contrary things—cannot in good faith agree to "get along," or to practice genuine mutual respect. Insofar as their antagonistic beliefs are sincere and not merely habitual or cosmetic, the critics suggest, true believers are bound to be intolerant of each other. Consequently, a political community has only two ways of meeting the challenge of intolerance: it can impose an orthodoxy (perhaps in disguise) and suppress dangerous deviations, or else it can hope and work for a diminution of belief and an increase in indifference among the creedal combatants, thereby dissolving their motivation to fight with each other.

So *is* toleration an impossible ideal? In chapter 7, I argue that the case for intolerance (and hence against tolerance) is indeed stronger than contemporary theorists and judges typically suppose. In some respects it is stronger than even critics of tolerance like Fish suppose. Fish charges that liberal theorists routinely "fail . . . by underestimating and trivializing the illiberal impulse."[5] He is right, but the charge is mildly ironic, because Fish himself to some extent underestimates and trivializes the illiberal impulse.

But Fish and like-minded critics are also wrong insofar as they assert that the case for intolerance is incorrigible, and that the only alternatives are either an imposed orthodoxy or a cultivated indifference. The historically relevant possibility that these critics overlook, chapter 8 will argue, is a theistically grounded tolerance that affirmatively promotes respect for difference—respect not only among those who ostensibly share a (probably illusory) common religion, but also toward those who in good faith adopt radically different and even nontheistic positions. Theism, I will argue, allows for a pluralism based on genuine mutual respect that goes beyond either the grudgingly granted tolerance of practical necessity or the thin, manipulable pretense of "equal concern and respect" apparent in so much modern case law and contemporary liberal theory.

I will not contend that theism necessarily or inevitably culminates in tolerance; that contention would be preposterous. But tolerance and mutual respect are the natural consequences of a particular theological twist—I will call it the "ultra-protestant turn"—that theism can plausibly take. By extending the central Protestant doctrine of "justification by faith," the ultra-protestant turn seeks to do what might seem impossible—to provide a sort of qualified validation for diverse and seemingly incompatible religious belief systems without dissolving them or compromising their integrity.

7

The (Compelling?) Case for Religious Intolerance

TO THE MODERN mind, at ease in a pluralistic culture, religious intolerance seems an anomalous and anachronistic vice, like dueling or racial bigotry. Human association is a presumptive good, after all, so why on earth *should* anyone be reluctant to accept and associate with others merely because they happen to adhere to different faiths (or to none)? How does it hurt me if you profess a different creed than I do? The classic expression was Jefferson's: "[I]t does me no injury for my neighbor to say there are twenty gods, or no God. It neither picks my pocket nor breaks my leg."[1]

From this perspective, religious intolerance seems a manifestation less of outdated thinking than of a failure to think at all; intolerance is an expression of that quintessential (although unexpectedly resilient) modern vice—"irrational prejudice."[2] It is nonetheless important that we understand the case for religious intolerance, in part because an understanding will help us appreciate the development by which tolerance can evolve from a character flaw into a virtue, and in part because toleration is not a completely secure achievement; it is something that still needs defending. Indeed, if critics like Stanley Fish are right, tolerance is something we have not yet achieved, even imperfectly (and perhaps could not achieve); our self-image as a tolerant people is a self-gratifying delusion.

So, with the help of critics like Fish, we need to examine the case for intolerance more closely. That case turns out to be much stronger than many of us would have supposed.

THE "SACRED RIGHT TO KILL THE OTHER FELLOW WHEN HE DISAGREES"

We can begin by noticing a view asserted in characteristically blunt fashion by Justice Holmes. In conversations and correspondence with

Judge Learned Hand, Holmes defended what he described as the "sacred right to kill the other fellow when he disagrees."[3] In a similar vein, Holmes in a renowned opinion declared "[p]ersecution for the expression of opinions" to be "perfectly logical."[4] Holmes was not exactly exulting over this "sacred right"; on the contrary, he was pondering strategies for containing it. But he evidently thought the logic of persecution unassailable; consequently, his remedy for the fearful consequences of this logic was in part a skepticism calculated to induce believers to "doubt [their] premises."[5] In this way, the "sacred right to kill the other fellow when he disagrees" would remain intact; but a judicious skepticism would remove the motivation for exercising it.

But was the logic tersely approved by Holmes truly inexorable, or was Holmes himself guilty of a non sequitur? We can consider the question by examining the argument for intolerance in small steps.

Truth Entails Falsity

For help in understanding Holmes's position, we can turn to Stanley Fish's recent argument for a similar position. Fish contends that tolerance can immediately be seen to be an incoherent and practically useless ideal.[6] This conclusion follows of necessity, he thinks, from the simple truism (which, Fish observes, "modern theorists try in every way possible to avoid") that "[i]f you believe something you believe it to be true, and perforce, you regard those who believe contrary things to be in error."[7]

Standing by itself, though, this truism need not culminate in intolerance, as Fish supposes. Fish seems to be right about what it means to believe something. If x and y are contradictory propositions, then it follows (in ordinary logic, at least) that if x is true, y is false. So if I believe x is true, then unless I am confused, I will believe that y is false; and if you happen to believe y then I will conclude that you are mistaken.

But this logic by itself does not support any particular *practical* conclusion—any conclusion, that is, about *how to act* or what attitude to take toward those who hold false beliefs. Instead of adopting an intolerant stance toward you for believing y (which I hold to be false), I might gently try to convince you of x. Or I might pity you for holding a false belief. Conversely, I might actually rejoice that you hold a false belief—because I don't like you, or because your error makes me look better by comparison, or because I believe (with Mill) that falsity makes truth shine all the brighter.[8] Or, as seems most likely, I might simply be indifferent—*not,* it is important to note, to the truth of *x,* but to *you.* What business is it of mine if your mind harbors nonsense?

If *y* is false, in short, then it will remain false whether you believe it or not; my shunning or banishing or punishing you will not make that proposition any less (or more) false. So believing *x,* even passionately and unreservedly, merely puts me in opposition to *y*—not to persons who happen to hold *y.*

Fish's claim, in sum, slights the case for intolerance by making it too abstract—too much an exercise in theoretical rather than practical reason. In order to turn Fish's claim about what it means to believe into an argument for intolerance, we would need to supply an additional, more practical premise. Is such a premise available? Consider two candidates for the role, which we might call the "altruistic" premise and the "self-protection" premise.

Promoting Truth

The altruistic premise asserts that *I ought to promote truth,* or that I ought to work to induce other people to hold true beliefs. If I am my brother's (and sister's) keeper, then I should not look on with indifference as they go through life holding false beliefs. Rather, I should strive to enlighten them.[9]

Perhaps Fish implicitly presupposes the altruistic premise. In any case, that premise adds practical force to Fish's more abstract proposition that to believe something is to believe it is true and its contrary is false. Moreover, the altruistic premise is one that many people seem to embrace: political zealots and religious missionaries are perhaps the clearest cases.

It seems more doubtful, though, that *inquisitors* embrace that premise—or at least that the premise provides plausible support for their intolerant measures. That is because the measures usually associated with intolerance—shunning, criminal sanctions, persecution, exile, sometimes execution—seem ill-conceived as ways of inducing the unconverted to accept true belief. Advocates of religious tolerance from Lactantius to Locke to many a modern friend of the First Amendment have explained that intolerance is futile as a way of discharging one's altruistic obligation to promote true and efficacious belief in one's neighbor.[10] Only a sincere belief is efficacious, the proponents of religious toleration insist, or indeed is even accurately described as "belief" at all; and external pressure or punishment cannot produce sincere belief.[11] For modern liberals the point may seem so obvious that it becomes hard to understand how the intolerant could ever have believed otherwise.* So if *this* is the premise upon which intolerance rests, then once again intolerance seems irrational—an expression not so much of logic as of unthinking prejudice.

Protecting the Faith

Whatever its practical implications, though, the altruistic premise is not essential to the argument for intolerance; indeed, as a historical matter it probably has not been at the heart of what Fish calls "the illiberal impulse." Timothy Hall's recent study[12] of Roger Williams, the first great American apostle of religious tolerance, illustrates the point. Hall begins his account of Williams by describing the mind-set of the Massachusetts Puritans who banished Williams for his doctrinal deviations. The Puritans acted from "logic as much as passion," Hall explains: the "zeal that harries an unbeliever with scourge and banishment is rooted in a syllogism of premises and deductions." And what were those premises? In part the Puritans acted on altruistic grounds, seeking "to rescue deviant souls and restore them to the bosom of the community." But their altruistic concern for religious correctness was severely

---

* The issue is actually more complicated. Coercion conceivably *might* help to induce belief, perhaps by forcing people to be exposed to and to consider particular beliefs, perhaps by producing a situation in which the psychological aversion to cognitive dissonance would lead people to embrace a belief in order to establish congruity between internal belief and external (coerced) professions and actions. Objections of this kind to the Lockean "futility" argument have been persuasively advanced by critics from Locke's own sparring partner, Jonas Proast, to modern philosophers like Jeremy Waldron. See Richard Vernon, The Career of Toleration: John Locke, Jonas Proast, and After 18–30 (1997); Jeremy Waldron, Locke: Toleration and the Rationality of Persecution, in John Locke: *A Letter concerning Toleration* in Focus 98, 115–19 (John Horton and Susan Mendus eds. 1991). Waldron explains that

> [c]ensors, inquisitors and persecutors have usually known exactly what they were doing, and have had a fair idea of what they could hope to achieve. If our only charge against their enterprise [is that it was] hopeless and instrumentally irrational from the start, then we perhaps betray only our ignorance of their methods and objectives, and the irrelevance of our liberalism to their concerns.

(Id. at 120)

limited. In reality, the Puritans "launched no inquisition to ferret out heresy from its hiding places in the hearts of Massachusetts inhabitants"; they were for the most part perfectly content to leave heretics in peace so long as their errors were not publicly promoted.[13]

So then what "syllogism of premises" *did* move the Puritans to banish and occasionally even execute the religiously heterodox? Hall explains that Massachusetts authorities acted primarily upon what they regarded as a policy of self-protection. They believed, quite plausibly, that vocal heretics would corrupt the faith of some who would otherwise accept orthodox beliefs. John Cotton, the prominent Puritan divine and Williams's leading antagonist, offered a clarifying comparison. If a member of the community were found with leprosy or some other highly contagious disease, the only responsible course would be to protect others against contamination by quarantining the infected person. Spiritual disease called for a similar remedy, Cotton explained: pernicious heresies, like infectious germs, needed to be removed for the good of others.

> It is not want of mercy, and charity, to set such at a distance: It is a merciless mercy, to pity such as are incurably contagious, and mischievous, and not to pity many scores or hundreds of the souls of such, as will be infected and destroyed by the toleration of the other.[14]

Cotton's statement suggests that Jeremy Waldron is off the mark when he suggests that the error in the classic "futility" argument for toleration advanced by Locke and others is that the argument appeals only to "the interests of the persecutors," and that what was needed was an argument based on "the interests of the victims of persecution."[15] As Cotton's statement indicates, intolerant governors will typically see themselves as acting precisely in the interest of the governed—of vulnerable citizens whose souls would be endangered by heresy (and perhaps in the interests of the heretics themselves). Brad Gregory's prize-winning history of martyrdom in early modern Europe explains that persecuting authorities were animated by "concern for heretics' and others' souls"; they believed that "[c]oddling heretics expressed a misplaced mercy that placed others at risk."[16] So the question was—and *is*—not *whose* interests are being invoked, but rather what those interests are and how they can be secured.

In short, the logic of intolerance as understood and practiced by the

Massachusetts Puritans included but went well beyond Fish's contention that to believe something is to believe it is true and its contrary false. The Puritans added to that contention additional and practical considerations—in particular, that true belief is vital to the health of one's very soul, and that exposure to publicly promulgated heresy is likely to undermine true belief in some of those who would otherwise hold it. Given this constellation of beliefs, persecution was, as Holmes would later put it, "perfectly logical." Indeed, persecution was more than merely "logical"; it was a religious imperative calculated to protect a sacred faith, as well as those who embraced that faith, from deadly contamination.

RELIGIOUS PLURALISM AND THE DEVOUT BELIEVER

An appreciation for the force of this logic is crucial in understanding the prevalence of religious intolerance through much of Western history and the appeal of intolerance even today. But measured against current attitudes, at least in academic circles, the logic of intolerance when explicitly laid out may seem counterintuitive; it may have a musty, archaic feel to it. So it may be helpful to flesh out the argument from the standpoint of the religious believers who may actually favor, and practice, intolerance. It will also be helpful at this point to talk not so much about "religion" in generic terms, but rather about a particular kind of religion: Christianity. That is because, as non-Christians may appreciate better than Christians,[17] the phenomenon of intolerance has in much of the Western experience been associated with societies populated predominately by people who have been, or have pretended or aspired to be (in varying forms and degrees), Christians. So it is important to consider how the question of intolerance may look from a Christian perspective.[18]

The Christian Framework

For present purposes, we can appreciate some central and relevant elements of the distinctively Christian perspective by noticing three terms that do not figure prominently in ordinary, nonreligious talk but that are pervasive in the Christian vocabulary: *salvation, righteousness,* and *creed.*

The Christian religion typically has taught that the overarching goal to which human beings should aspire is the salvation of the soul[19]—a goal that Christians (and others)[20] may understand in different ways but that typically has been projected into an afterlife. No merely temporal or this-worldly interest—not wealth or worldly happiness, and certainly not "civil peace"—even approaches this value in importance. "For what shall it profit a man," Jesus asked, "if he shall gain the whole world, and lose his own soul?"[21] Centuries later, Miguel de Unamuno expressed the same valuation:

> A human soul is worth all the universe. . . . A human soul, mind you! Not a human life. Not this life. And it happens that the less a man believes in the soul . . . the more he will exaggerate the worth of this poor transitory life.[22]

So our overarching concern should be for the salvation of the soul. Salvation, in turn, is a benefit deriving from God's "righteousness"; and it is in some difficult and controversial sense—I will briefly note some of the controversies surrounding this idea later—a reward for human righteousness. The term "righteousness," meaning (as the OED explains) "justice, uprightness, rectitude," may seem quaint; and indeed it hardly ever appears anymore outside religious contexts—except in the pejorative compound "self-righteous." But the term serves to convey the blend of "truthful" and "virtuous" that is urged on Christians.

The righteousness that is a means to salvation encompasses, for Christians, not only virtuous conduct but also—the point is crucial—correct *belief*. "Faith" is the first of the three traditional Christian virtues; and faith is usually understood to include, even if it is not identical with, true belief in essential theological matters. So Christianity has given rise to a remarkable outpouring of formal creeds, or statements of basic beliefs.[23] Some Christians place great weight on these creeds, reciting them regularly in worship services. Other Christians attach less value to formalized and recitable statements, or even view them with disdain,[24] but these Christians may nonetheless accept the central importance of belief—of the act or fact of *believing*, or the "I believe" of the "credo." Thus, a New Testament verse cited on posters at seemingly every televised athletic contest in America declares "everlasting life" to be the reward of "whosoever *believeth* in" Jesus.[25] A subsequent chapter in John's Gospel elaborates the point. "What shall we do, that we might work the works of God?" Jesus's interlocutors ask, and Jesus enjoins: "This is the work of God, that ye *believe* on him whom he hath sent."[26] It would hardly be an overstatement to say that the subsequent tradition of Christian creeds and doctrine simply reflects an effort to take that injunction seriously—*very* seriously.

A standard Christian creed expresses the fearsome negative implication of this emphasis on correct belief (albeit in terms that might embarrass many Christians, today at least).[27] The Athanasian Creed, widely accepted by Protestants as well as Catholics, is devoted to formulating basic trinitarian and christological doctrines, but it begins with an ominous warning:

> Whosoever will be saved: before all things it is necessary that he hold the Catholic [or universal] Faith: Which Faith except every one do keep whole and undefiled: without doubt he shall perish everlastingly.[28]

Though benignly absent from other classic Christian creeds,[29] these warnings are reminiscent of some passages from the New Testament itself,[30] and they foreshadowed what has probably been the most common Christian view in the centuries since. Francis Sullivan explains:

> St. Thomas and the whole medieval tradition had taught that there was no salvation for anyone in the Christian era without explicit faith in Christ. They were convinced that anyone who had heard about Christ and did not believe in him must be guilty of the sin of unbelief, for which he would be justly damned.[31]

Dying—and Killing—for the Truth

The conjunction of beliefs I have just described (in the surpassing importance of salvation and in the imperative of correct belief as one qualification for salvation) helps to explain why thousands of believers would cheerfully suffer death rather than consent to embrace heresy[32]—even when the differences between "heresy" and "orthodoxy" might to an outsider seem to amount to petty doctrinal quibbles. Brad Gregory notes in modern scholars and theorists "a tendency to condemn the virulence of the [early modern] period's doctrinal disputes as disproportionate to the issues involved." Conversely, he detects in modern treatments "assumptions that regard self-preserva-tion and the prolongation of one's life as the greatest of all values." But to the devout believer, this inversion of values will seem perverse and irrational. "Catholics as well as varieties of Protestants and Anabaptists concurred," Gregory explains, "that scripture was the word of God, that it was true, . . . and that correct faith was necessary for eternal salva-tion." On the basis of these premises, "martyrs measured temporal pain against eternal gain and drew the logical conclusion. Torture and death were surely horrific—but incomparably less so than eternal suffering." Consequently, "[i]n dying for their religious convictions, the new mar-tyrs proclaimed the transcendent importance of their beliefs."[33] One critical contemporary observer described the attitude of Anabaptist martyrs, for example: "[S]ooner than recant one article they would suf-fer another hundred deaths."[34]

If we understand why believers would willingly *suffer* death to avoid heresy, we may begin to understand why they might also be will-ing to *inflict* it—for a similar purpose. In the early modern period, as Gregory explains, religious martyrdom and religious persecutions were simply different corollaries of the same premises applied to different situations:

> [T]he willingness to die for one's beliefs was not necessarily the sim-ple opposite of the willingness to kill for them. Both dispositions em-braced central Christian notions about truth, faith, the afterlife, an-swerability to God, and responsibility to others. . . . Just as men and women interrogated about their faith were answerable to God, so were rulers responsible to God (and their subjects) for maintaining true religion. The issue was not suffering as opposed to meting out punishment, but rather what commitment to the truth called for in di-vergent circumstances.[35]

The Spiritual Hazards of Religious Pluralism

It might seem that this logic is no longer relevant to our modern sit-uation. After all, most of us do not typically think of our government of-ficials as answerable to God. And most of us may be quite comfortable with a condition of religious pluralism. But to a person with the kind of commitments I have just described, that condition may still, and very plausibly, seem to present grave dangers. Consider, to begin with, two matters that have arisen directly or indirectly in the lives of nearly all human beings in all times and places: marriage, and the education of children. At least to the devout, a religiously pluralistic society can present deadly risks in both these crucial concerns.

To appreciate these risks, imagine that you hold to a faith (Christian or not) that teaches that the whole point of life on earth is to attain salvation and that salvation depends on careful adherence to a particular creed, a particular pattern of worship, and a particular code of behavior. Imagine also that you belong to a religiously homogeneous society faced with the question whether to accept people of other faiths. With just a bit of foresight, you will anticipate that if nonbelievers are welcomed, over time a situation of pluralism is likely to develop. Eventually, many or even most of the people in the community will no longer understand—or will consciously reject—what you regard as vital religious beliefs and commitments. It is readily foreseeable that under those circumstances, you and your fellow religionists (or your children) will interact constantly with nonbelievers at school, at work, in the marketplace, and in various public functions. Only by studiously blinding yourself to human experience—by refusing to watch or learn from films like *Fiddler on the Roof,* for example—could you overlook the likelihood that in the course of these constant, daily interactions, you or your fellow believers may form relationships, including marriage, that will lead (if not immediately, then in later generations) to the compromising of what you regard as the most crucial commitments—commitments that for you constitute the essential point of human life.

A vivid expression of this specific concern occurs in the Hebrew scriptures, adopted by Christians as the Old Testament. As the people of Israel prepare to enter the land of Canaan, God warns them that interaction and especially intermarriage with the people currently living in that land will subvert their faith. "For they will turn away thy son from following me, that they may serve other gods: so will the anger of the Lord be kindled against you." As a way of preventing this grave evil, the people of Israel are enjoined to annihilate the current inhabitants. "[T[hou shalt smite them, and utterly destroy them; thou shalt make no covenant with them, nor show mercy unto them."[36] The sentiment may seem barbaric, but the underlying logic has not lost its validity.

Nor is marriage the only danger. If your children are educated in common schools, you have every reason to expect (even assuming, perhaps implausibly, an utter absence of conscious opposition to your faith) both that your children will *not* be instructed in what you regard as the indispensable truths necessary to salvation, and that they *will* be instructed in ideas and values that are subtly corrosive of, or even overtly contrary to, those truths. You might respond to these risks, of course, by developing a separate, compensatory program of religious instruction to be conducted at church or at home. Even so, the risk posed by constant, daily, extended exposure to contrary beliefs and values might well be a major concern.

Marriage and education are merely among the more conspicuous and specific contacts through which pluralism bids to undermine faith. More generally, the challenge that pluralism creates for faith lies in the simple, constant fact of association with nonbelievers. Such association threatens belief in several related ways. One kind of challenge arises because, as sociologist Peter Berger explains, "pluralism undermines the taken-for-grantedness of beliefs and values" that has prevailed through most of human history.[37] Historically, that is, most people have held particular religious beliefs because in a given cultural setting these beliefs seem to be almost automatic; they are inherited and accepted as uncontroversial statements of the way things just obviously are. But association with people who conspicuously do not share a set of beliefs will tend to make those beliefs less automatic, and therefore more optional; and at least some people will exercise their option by discarding formerly held religious beliefs—or by declining to embrace them in the first place.[38]

Having rendered religious beliefs optional, pluralism may also create new *epistemological* obstacles that hinder individuals from opting to retain or embrace religious beliefs. Comparing beliefs with friends and associates, you may discover that they explain and justify their own faiths on pretty much the same kinds of grounds that you offer for yours. Some of these individuals will likely be decent, thoughtful people who are at least as intelligent and as devoted to their faith as you are. So how can you be confident that your creed is right when other people adhere to other creeds with the same fervor—and seemingly on many of the same grounds—that you claim? In this vein, Martin Marty notes that "[t]o believe in God in one way and then to find my neighbour disbelieving, or believing in another God or in another way, and still being a fine, moral functioning member of society—this can be a challenge to the grip I have on my faith."[39]

But inclusiveness and pluralism may also threaten faith in an even more telling and indeed *theological* way that can turn a theistic creed against itself. Your religion teaches you to believe, let us suppose, in a benevolent and just God. Perhaps the conditions of pluralism do nothing, intially at least, to disturb this belief; after considering objections and contrary views, you introspect and find your belief in God unshaken. Even so, a delicate question arises: Would a loving, just God reward *you* with salvation while condemning someone whom you have come to know and respect, even though it may appear after discussion and candid reflection that she differs from you mainly in having been raised and educated in a different religious tradition? In this spirit, Paul Badham worries that Christian "exclusivism" implies an "appalling picture of God."[40] John Rawls observes in the same vein that "it is difficult, if not impossible, to believe in the damnation of those with whom we have, with trust and confidence, long and fruitfully cooperated."[41] The observation is cogent, but while Rawls offers the observation cheerfully, from the perspective of a devout believer the phenomenon presents a subtle but powerful hazard. Insofar as your creed teaches that damnation *is* the fate of nonbelievers, this charitable conclusion suggests that your creed is in error. And if the creed is mistaken in one important matter, then . . . well, who knows?

In an autobiographical reflection, Sanford Levinson offers a concrete illustration of these challenges. Levinson recalls how, growing up as part of a small Jewish minority in Hendersonville, North Carolina, he attended public schools and had lengthy discussions about religion with friends he made there. During his high school years, he reports,

> [a] fairly typical evening, especially in summers, would be to drink beer or play poker while at the same time energetically debating the basic questions of religion, especially those involving *theodicy* and the presence of an after life. My friends included a Catholic . . . , several Southern Baptists, a Methodist, a Presbyterian. . . . We argued with the particular intensity of teenagers, though never, so far as I recall, acrimoniously.[42]

Levinson explains the challenge that these friendly discussions created for those participants who held to a strict or exclusive faith:

I particularly remember my Southern Baptist friends expressing seemingly genuine regret that my failure to acknowledge Jesus as my Savior condemned me to eternal torment in hell. They would have preferred knowing that I would join them in heaven. . . . I do not censure them for their concern, especially given their general courtesy and willingness to tolerate my response to their entreaties that, as a Jew, I just did not see any reason to accept Jesus as divine. . . . Moreover, I added that I did not believe that a God worth worshipping (or even respecting) would condemn anyone to the torments of eternal punishment.[43]

Levinson does not say whether these arguments led to any change in the views of his Baptist friends (though he mentions that their parents were concerned about the effects of the discussions).[44] His reflections on these experiences, however, prompt him to oppose an overzealous application of "strict separation" principles to the public schools, and for a revealing (and candidly expressed) reason: Levinson fears that aggressive secularization will drive some religious students out of the public schools, thereby depriving them of the pluralistic interactions that he himself experienced. And he thinks this deprivation would be unfortunate precisely because such interactions tend over time to subvert religious beliefs, thereby bringing religious students around to beliefs that he regards as more plausible and salutary. Thus, Levinson contends that "[religiously trained] children, by attending public schools, will in fact meet and begin talking with (and learning from) more secular students." To be sure, such conversations might convince some initially secular students to accept religion, but Levinson is confident that "the transformation is far more likely to run from the religious to the secular than vice versa." His "desire to 'lure' religious parents back to the public schools thus has at least a trace of the spider's web about it."[45]

In this respect, Levinson simply contemplates—though with opposite valences—the same social and psychological dynamic that devout critics of tolerance have long anticipated. Nathaniel Ward (the Cambridge-educated, Latin-spouting, but self-styled "simple cobbler" of Puritan Massachusetts) deplored religious pluralism as a kind of "Hell above ground." Ward recalled "a City where a Papist preached in one Church, a Lutheran in another, a Calvinist in a third"; and he described the natural consequence of such pluralism: "the Religion of that place was but motley and meagre, their affections Leopard-like."[46]

Stanley Fish misconceives the matter, I think, when he writes that "persons grasped by opposing beliefs will be equally equipped ('on both sides equal') with what are, for them, knockdown arguments, unimpeachable authorities, primary, even sacred, texts, and conclusive bodies of evidence."[47] No doubt many believers will think in much this way, but others will notice the same thing that Fish here notices, and will realize that a rough equality of epistemic authority on all sides of an issue undermines the authority for every side. Surely a weakening of belief as a result of such encounters is a common human experience. Indeed, if believers were as secure in their faith as Fish suggests (and as he himself typically seems in his own professions), they would presumably not fear contact with the differently minded (as he himself evidently does not), and would therefore be less motivated to adopt exclusionary or intolerant measures. In this respect, Fish himself misunderstands and "underestimates the illiberal impulse."

From one standpoint, of course, the dilution of faith that may accompany pluralism will appear to be a positive benefit, in both social and epistemic terms. Thus, secular liberals like Rawls, Levinson, and Stephen Macedo treat the dynamic described here in sanguine tones. But from the standpoint of the devout Christian in particular, these risks associated with pluralism may seem to be mortal hazards that threaten one's very salvation, or the salvation of one's children and other loved ones. So those who in earlier eras deplored religious toleration and dreaded pluralism—who perceived "[t]he spreading of heresy" as "religious reckless endangerment by spiritual serial killers"[48]—were in this respect not being timid or narrow-minded or officious, as we may like to suppose; they were simply being realistic.

So it is little wonder that people with such religious commitments have sometimes thought it imperative to prevent the integration of nonbelievers into their communities,[49] or why, failing in that, believers have fled from pluralistic society through the formation of separate, more monistic communities. This separatist and anti-pluralist impulse played a role in the formation of this country, of course—indeed, each Thanksgiving we remember affectionately a people who left tolerant Holland, in part precisely because of its indulgence of alternative faiths—and it is still evident in legal controversies involving, for example, the Amish, the Satmar Hasidim or, more amorphously, the home schooling movement. Very recently, some prominent leaders of the "religious right" seem to have concluded that American politics and culture are so corrupt that the best strategy for religionists is with-drawal and the development of separate institutions.[50] Though liberal thinkers or jurists like Justice Stevens or Justice Douglas sometimes ex-hibit an almost childlike insouciance in the face of this separatist im-pulse[51]—why should anyone have a problem with pluralism so long as all citizens are free to believe and live in the way they choose?—their in-sensibility evinces a magnificent failure of imagination and empathy. In reality, given a historically very common kind of religious outlook, the rejection of a tolerant pluralism seems the only responsible course.

THE FUTILITY OF THE "COMMON GROUND" STRATEGY

Contemplating religious pluralism from the standpoint of a devout be-liever thus shows the case for intolerance to be much stronger than modern thinkers in a liberal society commonly suppose. Stanley Fish's articulation of the logic of intolerance may be unduly academic and his diagnosis partly mistaken, but his conclusion that a true believer cannot in good faith tolerate publicly expressed error begins to seem at least prima facie compelling. Conversely, one who does tolerate error will seem to be, as critics from Ward to Holmes to Fish have argued, weak or insincere in his faith.[52]

Proponents of pluralism and tolerance have typically tried to over-come this logic by finding—or constructing—common ground among those of different faiths; such efforts feature prominently in contempo-rary political theory by notables such as John Rawls, and also in reli-gious ecumenical efforts. But whatever their positive virtues, common ground proposals are deficient as a response to the logic of intolerance, as critics like Fish effectively show.

Three main problems deserve notice. First, the ostensible common ground will often be largely artificial and semantic in character, and therefore illusory as a practical matter. Michael Zuckert notices this problem in his analysis of Rawls's political liberalism. The entire edifice of Rawls's imposing theoretical structure is grounded in a presumed common commitment to "equality." But, as is well-known, equality means very different things to different people. So even among those who share a commitment to the *concept* of equality, Zuckert explains, "there is . . . a wide range of disagreement over what about persons makes them equal, and over what the claim of equality entitles them to." Nonetheless, "when Rawls brings the agreement on the concept of equality into his system he treats it as if it were an agreement on a conception," and no such agreement exists. So "the shift from concept to conception is simply arbitrary and illegitimate within the terms of Rawls' own thought."[53]

Rawls's position can also illustrate a second problem with "common ground" proposals: even if we take a proposed common ground uncritically and as formulated, the ground will be less than—indeed, very far from—universal. Rawls, for example, advocates a "political conception of justice" based on an ostensible "overlapping consensus" among people of diverse "reasonable comprehensive views."[54] But even Rawls must acknowledge that the "overlapping consensus" does not include *all* citizens. Some citizens—perhaps many, or conceivably even most—will hold what from a secular liberal perspective are *unreasonable* comprehensive views.[55] And many particular religions and specific religious tenets will be excluded from the liberal "consensus." Thus, in an essay enthusiastically expounding Rawls's position and its implications for religion, Edward Foley candidly acknowledges that Rawls's political liberalism not only permits but requires government to reject and discriminate against "illiberal religions."[56] Rawls soft-pedals this implication of his view, but Foley concedes that the implication is simply unavoidable.[57] And Foley catalogs other, more specific religious beliefs that a liberal regime will likely reject as false, including antidemocratic tenets, a commitment to faith healing (at least when children are at risk), and various religious notions about the education of children.[58]

These two problems—that the "common ground" is illusory and that even the illusion is not fully inclusive—will often run together because, as Stanley Fish explains, the ostensible common ground is typically presented with "a conceptual sleight of hand" that involves "defining 'everyone' in a way that excludes (or marginalizes) those" who do not share the central commitments. To put the point differently, "the views supposedly rejected by everyone will always have supporters," and these supporters "must then be eliminated or declared insane so that the common ground will appear to be really common."[59] Fish deftly exposes this "sleight of hand" in a variety of contemporary liberal theorists. In particular, he shows, citizens who place more faith in revelation or scripture than in modern scientific rationality as sources of truth are routinely marginalized so as not to disturb the "common ground."[60] Fish comments caustically on a book by Ronald Thiemann, former dean of the Harvard Divinity School, that advocates a familiar common ground strategy:

> Once outliers like religious fundamentalists have been cast out into the wilderness, you can then prate on blithely, as Thiemann does, about "common bonds," "common goals and values," "public good," and "underlying beliefs" (all on a single page), and casually stigmatize those you have exiled as adherents of "fanaticism."[61]

Moreover, Thiemann is in this respect entirely typical of "common ground" theorists, who can maintain the pretense of consensus only by asserting or assuming that "those who disagree with us, those who begin from a different conception 'of the good life or of what gives value to life,' are obviously beyond the pale, barely human, and deserve minimal consideration or perhaps no consideration at all."[62]

The discussion to this point has suggested that the "common ground" strategy is not a satisfactory response to the problem of pluralism because, in reality, there is no common ground. But there is a third and even more serious difficulty, which is that the "common ground" strategy simply fails to perceive and address the real nature of the challenge that pluralism poses for faith. Even if a common ground were real and universally inclusive, that is, the discovery of common ground simply does not eliminate the spiritual hazards created by pluralism. From the believers' standpoint, after all, pluralism is threatening not so much for what it *lacks* as for what it *is*: the problem, as discussed above, is not the absence of any common ground, but rather the existence of positive differences that jeopardize the faith of the believer or her loved ones.

Indeed, it is precisely the presence of limited common ground—of episodic occasions for mutual interaction and cooperation—that makes these differences in faith threatening. Nathaniel Ward, the "simple cobbler of Aggawwam," explained regarding the adherents of error that "their breath is contagious, their leprey spreading": the devout should thus avoid meeting with, speaking with, or even hearing such "Errorists."[63] But "common ground" is by definition and design the public space where such dreaded interactions will occur—where the contagion of heresy finds its opportunity to spread. Remember John Cotton's "disease" analogy. Suppose we tell a political community that is acting to quarantine people with a devastating and highly communicable disease—a plague of medieval proportions, say—that the afflicted persons have common interests with those who are not (yet) infected. The observation seems wholly inapt. *Of course* there are common interests, but how does that fact alleviate the concern about spreading a lethal disease?

A comparative conjecture may help to make the point. Suppose, for example, that we were to point out to diverse believers in religiously troubled parts of the world today—to Hindus and Muslims in India, or to Muslims and Jews in the Middle East, or to Muslims and Christians in southern Europe, or to Catholics and Protestants in Ireland—that their religions have important common elements and, furthermore, that in any case they do not need a common religion to unite them. There are plenty of other factors and interests that might serve as a basis for mutually beneficial association: common economic or military interests, perhaps, or a shared history (including a history of oppression by outsiders), or a common language and geographical proximity. This sort of pacifying argument is familiar enough, but in many situations it may also seem obtuse. The problem *for the devout believers* is not so much one of finding common interests—those may be obvious enough—but rather of associating with people whom they may regard as heretics or infidels. Once again, it is precisely the fact of shared interests that makes religious pluralism worrisome to believers because, as discussed above, those interests will bring differently minded believers together in ways likely to lead to conversation, frequent association, and perhaps intermarriage—interactions that over time threaten to undermine their faith.

A DESPERATE PROGNOSIS?

The discussion in this chapter has suggested that Learned Hand was right: religious faith and tolerance seem to be incompatible. This conclusion leaves our situation looking very bleak. Indeed, the conclusion is so bleak that we may become suspicious. Doesn't the American experience with pluralism provide an empirical refutation of the logic of intolerance described above? Haven't we managed in fact to achieve a limited but still significant amount of mutual respect among people of competing faiths?

Critics of tolerance such as Fish have an answer to this observation, of course. Much of what goes under the heading of tolerance, the critics will suggest, is in reality a form of politics on behalf of (disguised) orthodoxies. And much of it reflects a simple loss of genuine belief: when prompted, people may continue to mumble the old creeds, but the belief—the fervor, the real conviction—is no longer there. But even if this assessment contains a measure of truth (and indeed a truth that the devout themselves may sometimes insist on),[64] is it a fully satisfactory account of our situation? Or have the critics of tolerance overlooked something?

I will argue in the next chapter that they have. More specifically, the critics of tolerance have failed to notice the possibility of a theologically based mutual respect among people of conflicting faiths.

8

Theism and Tolerance

FROM THE OUTSET, Christian thinkers worried about—and devised subtle ways of avoiding—the conclusion that God would condemn those who blamelessly fail to accept the orthodox Christian faith. For example, early Christian thinkers like Justin Martyr, Irenaeus, and Clement of Alexandria developed a "logos theology" in which the "Logos" or Word of God, incarnated in Jesus, had also manifested itself in Greek philosophy and pre-Christian religion, so that adherents of these traditions had in fact accepted Christ without knowing it. More recently but in similar vein, Karl Rahner has argued for the possibility of an "anonymous Christianity."[1]

As a result of these efforts, there may be more than one theological road to religious tolerance within a community significantly rooted in various ways in Christian faith and tradition. The route that I intend to explore in this chapter is less theologically ambitious than many but perhaps (and just for that reason, I suspect) more accessible to ordinary believers on an intuitive level. I will call the rationale to be developed here "ultra-protestant" not because it is peculiarly available to Protestants, or even to Christians, but because it reflects an extension of the idea of justification by faith that was strongly emphasized by historic Protestantism and in particular by Martin Luther.

THE ULTRA-PROTESTANT TURN

Martin Luther's discovery of the idea of justification by faith came as the culmination of a personal spiritual crisis, in which he was "driven by his desire to find the merciful God."[2] Luther did not invent the idea of "justification by faith"—it was a long-standing Christian doctrine, as he himself insisted,[3] and it was a theme available in late medieval Christian thought, as he seemingly did not realize[4]— but his personal discovery and exuberant defense of the principle precipitated the

Protestant Reformation. So we can usefully begin by recalling the sort of spiritual crisis that led Luther to his crucial discovery.

The Goodness of God and Justification by Faith

As discussed in chapter 7, the Christianity that constituted Luther's spiritual and intellectual world demanded of the Christian righteousness in both belief and conduct. It was the latter demand that particularly troubled the lively, accusing conscience of the young Luther. *Believing*, it seems, was less of a problem. Luther exhibited no lack of confidence in his ability to discern the truth, primarily through the study of scripture; his famous "Here I stand!" speech exudes what might be (and most emphatically *was*) regarded as an inordinate self-confidence in this respect.[5] His biographer notes that "Luther rarely used the commonly employed scholarly qualification 'if I am not mistaken'—*ni fallor*—but made generous use of his favorite expression, 'certainly'—*immo*."[6] Nor did Luther hesitate to endorse the traditional Christian creeds, especially the Athanasian Creed with its ominous pronouncements of damnation on any who might disbelieve its contents.[7]

But Luther experienced a different sort of difficulty: despite his struggles, he could not bring himself to suppose that his conduct, or perhaps his character, was sufficient to render him acceptable to God. Thus, Luther early on abandoned the legal career that his father had projected for him, and opted instead for a more pious life in an Augustinian monastic order.[8] The condition of admittance to that order, Heiko Oberman explains, was acceptance of a strict discipline:

> What conversion meant in practice was explained very clearly to the candidate during his first questioning by the prior: killing off one's own will, meager meals, coarse clothing, hard work during the day, keeping vigil during the night, chastising the flesh, self-mortification by begging, extensive fasting, and an uneventful monastic life in one place. Only when the aspirant said yes to all this was he admitted to the novitiate.[9]

Luther accepted these vows, and he kept them (at least in his own estimation). According to his later report, he lived "an irreproachable life as a monk,"[10] and he "did not think about women, money, or possessions."[11] Nonetheless, he continued to feel condemned for his unworthiness. His heart "fidgeted and trembled," he said, and he "could not but imagine that I had angered God."[12] God seemed to him an unrelenting, insatiable taskmaster who demanded of humans what they could never give. "I did not love—in fact I hated—that righteous God, the God who punishes sinners," he confessed.[13] And the verse in *Romans* that spoke of "iustitia dei"—the justice or righteousness of God— became hateful to him. "Thus I drove myself mad," he recalled, "with a desperate disturbed conscience."[14]

Luther escaped from this spiritual despair only when he came to understand and embrace the principle of "justification by faith." It was true, he concluded, that human righteousness will always fall far short of divine requirements; no amount of human exertion can earn salvation. But we are not thereby condemned to damnation. Rather, a loving God has provided for us to be freely justified by the exercise of faith. The faithful will enjoy the benefit of what was sometimes called "imputed righteousness"[15]—a quality that Luther contrasted with "works righteousness." Because persons of faith are justified through imputed righteousness while continuing to pursue lives partially characterized by sin, they are *"simul justus et peccator"*—simultaneously justified and sinners.

These concepts—justification by faith, imputed righteousness, and the idea of *simul justus et peccator*—were central to the "good news" of the Gospel as Luther understood it, and they permitted the believer to accept God as a loving Father, rather than a merciless master more deserving of hatred than love. The doctrine of justification by faith, Luther's biographer says, restored his "trust in the reality of God's unshakeable love."[16] And the scriptures that he had come to loathe—those that speak of the "righteousness of God"—now became, as he put it, "the very gate of paradise."[17]

Two-Tiered Religion

An emphasis on justification by faith has always posed an obvious risk of antinomianism, or moral lawlessness. The problem is this: a believer might reason that if righteous works are neither necessary nor sufficient for salvation, there is little reason to strive for good works at all. Why not live as we please, indulging our various appetites, and trusting (as we must in any event) to faith and God's imputed righteousness to save us? This tempting deduction would pose an ongoing concern not only to Luther but to Protestants generally (as it had done to their New Testament mentor, the apostle Paul),[18] and they made strenuous efforts to refute the antinomian inference. The latter part of Luther's famous essay on "The Freedom of a Christian" is largely devoted to explaining why the believer must strive to do good works even though works are not the basis of justification. John Calvin similarly denounced the criticism that the doctrine of justification by faith would undermine good works as an "impudent calumny."[19]

The Protestant response to the danger of antinomianism eventually led to, among other things, intricate intellectual meanderings through and around the contrasting concepts of "justification" (which might be secure through and upon the exercise of faith) and a more visible "sanctification" (which could be the struggle of, and beyond, a lifetime). The anti-antinomian arguments may not have been wholly persuasive; consequently, various forms of the heresy continued to surface from time to time (as with Anne Hutchinson in the Massachusetts colony). But as a practical matter, Luther and his Calvinist allies and their successors managed—perhaps, some would say, *too* successfully—to fend off lawless impulses. Thus, the most important Protestant influence in this country's early period was "Puritan," a label that has come to be, in some usages at least, a pejorative term—but *not* because it is equated with moral laxity or self-indulgence. On the contrary.

In stressing faith but also resisting antinomianism, Protestant thinkers in effect advocated what we might think of as a two-tiered religious life. Outwardly, one must strive for good works. God asks—and humans owe—a righteous life. On one level, therefore, Christians should behave much in the way they would if they were actually earning salvation through their good works. At the same time, they must realize that this striving in itself will always be insufficient. So on a different, more inward level, Christians should recognize the ultimate spiritual futility of their labors in "works righteousness," and they must trust in faith and "imputed righteousness" as the means for attaining salvation.

Extending Luther

As noted, Luther's spiritual crisis arose out of his inability to feel that he had satisfied God's demands for righteous *conduct* (or righteous *character*); he seems to have been less troubled by the problem of what or whether to *believe*.[20] So the idea of "justification by faith" was not directed to the requirements of belief—or to what we might call the creedal component of Christian righteousness. By contrast, for many people, especially today, *believing* may pose as great a challenge as *behaving*. Luther's trust in his ability to discover the truth through study of the scriptures (hence the Protestant idea of *sola scriptura*) may not be replicable for others, and especially for those whose confidence has been corroded by the biblical criticism that in the ensuing centuries has rendered historically doubtful much that seemed secure to Luther and his generation. Other modern developments—reductionist or materialistic science, for example, and in particular the theory of Darwinian evolution—may make religious belief much less natural or accessible for many.[21] In addition, the possibility of secure belief has been undermined by the development of a rampant religious pluralism. As discussed in chapter 7, pluralism eliminates the "taken for granted" quality of religious belief, and also creates both epistemological and theological obstacles to the confident acceptance of any particular religious creed.

A recent essay by Peter Berger explores this problem and suggests a "Protestant" remedy. Religious believers, like human beings generally, have a craving for certainty, Berger observes, but in the modern world an honest certainty may be hard to come by. In matters of religion, seekers after certainty have typically turned to three sources: authoritative institutions ("the church"), authoritative scripture ("no creed but the Bible"), and inner personal experience or revelation. But both the existence of pluralism and developments in modern science and scholarship have destroyed the power of these sources to deliver a plausible certainty. As a result, Berger detects in the modern world a tendency for people to vacillate between a nihilistic relativism and an artificial certainty. Relativism leaves the need for certainty unsatisfied, thereby pushing people toward "fundamentalist" religions or other sources of certainty; but the certainties achieved in this way are implausible and constricting, so that the believers are always in danger of "losing the faith" and careening toward nihilism or relativism.[22]

And what is the remedy for these disorienting vacillations? Berger proposes that Protestantism—and in particular the Protestant doctrine of *sola fide* (faith alone)—offers a viable and honest alternative. But Berger's own depiction of that alternative seems problematic. Berger's essay does not describe his proposal in detail, so it is hard to be sure just what he intends, but he at least seems to contemplate something like a noncreedal "faith" largely devoid of specific beliefs—a "mellow synthesis of skepticism and faith," as he puts it. In this way, Berger thinks, "one can live with uncertainty"—indeed, one scrupulously "refuses the various offers of certainty with which our situation abounds"—but "without succumbing to a corrosive relativism." Arguably, though, Berger's "mellow synthesis" has too *little* content to satisfy the perennial human questions to which faith attempts to respond, and it also has too *much* content to avoid the false certainty he eschews.[23]

A different approach would more closely parallel Luther's two-tiered, faith-grounded religion. At the level of conduct, recall, Luther held that Christians must strive to practice righteousness but that their works will in fact always be deficient; consequently, a loving God will "impute" righteousness to those who accept this gift in faith. Might not a similar pattern of reasoning apply to the *creedal* demands imposed on Christians? In this view, human beings are obligated to hold correct beliefs—and to do what is possible to arrive at and embrace those beliefs. Epistemic obstacles are no license for an indolent agnosticism—or for what we might think of as *creedal* antinomianism—any more than the impossibility of *behaving* perfectly excuses *behavioral* antinomianism, or moral laxity. At the same time, given human fallibility and the difficulty of grasping the truth, it is also inevitable that humans will fail to achieve the proper kind of belief; indeed, in many instances they will fail miserably. And despite these failings, God will nonetheless justify—he will impute a kind of "creedal righteousness"—to those who accept this gift in faith. So the faithful will be simultaneously justified and, often or always, in error.

This theological position, in short, would apply the same concepts that Luther used with respect to conduct—justification by faith, imputed righteousness, *simul justus et peccator*— but in the realm of belief itself. Its underlying spiritual motivation would be similar as well: the position reflects a fundamental sense that a good and just God would not ask of us more than we are capable of giving (righteous conduct, correct belief) without providing a remedy for our inadequacies.[24] And the position would produce the same kind of two-tiered religion with respect to belief that Luther's views supported with respect to conduct. At one level (or what we might call the level of *creed*), Christians would adhere to what they believe to be the true creed just as Christians have done from the early stages of the religion. They would continue to confess and profess—to reflect, witness, debate, formulate, revise, cate-chize, and proselytize. But at another level (which we could call the level of *faith*), Christians would acknowledge their overwhelming falli-bility and their need for divine assistance and mercy. So they would admit the likelihood that much of what they currently believe will turn out to be in need of drastic revision—and that much of what they cur-rently reject in the creeds of other-minded believers may turn out to contain truth. In the end, whether we are Christians or non-Christians, we must all believe as well and as truly as we can; and in addition, given our formidable epistemic limitations, we must also trust ulti-mately to an "imputed creedal righteousness" for our salvation.

This theological position is aptly called "ultra-protestant" because it tries to apply the Protestant principles of justification by faith and im-puted righteousness to the problem of belief itself. But the term is not meant to suggest either that "ultra-protestantism" is necessarily con-genial to all Protestants—it surely is not, and was not[25]—or that it is available *only* to Protestants.[26] In fact, ultra-protestantism goes *beyond* Protestantism and offers itself as a possibility to a wide range of believ-ers—certainly to all theists, including Christians, Jews, and Muslims.

It might seem that the position would at least exclude faiths that at-tribute infallibility to some source or authority—to a scripture regarded as inerrant, for instance, or to select papal pronouncements.[27] But the exclusion is far from inevitable. Though the idea may at first seem par-adoxical, it is entirely possible to believe in inerrancy or infallibility but to do so undogmatically. There is no logical contradiction, that is, in a believer's assertion: "I sincerely *believe* that the Bible is inerrant (or that the pope's ex cathedra pronouncements are infallible); but I also recog-nize that *my belief might be mistaken,* and I am ready to discuss and con-sider the validity of that belief." No doubt many reflective evangelical or Catholic Christians *do* hold something like this view. In short, the two-tiered approach is available even to those who sincerely believe in an infallible religious authority.

Consequently, ultra-protestantism could harbor both an orthodox Roman Catholic with extensive theological and creedal commitments and a Unitarian whose theological affirmations include very little be-yond a deity who is love and seeks justice. At the level of *creed,* both the Catholic and the Unitarian could think the other's beliefs mistaken or inadequate—perhaps egregiously so. But at the level of *faith,* each be-liever could accept the overarching fallibility of all human endeavors—

including the effort to grasp and state religious truth—and the conse-
quent need for divine grace, received in faith, to save us from our
(creedal) errors.

It should be clear that ultra-protestantism is not at all equivalent to
the sort of creedal minimalism or latitudinarianism that is often associated with eighteenth-century deism and that Berger's essay may contemplate. The position might be capacious enough to *include* that sort of
creed—or anticreed—when it is honestly come by. But it does not in itself require or even provide support for a gingerly or parsimonious
faith. On the contrary, ultra-protestantism is compatible with a full-
blown, highly developed set of doctrinal or theological commitments.

Ultra-Protestant Heresies

Every theological position with any content will have its characteristic heresies, and identifying those heresies can help to clarify the position itself. John Knox has observed that "the identification of the 'heretical' may be, not only a way, but even the indispensable way, to the
identification of orthodoxy."[28] The two-tiered approach of ultra-protestantism allows for heresies in two different senses. The traditional heresies will be, potentially at least, heresies still. But these traditional heresies will be contingently, not intrinsically, heretical; they will be a heresies *within* ultra-protestantism, so to speak, not *in opposition* to it. So
orthodox trinitarianism and the nineteenth-century unitarianism of a
William Ellery Channing might both pitch their tents securely within
the broad camp of ultra-protestantism; and each will also continue to be
heretical from the standpoint of the other.

More distinctively, ultra-protestantism also recognizes two kinds of
heresy that are intrinsically in error relative to ultra-protestantism itself.
More specifically, if ultra-protestantism reflects a two-tiered approach
to religious belief, then it will regard as heretical all religious positions
that deny the two-tiered structure by rejecting one or the other of the
levels. Consequently, intrinsic heresies will fall into two general categories, depending on which of the levels—the level of "faith" or the
level of "creed"— they reject. We might describe these categories of
error as "dogmatism" and "vacantism."

The first kind of error is familiar enough. This way of thinking operates entirely on the level of creed but does not recognize the level of
faith in the way ultra-protestantism understands it. In other words, a

dogmatist in this technical sense is someone who insists on the correctness of a particular set of beliefs without acknowledging the possibility of error or, more importantly, the possibility of "imputed creedal righteousness" or justification by faith. Though this sort of heresy may be common, discerning it is a delicate and sometimes impossible business since, as discussed above, *every* belief system at one level *will* necessarily assert its own correctness; if it did not, it could hardly be called "belief" at all. But even the person or religion that appears "dogmatic" in a conventional sense *may*, upon closer investigation, allow for the possibility of error—and of divine mercy in forgiving good faith mistakes. And, conversely, even the person who holds to a very lenient and minimalist creed might be dogmatic in maintaining it: the dogmatic latitudinarian is hardly an unfamiliar figure.

The second and opposite kind of error that I have called "vacantism" reflects a greater conceptual ingenuity. This heresy consists of evacuating the level of creed altogether while continuing to attempt to maintain some sort of faith. So the vacantist is someone who holds fast to a sincere faith in . . . nothing. Faith becomes merely an attitude without an object; it degenerates into something like cheerfulness, or optimism, or perhaps "the power of positive thinking." Robert Wilken observes this phenomenon when he describes an "impoverishment of Christian speech in our time" in which "the term 'faith' has been emptied of its cognitive dimension."[29]

The heresy of vacantism suggests that it would not be quite accurate to describe ultra-protestantism as distinguishing between *belief* and *faith*.[30] Faith itself, though frugal with its propositions, nonetheless entails at least one belief—a belief, that is, in a deity who is able and willing to impute creedal righteousness to those who believe mistakenly but in good faith. Without this belief—a belief that will appear on, and will serve to link, *both* "levels" (of creed and of faith)—the faith itself would self-destruct; it would no longer be "faith" in any substantial sense, but merely something like an unmoored, temperamental optimism without the intellectual wherewithal even to account for itself.

Like dogmatism, the heresy of vacantism is difficult to identify with confidence. Believing that the God in whom we are to have faith transcends created reality and hence exceeds any human description, religious seers and mystics have often resorted to the language of darkness, emptiness, and negation in an effort to convey some (admittedly inadequate) sense of God's nature.[31] This language of negation, however, is not intended to evacuate the level of belief, but rather to fill it with the most adequate terms and images accessible to humans. Spoken by someone else, however, the same language might well express a kind of vacantism. So religious language can be a slippery guide to the substance of a believer's faith. Alasdair MacIntyre has charged that the "theism" of twentieth-century theologians like Paul Tillich, by reducing faith to a matter of subjective psychology, is substantially identical to the atheism of nineteenth-century skeptics like Feuerbach.[32] Whether the charge is warranted—and, if it is, whether the conclusion ought to be that Tillich was "really" an unwitting atheist or that Feuerbach was "really" an unwitting theist—are questions about which perhaps not even Tillich or Feuerbach could have given completely authoritative answers.

ULTRA-PROTESTANTISM AND THE POSSIBILITY OF TOLERANCE

The two-tiered approach to religious belief permits a distinctive and respectful approach to religious pluralism; but it is important to note at the outset how this approach differs from other enterprises that share this objective. In the first place, ultra-protestantism's response to pluralism is not exactly *ecumenical* in the most familiar sense. It does not, that is, try to promote the actual merger of faiths or denominations by overcoming or dissolving doctrinal discrepancies, or by seeking the "least common denominator" among different religions. Neither does ultra-protestantism join in the project of Enlightenment thinkers like Voltaire and of many modern scholars of the "theology of religions" to promote mutual respect by convincing believers that their varied faiths are at bottom merely different symbolic or metaphorical manifestations of a common, pre-propositional apprehension of "the numinous,"[33] or of "an ultimate ineffable Reality which is the source and ground of everything."[34] The two-tiered approach need not condemn this project, to be sure, but it is also perfectly content to let believers regard their diverse creeds as "objective" statements of truths that can be set against contrary creeds with all the force of—and all the possibilities for error and contradiction available with—everyday or scientific propositions.[35]

There is no effort, in short, either to negotiate away religious differences or to transcend them by denying the ordinary propositional content of religious creeds. On the contrary, ultra-protestantism is fully compatible with a large variety of flourishing faiths that differ dramatically on the level of belief—and that exhibit no inclination to downplay differences or to achieve overt creedal unity. Nonetheless, ultra-protestantism allows for a kind of mutual respect that a one-level approach to religion does not permit.

In the usual course of things, that is, differently minded believers might agree out of necessity to "put up with" each other. But insofar as creeds are inconsistent in their declarations, a believer in one creed would have to regard other, incompatible creeds as simply *wrong* and, as such, unworthy of actual respect. Error has no rights, as the old Catholic slogan asserted—or at least it has no rights if regarded simply *as error.* Moreover, insofar as correct belief or a true confession of faith is held to be necessary to a person's salvation, believers in erroneous creeds will seem ineligible for that blessed reward. As discussed above, the presence of persons professing such exquisitely dangerous errors—dangerous to one's soul and to the souls of one's friends and family—will therefore be a hazard jeopardizing the maintenance of a condition of tolerance.

The two-level approach alters this outlook. Believers in a particular creed will still regard those who hold contrary beliefs as mistaken; they will have no cause to evade Fish's truism, noted in chapter 7, that to believe something means to believe it is true and its contrary false. But insofar as these various believers are sincere, the possibility of justification by faith softens the consequences of these disagreements. The heterodox may still be wrong, but ultra-protestantism teaches that if they are in good faith then God will impute a true belief to them. Consequently, souls—the souls of the unconverted, and of one's children, and even of oneself—are not in danger of being forever lost because of an honest creedal mistake. A sort of reciprocity of respect becomes possible. I still believe you are wrong, and you still believe I am wrong; but if we are believing in good faith then I can grant that a true belief can be imputed to you, and you can concede the same to me.

To put the point differently, ultra-protestantism prizes good faith above creedal correctness—though good faith, to be sure, entails an effort to achieve creedal correctness—and the position thereby permits a genuine respect among different kinds of good faith believers. Differently minded believers can respect each other, that is, not only in the weak sense of acknowledging each other's sincerity, but in the much more substantial sense of acknowledging the salvific possibility in the other's beliefs (even as they continue to reject those beliefs).

Nor need this respect be limited to religionists who themselves take (or are capable of taking) the ultra-protestant turn. Consider the challenge posed by nontheistic religions, for example—such as some forms of Hinduism, Buddhism, or Taoism, or even Marxism or "secular humanism" regarded as a sort of creed or faith. Insofar as their adherents believe devoutly in these faiths, the ultra-protestant position suggests that a good God would not condemn these adherents for their good faith beliefs.[36] Thus, conscientious nontheists as much as devout theists may be the beneficiaries of imputed creedal righteousness.

To be sure, insofar as someone does not believe in the essential premise of ultra-protestantism—in the existence of a good God, that is—the same *reciprocity* of respect may not be available. The nontheist may have different resources within her own theological or intellectual tradition that support respect for other faiths. But even if she does not, so that *reciprocity* of respect is not possible, the theist of an ultra-protestant persuasion can still extend a unilateral respect—can allow for the possibility of "justification by faith," that is—to all good faith believers.

Beyond permitting mutual respect among different faiths, ultra-protestantism actually allows believers to look upon pluralism as a valuable spiritual opportunity, rather than as a threat to be endured and defended against. After all, if the goal is not so much to avoid holding erroneous beliefs (a fate that our finitude and fallibility make highly likely in any case) but rather to believe as well and honestly as we can, then the opportunity to compare and defend our faiths with and against persons holding other beliefs should be understood not as a danger, but instead as a chance to refine and test and ultimately improve our beliefs.[37]

Indeed, from this perspective, an anti-pluralistic aversion to entering into such dialogue might well indicate suppressed doubt about one's own creed, and hence a lack of the sincere "good faith" that in an ultra-protestantist understanding God prizes above mere correctness. So the ostensible "true believers" who profess unqualified certainty in their creeds and therefore eschew pluralistic interaction may be suspected of having *less* of the requisite faith, not more. For them, as Reinhold Niebuhr observed, "[f]rantic orthodoxy is a method for obscuring doubt."[38]

In sum, ultra-protestantism permits believers affirmatively to welcome pluralism as a valuable resource for perfecting faith, and not to fear it, or even to regard it (as ecumenism sometimes does) as a misfortune to be overcome as expeditiously as possible through the dissolution of creedal differences.

ULTRA-PROTESTANTISM IN AMERICAN HISTORY?

The preceding discussion has suggested that by taking the ultra-protestant turn, theism (which is to say, belief and trust in a righteous God) can support the kind of mutual respect among faiths that the critics of tolerance like Justice Holmes and Professor Fish have thought to be practically and even logically impossible. But has this theology of tolerance actually been operative in American history? Has ultra-protestantism been the ingredient that has made the American achievement in domesticating religious pluralism possible?

The question is not susceptible of any clear, simple answer. On the one hand, it seems plausible that the thinking of Americans *might* often have traveled along ultra-protestant routes. The colonial and founding periods provided an ideal setting for the development of ultra-protestantism in several respects. The country's inhabitants were mostly Protestant in varying degrees and in one form or another, and hence were at some level committed to the ultra-protestant premise—that is, to the idea of justification by faith. But not *all* citizens were Protestants, of course; and even within the broad canopy of Protestantism a vigorous religious pluralism prevailed from the outset.[39] So the question of how to regard people holding different creeds constantly presented itself. Moreover, the colonial and founding experience provided recurring occasions of interaction and cooperation among citizens of different faiths—in economic associations, in politics, in the revolutionary struggle itself—and thus created both the incentive and the opportunity to develop mutual respect. In sum, conditions in this country offered both the material and the occasion for Americans to take the ultra-protestant turn in developing a tolerant pluralism.

On the other hand, if Americans have adopted ultra-protestantism, their adherence to that faith will necessarily have been mostly tacit. American religious convictions have been much more the product of ordinary believers than of professional theologians,[40] and ordinary believers are typically not given to intense theological reflection, or to careful expositions of their theological presuppositions. Moreover, even when ordinary people *do* make explicit statements of their religious beliefs, it would not be easy to say with any confidence whether these beliefs reflect an ultra-protestant orientation, as opposed to one or another ultra-protestant heresy—dogmatism or vacantism. Everyday religious conversations will often operate on what I have called the level of creed, as different individuals explain and defend what they believe. It may be hard to know whether those who reveal their beliefs in this way *also* accept ultra-protestant notions of justification by faith, or imputed creedal righteousness, just as it may be hard to know whether a person who struggles to perform good works thinks she is earning her salvation or believes in the doctrine of justification by faith.

An individual might focus on specific beliefs on many occasions (affirming a creed during worship services, for example, or explaining her religion to a friend) while consciously or intuitively groping for a notion of creedal justification by faith on other occasions (perhaps in wondering, at a wedding or a funeral, about the fate of a respected friend or relative of a different religion). Such a person would reflect a sort of ultra-protestantism-in-the-aggregate, perhaps without ever being fully conscious of accepting that (or any other) overall theological position at all.

So if we ask whether Americans have in fact been brought to the practice of tolerance through ultra-protestant convictions, it seems unlikely that any straightforward empirical investigation will supply the answer. In any case, I will not attempt any such investigation here. The hypothesis that a conscious or tacit ultra-protestantism has affected the thinking of large numbers of Americans, influencing them to develop a mutual respect among the variety of faiths that flourish here, will remain just that—a hypothesis. Instead of making claims about the general culture, I want to focus on a carefully meditated statement by a man who is probably the most revered political leader in our nation's history, and who has sometimes been regarded as our leading public theologian. Abraham Lincoln's Second Inaugural Address has come to be viewed as a landmark in a national effort to establish inclusive unity and mutual respect amidst a potentially incendiary pluralism. And that Address reflects and indeed depends on (or so I will argue) an ultra-protestant orientation.

Abraham Lincoln and the Crisis of the Union

The Civil War was the greatest challenge to national unity arising out of American pluralism. To be sure, neither the war itself nor the problem that was the principal cause leading to the war—slavery—was a direct manifestation of *religious* pluralism per se, but both evils sounded in, and had obvious implications for, religion and religious differences. In the antebellum years, the institution of slavery was attacked—and defended—largely on explicitly religious grounds.[41] Consequently, the crisis of slavery and union had the effect of splitting many of the country's leading religious denominations.[42] And of course the Civil War was understood and justified by many in overtly and even stridently religious terms;[43] Julia Ward Howe's "Battle Hymn of the Republic" ("Mine eyes have seen the glory of the coming of the Lord; . . . Glory! glory! Hallelujah!") was probably the most powerful and influential religious interpretation of the war.

Nonetheless, the war was not fought primarily for the salvation of individual souls, but rather over the salvation or preservation of the union; and its aftermath did not call for religious toleration only, but instead for a more encompassing mutual respect among Americans divided by a constellation of factors including religion, race, culture, regional history, and recent military struggle. In pleading with Americans to develop such inclusive attitudes, therefore, Abraham Lincoln was not invoking ultra-protestantism in any narrowly or traditionally religious way. Nonetheless, the position that Lincoln urged upon the nation displayed important parallels to an ultra-protestant theology, and it grew out of Lincoln's own profound (and, I will suggest, idiosyncratically ultra-protestant) religious struggles.

Lincoln's Elusive Faith

Because of his epic stature in American history and mythology, it was probably inevitable that partisans—and critics—of a variety of religious positions would try to claim Lincoln for their causes. Consequently, as Merrill Peterson reports, "millions of words [have been written] on the subject."[44] On dubious evidence it has been claimed that Lincoln was secretly a Quaker, a member of the Disciples of Christ, a Methodist, a Roman Catholic, and a Spiritualist, and also that he had privately disclosed an intention to join the Presbyterians on Easter

1865.[45] But though we can be skeptical about these claims, it is harder to be more affirmative in our descriptions. Much about Lincoln's religious views and commitments will probably remain indecipherable. A recent biography notes that "there were wild fluctuations in what even Lincoln's closest friends thought his religion, if any, had been like."[46] And it seems that his friends'—and, later, the historians'—perplexities in this respect mirror Lincoln's own.

On the one hand, the evidence indicates that Lincoln was never baptized, never took communion, and never joined a church.[47] As a boy, he entertained his siblings with skillful parodies of the sermons given at the Baptist church to which his parents belonged; later, as a young man, he enjoyed associating with "freethinkers" and was impressed by the critics of conventional religion such as Thomas Paine and Constantin de Volney.[48] He was thought by some who knew him to be a deist, a skeptic, or an "infidel"; and he once wrote (but burned without publishing) a short book attacking Christian scripture and pieties.[49] Though he evidently became more devout later in life and especially after assuming the presidency, he was never, as his wife delicately put it, a "technical Christian."[50] But throughout his life Lincoln also pored over the Bible and other religious writings and wrestled with the religious issues that were ubiquitous in the religious culture in which he lived;[51] he reportedly prayed, talked substantively and at length with clergy and religionists of a variety of faiths, and rented a pew and attended church services frequently both in Springfield, Illinois, and in Washington.[52] His religious struggles seem to have produced in him an uneasy mixture of conviction and doubt that he could never wholly reconcile.

This inner turmoil, not surprisingly, left Lincoln ambivalent about religious creeds. He seems never to have found a traditional creed that he could fully embrace, and he is said to have remarked that he would join the church that required as a condition of membership only acceptance of Jesus's commands to love God and to love one's neighbor.[53] But Elton Trueblood, the Quaker philosopher and historian, explains that this remark, evidently made partly in jest, is far from a complete expression of Lincoln's theological perspective. In fact, Lincoln's religious views were more specific and developed, but also paradoxical and prone to perplexity.[54] Far from finding creeds and sects objectionable, Lincoln regarded the large number of Christian denominations as a positive benefit so long as they were willing to listen to each other. Thus, when a friend once lamented the fragmented state of Christianity, Lincoln disagreed. "My good brother," he was reported as saying, "you are all wrong. The more sects we have the better. They are all getting somebody in that the others could not."[55] But while respecting the variety of religions, Lincoln was also disturbed by faiths that were too sure of themselves,[56] and as President he lamented the "opposite opinions and advice [coming from] religious men, who are equally certain that they represent the Divine will."[57]

Trueblood concluded that "Lincoln's mature theology was what we may truly call a sophisticated ecumenicity."[58] This ecumenicity had obvious political value. Thus, Lincoln was highly regarded by American Jews;[59] he could converse freely and respectfully with Protestants of all types; he conferred repeatedly and profitably with Quakers; and he took the initiative in appointing Roman Catholic chaplains in government hospitals.[60]

After his election to the presidency, and under the pressure of politics, war, and personal tragedy,[61] Lincoln's religious reflections intensified, and he seems to have arrived at a complex theological position that carefully avoided the heresies of both vacantism and dogmatism. At one level, Lincoln was convinced of certain specific propositions that were political but also for him at least quasi-religious—the immorality of slavery,[62] the value of democracy, and the providential role of America in preparing the world in general for freedom. He was convinced as well of the need to act in accordance with these beliefs. These themes were emphasized in, for example, the Gettysburg Address. At the same time, Lincoln was also profoundly aware of his own fallibility, and of the fallibility of human beings generally.[63] And beyond his more specific beliefs Lincoln became increasingly assured of an active, divine design that was directing both the nation and himself to fulfill some beneficent plan that neither he nor his adversaries could fully grasp. Over time, this conviction gradually led Lincoln to a conclusion that he had initially stoutly resisted—that the ultimate purpose of the war must be, in some not fully fathomable way, to bring about the end of slavery.[64]

In a written meditation from 1862, apparently prepared purely for his own clarification but "contain[ing] the most radically metaphysical question ever posed by an American president,"[65] Lincoln related this complex theological perspective to the war:

> The will of God prevails. In great contests each party claims to act in accordance with the will of God. Both *may* be, and one *must* be wrong.

God can not be *for,* and *against,* the same thing at the same time. In the present civil war it is quite possible that God's purpose is something different from the purpose of either party—and yet the human instrumentalities, working just as they do, are of the best adaptation to effect His purpose. I am almost ready to say this is probably true—that God wills this contest, and wills that it shall not end yet. By His mere quiet power, on the minds of the now contestants, He could have either *saved* or *destroyed* the Union without a human contest. Yet the contest began. And having begun He could give the final victory to either side any day. Yet the contest proceeds.[66]

This position left Lincoln simultaneously committed to carrying out God's will as well as he could discern it, yet also suspicious of those who were overly certain that they knew what the will of God was. Paradoxically, but consistent with an ultra-protestant insight, Lincoln even suggested that those who were overconfident about what God wants were not merely misguided or presumptuous, but in fact were lacking in faith; they were in effect demoting an infinite deity to their own finite level of understanding. Thus, months before the Emancipation Proclamation, Lincoln was accosted by an abolitionist who insisted that if Lincoln would simply free the slaves immediately, God would vindicate the decision and reward the Union with victory. Lincoln defended his own seemingly more vacillating position with a surprising and passionate declaration: *"My faith is greater than yours."* He went on to insist that although (or rather because) he believed in and struggled to follow the divine will, he also believed, as a biographer paraphrases his response, that "God will not abandon us to the foolishness of our own devices."[67] Lincoln's faith was greater than that reflected in the dogmatic, self-assured prescription of the abolitionist, in short, because he ultimately trusted in providence, not in his own understanding.

The Ultra-Protestant Dimension of the Second Inaugural Address

The culminating expression of these intense, agonized theological reflections occurred in the speech[68] inaugurating Lincoln's second, tragically truncated term in office. By that time, the Civil War appeared to be nearing its end (as he noted at the outset of the speech), and Lincoln used the occasion to reflect on the deeper significance of the conflict and on the course that lay ahead. What had the war meant in the overarching providential scheme of things? What larger purpose had it served? What were its political, moral, and religious implications? Lincoln's succinct meditation on these questions, containing within its twenty-five sentences "fourteen references to God, many scriptural allusions, and four direct quotations from the Bible," would come to be recognized as a "theological classic"; a London newspaper promptly described the speech as "the noblest political document known to history."[69]

Lincoln's meditation is searching and complicated; it proceeds on more than one level. Its complexity can be appreciated if we contrast his speech with what might easily have been said on the occasion by a similarly motivated but more dogmatic and single-minded speaker (such as almost any of the abolitionists, or perhaps the Radical Republicans who would soon be in control of the nation). We can easily imagine a speech, that is, that would unfold the following theme: slavery was an abomination and offense in the sight of God; the South practiced and defended that abomination; and God's judgment has therefore come upon the South (as the foreseeable imminent defeat of the Confederacy makes clear). Such self-gratifying and self-righteous assessments are common enough, especially in war; they might come with particular ease in a struggle fought successfully (but with horrifying losses) in large part over the institution of slavery.

And in fact this theme *is* discernible in Lincoln's address. He plainly expresses his belief that slavery is an "offence" in the eyes of God. And he intimates that the "scourge of war" may well be understood as divine retribution for "all the wealth piled by the bond-man's two hundred and fifty years of unrequited toil." But the moral condemnation and the assertion of divine retribution are counterbalanced in Lincoln's speech by two other and related themes: human fallibility, and the need to trust in an inscrutable divine righteousness.

Thus, Lincoln confesses his inability—and *our* inability as mortals—to fathom God's overall design. This incapacity is initially inferred from the fact of religious pluralism: Americans in both the North and the South "read the same Bible, and pray to the same God"; but they reach different conclusions and pray for different outcomes. So the fallibility of our religious investigations and deductions is apparent. As Lincoln had remarked in his 1862 reflection, contradictory beliefs about God may both be wrong but cannot both be right. Recognizing our fallibility, we should understand the frailty of our beliefs and commitments even as we continue to assert and to live by them.

Indeed, we should be cautious even in our condemnation of slavery, and of those who practiced and supported it. "It may seem strange that any men should dare to ask a just God's assistance in wringing their bread from the sweat of other men's faces; but let us judge not that we be not judged." For all we know, Lincoln observes, slavery might indeed be an "offence," but also one that in God's providential scheme "must needs come," at least for an "appointed time."

So beyond all our specific and fallible judgments about concrete matters and issues we must trust in the righteousness and justice of God. "The Almighty has his own purposes" to which we are not privy. Most strikingly, Lincoln suggests that even our fervent belief that it would be good for the war to come to a speedy end must defer to this larger faith. Consequently, "if God wills that [the war] continue, until all the wealth piled by the bond-man's two hundred and fifty years of unrequited toil shall be sunk, and until every drop of blood drawn with the lash, shall be paid by another drawn with the sword, as was said three thousand years ago, so still it must be said 'the judgments of the Lord, are true and righteous altogether.'" Lincoln here quotes a verse from Psalm 19 that conjoins divine justice with divine righteousness. This was the very same conjunction, expressed in the New Testament writings of Paul and in the idea of *iustitia dei*, that had tormented Luther and propelled him to discover the idea of justification by faith.[70]

Lincoln's address reflects the two-tiered character of ultra-protestantism, but with a communal rather than a personal application. Our fallibility does not support any skeptical or relativistic withdrawal from the issues of life: humans will—and must—continue to hold specific beliefs (such as the belief that slavery is immoral and offensive to God). We must avow and live by these beliefs even as we acknowledge their fallibility, acting "with firmness in the right as God gives us to see the right." More fundamentally, though, we must trust in and submit to God's justice, next to which all our efforts and our small certitudes are of little account: only by our submission to that larger, and largely unfathomable, design will our political order be redeemed.[71]

Promoting Tolerance

The address also displays the capacity of this ultra-protestant approach to uphold belief while accepting and respecting differences in basic beliefs. Thus, at one level Lincoln judges and eloquently condemns the institution of slavery, but at another level he can plead that we "judge not that we be not judged." Again, at one level Lincoln distinguishes between the causes of the North and the South. Indeed, he speaks officially and authoritatively as the leader of the Northern cause—one that has opposed the Southern cause at the cost of massive violence and destruction—and he urges that we "strive on to finish the work we are in." And he quietly implies that the South bears greater responsibility for starting the war.[72] But at another, deeper level he understands that Northerners and Southerners are in the same universal human predicament; both "read the same Bible, and pray to the same God," and both are similarly subject to error and offense.

Commenting on this dimension of the speech, Reinhold Niebuhr maintained that "[a]mong all the statesmen of ancient and modern periods, Lincoln alone had a sense of historical meaning so high as to cast doubt on the intentions of both sides and to place the enemy into the same category of ambiguity as the nation to which his life was committed."[73] The war, in Lincoln's understanding, is not so much punishment for the errors of *the South* as it is retribution for human error and sinfulness: God "gives to *both North and South,* this terrible war, as the woe due to those by whom the offence came." David Donald observes that the speech is "[n]otably lacking . . . [in] any attribution of blame."[74] And rather than "invok[ing] His aid against the other," as both North and South have heretofore done, Lincoln implores the combatants to recognize their common need for divine justice and mercy, and so to proceed, as the speech's most famous phrase implores, "[w]ith malice toward none; with charity for all."

In this way, Lincoln's reflection concludes, it may be possible to achieve peace among conflicting sides and views. Indeed, Lincoln contemplates such a peace not only as an end to the immediate civil war, and not only for this country, but as a more universal possibility. So we must "strive on . . . to do all which may achieve and cherish a just and lasting peace, among ourselves, and *with all nations.*" As Willard Sperry, dean of the Harvard Divinity School, later observed, Lincoln was "one of the few men in history . . . whose religion was great enough to bridge the gulfs between sects, and to encompass us all."[75] And that embracing capacity of Lincoln's "religion," I have argued, derived in large part from its ultra-protestant character.

CONCLUSION: THE TOLERANCE OF FAITH

If the pluralism that arose in the aftermath of the Protestant Reformation has been the distinctive political challenge of modernity, as theorists like John Rawls assert, then it would seem that perhaps the most notable achievement of our political order has been its ability, thus far, to maintain a measure of peace amid a volatile diversity. That achievement seems even more remarkable if we contemplate it in connection with the arguments of the critics of tolerance like Holmes or Stanley Fish. Their forceful critique, elaborated in the preceding chapter, contends that tolerance and mutual respect among people of different faiths is impossible. Our own actual history suggests a different conclusion: we at least *seem* to have managed—imperfectly, to be sure—to sustain a considerable degree of tolerance and mutual respect. So how has this achievement been accomplished?

The answer is no doubt multifaceted, involving a combination of political, legal, religious, and cultural factors, and probably a certain amount of plain good fortune. But this chapter has suggested that one ingredient has been the possibility of a theologically grounded tolerance arising out of an ultra-protestant elaboration of a theistic premise. Ultra-protestantism is crucial because it provides an escape from the logic of intolerance as propounded by thinkers like Holmes and Fish. As Lincoln's Second Inaugural Address so powerfully manifested, a theism that takes the ultra-protestant turn offers a way for believers to tolerate and respect contrary creeds without sacrificing, compromising, or diluting their own beliefs—and without pretending to a spurious and ultimately corrosive "equality" among the variety of diverse faiths.

Notes

NOTES TO THE INTRODUCTION

1. Michael J. Perry, Religion in Politics: Constitutional and Moral Perspectives 12, 15 (1997).

2. For a recent, brief defense of this argument against later criticism, see Steven D. Smith, The Religion Clauses in Constitutional Scholarship, 74 Notre Dame L. Rev. 1033 (1999).

NOTE TO PART I: HOW FIRM A FOUNDATION?

1. Michael P. Zuckert, The Natural Rights Republic 11 (1996).

NOTES TO CHAPTER I

This chapter is adapted from a paper presented at a conference on "Religious Freedom at the Dawn of a New Millennium" held at the University of Indiana-Bloomington in April 1999.

1. Martin E. Marty, The Virginia Statute Two Hundred Years Later, in The Virginia Statute for Religious Freedom: Its Evolution and Consequences in American History 1, 2 (Merrill D. Peterson and Robert C. Vaughn eds. 1988).

2. For a discussion of the more substantive character of discussions of religious freedom during the early colonial period, see Steven D. Smith, Separation and the Fanatic (review essay), 85 Virg. L. Rev. 213, 239–46 (1999). For an earlier period, see the various positions excerpted in Brian Tierney, The Crisis of Church and State 1050–1300 (1964).

3. For a laudatory review of Madison's contributions to the establishment of religious freedom in this country, see John T. Noonan, Jr., The Lustre of Our Country: The American Experience of Religious Freedom 59–91 (1998).

4. William Lee Miller, The First Liberty 5–7 (1986). For a discussion taking a similar view, see Noonan, supra note 3 at 69–71.

5. James Madison, Memorial and Remonstrance against Religious Assessments, reprinted in Robert S. Alley, The Supreme Court on Church and State 18, 20 (1988).

6. See Creating the Bill of Rights: The Documentary Record 13 (Helen E. Veit, Kenneth R. Bowling, and Charlene Bangs Bickford eds. 1991).

7. Peter Westen, The Empty Idea of Equality, 95 Harv. L. Rev. 537 (1982).

8. A Bill Establishing a Provision for Teachers of the Christian Religion, reprinted as appendix to Justice Douglas's dissent in Walz v. Tax Commission, 397 U.S. 664, 716, 718 (1970).

9. Madison, supra note 5 at 20.

10. For a lucid discussion of the question, see Michael W. McConnell, The Origins and Historical Understanding of the Free Exercise of Religion, 103 Harv. L. Rev. 1409, 1491–500 (1990).

11. Madison, supra note 5 at 18–19.

12. Christopher L. Eisgruber and Lawrence G. Sager, Unthinking Religious Freedom (review essay), 74 Tex. L. Rev. 577, 600–601 (1996).

13. Id. at 603.

14. As an example, consider the nonestablishment component of Michael Perry's "antidiscrimination norm." Under this heading, Perry argues that government must not take any action based on the view that any particular religious tenet is "truer or more authentically American or otherwise better" than any competing religious or nonreligious tenet. Michael J. Perry, Religion in Politics: Constitutional and Moral Perspectives 12, 15 (1997). Packaged in the language of "nondiscrimination," this prohibition may seem appealing, even compelling. Unpacked, the prohibition appears to be substantively equivalent to a familiar and quite extreme position in the by now voluminous debate about whether citizens, or legislators, or other government officials may permissibly rely on religious convictions in making political decisions. More specifically, the prohibition that Perry attaches to an "antidiscrimination principle" appears to reduce itself to the position in that debate that seeks to exclude religious convictions as a basis for political decisions, because to base a controversial political decision on a religious belief would surely be to treat that belief as "truer or more authentically American or otherwise better" than the opposing beliefs that would have dictated a different decision. To be sure, some scholars *have* taken that extreme exclusionary position in the "religious convictions" debate. But the exclusionary position has also been powerfully criticized—by, among many others, an earlier (and later) Perry. See, for example, the essays by Philip Quinn and Nicholas Wolterstorff in Religion and Contemporary Liberalism (Paul J. Weithman ed. 1997); Kent Greenawalt, Religious Convictions and Political Choice (1988); Michael J. Perry, Comment on "The Limits of Rationality and the Place of Religious Conviction: Protecting Animals and the Environment," 27 Wm. & Mary L. Rev. 1067 (1986). However one comes out in this debate, it seems clear that the exclusionary position is highly controversial and in need of serious justification; it cannot be rendered acceptable merely by being piggybacked onto an "antidiscrimination principle."

15. Michael Zuckert has cogently argued, for example, that the whole edifice of Rawlsian political liberalism rests on just such equivocations about the meaning of equality. Michael P. Zuckert, Is Modern Liberalism Compatible with Limited Government? The Case of Rawls, in Natural Law, Liberalism, and Morality 49, 75–78 (Robert P. George ed. 1996).

16. See James Madison, Federalist 51, The Federalist Papers 324 (Clinton Rossiter ed. 1961). See also id. at 84 (Federalist 10) ("A religious sect may degenerate into a political faction in a part of the Confederacy; but the variety of sects dispersed over the entire face of it must secure the national councils against any danger from that source.").

17. Robert Wiebe, The Opening of American Society 25 (1984).

18. See Steven D. Smith, Foreordained Failure: The Quest for a Constitutional Principle of Religious Freedom 17–43 (1995).

19. See Paul E. Johnson and Sean Wilentz, The Kingdom of Matthias (1995).

20. See Stephen Toulmin, Cosmopolis: The Hidden Agenda of Modernity 100 (1990) (discussing Leibniz's "vision of a universal language in his panacea for both political and theological ills").

NOTES TO CHAPTER 2

This chapter is adapted from a paper presented at a conference on "Religion in the Public Square" held at the College of William and Mary in March 2000.

1. Sanford Levinson, Religious Language and the Public Square, 105 Harv. L. Rev. 2061, 2077 (1992).

2. See generally Immanuel Kant, An Answer to the Question: What Is Enlightenment? reprinted in What Is Enlightenment? Eighteenth-Century Answers and Twentieth-Century Questions 58 (James Schmidt ed. 1996).

3. Onora O'Neill, Vindicating Reason, in The Cambridge Companion to Kant 280, 298–99, 305 (Paul Guyer ed. 1992).

4. Gerald Dworkin, The Theory and Practice of Autonomy 8 (1988). See also William A. Galston, What Is Living and What Is Dead in Kant's Practical Philosophy? in Kant and Political Philosophy: The Contemporary Legacy 207, 216 (Ronald Beiner and William James Booth eds. 1993) (observing that for Kant, only "rational being has 'absolute worth.'"). Cf. Immanuel Kant, Groundwork of the Metaphysic of Morals 96 (H. J. Paton tr. 1964) ("Persons, therefore, are not merely subjective ends whose existence as an object of our actions has a value *for us*; they are *objective ends* . . . ; for unless this is so, nothing at all of *absolute* value would be found anywhere."). Cf. Robert Paul Wolff, In Defense of Anarchism 72 (1998 ed.) ("When I place myself in the hands of another, and permit him to determine the principles by which I shall guide my behavior, I

repudiate the freedom and reason which give me dignity. I am then guilty of what Kant might have called the sin of willful heteronomy.").

5. See id. at 14 ("[Man] is *autonomous*. As Kant argued, moral autonomy is a combination of freedom and responsibility; it is a submission to laws which one has made for oneself.").

6. See Vittorio Hösle, Objective Idealism, Ethics, and Politics 49 (1998) (arguing that "[o]nly Kant's conception of freedom can give dignity to human beings.").

7. J. B. Schneewind, Autonomy, Obligation, and Virtue: An Overview of Kant's Moral Philosophy, in The Cambridge Companion to Kant, supra note 3 at 309, 310. See also Hösle, supra note 6 at 41:

> Kant's thought implies a Copernican revolution not only in theoretical, but also in practical philosophy: all heteronomous attempts at founding ethics are rejected, and ethics is grounded in the autonomy of the subject. The indissoluble link between freedom and ethics tries to bring the Enlightenment into its truth: no external validity claims are accepted; every authority has to justify itself before reason.

8. See Wolff, supra note 4.

9. Cf. John E. Hare, The Moral Gap 7 (1996) ("Kant is like other great philosophers; the basic components of his theory are in dispute between interpreters, and so all the parts of the theory relying on these components become controversial.").

10. Cf. Bolling v. Sharpe, 347 U.S. 497 (1954).

NOTE TO CHAPTER 3

This chapter is adapted from a presentation to the Law and Religion section, national conference of the Association of American Law Schools, Washington, D.C., January 6, 1997.

1. John Rawls, Political Liberalism xxxix (1996 ed.).

2. Galatians 5:17.

3. Walter Ullmann, Principles of Government and Politics in the Middle Ages 33 (1974 ed.)

4. Id. at 34. See also id. at 73:

> However much a thing may be purely "temporal" it nevertheless had to serve a Christian end, because in papal doctrine the "temporal" had no indigenous value, had no autonomous standing, but was simply a means to an end. . . . The "temporal" . . . had no value in itself but assumed value if it was harnessed to the purpose and end of the Christian's life and consequently of Christian society.

5. "Precisely because this Church was an entity that existed on this earth its direction concerned therefore the doings of its members on this earth. The vital point was that these earthly activities of the Christians must be directed by Christian norms, which meant that they must be guided, orientated, directed." Id. at 35.

6. Id. at 55. In this allocation of powers, the specific function of the secular prince was the suppression of evil, including heresy, by force. Id. at 64–66, 79–82. It was for the church to judge what was evil—full authority or sovereignty lay only with the pope—and it was for the prince to act upon and enforce that judgment. Id. at 67, 72, 87.

7. Id. at 65.

8. "It meant that each office-holder should fulfil the functions contained in his office, and no more. The king should not interfere in the functions of the bishop, because he was not created for this purpose; the archdeacon should not meddle with matters pertaining to the sheriff, and so forth." Id. at 67.

9. Id. at 88.

10. Id. at 61.

11. Id. at 97. "[D]ualism of government was to be the panacea of royal governments from Henry IV in the Investiture Contest, who actually coined the term and invented the idea, down to the Reformers and beyond." Id.

12. Id.

13. Cf. Suzanna Sherry, Outlaw Blues, 87 Mich. L. Rev. 1418, 1427 (1989) (asserting that "such things as divine revelation and biblical literalism are irrational superstitious nonsense").

14. See, e.g., Daniel O. Conkle, Toward a General Theory of the Establishment Clause, 82 Nw. U.L. Rev. 1113 (1988).

15. The "conscientious objector" draft exemption cases illustrate this progression. They started with statutory language that plainly exempted only persons whose objection to war arose from a set of beliefs centered on faith in a "Supreme Being"—that is, God. But in the modern climate of legal opinion this sort of focus seemed incongruous or unacceptable. Hence, the cases first expanded the definition of what would count as a religious objection and then made it clear that the expanded definition would apply even to a belief that the conscientious objector himself did not regard as a religious belief. See, for example, Welsh v. United States, 398 U.S. 333 (1970). In *Welsh,* Justice Harlan went even further, explicitly asserting that the availability of the exemption could not depend on religion per se at all, but would have to be tailored to something else, such as a sincere *moral* objection to war.

16. William Marshall is a prominent religion clause scholar who tends to reduce religious freedom commitments into free speech principles. See, for example, William P. Marshall, Religion as Ideas: Religion as Identity, 7 J. Contemp. Legal Issues 385 (1996); William P. Marshall, Solving the Free Exercise Dilemma:

Free Exercise as Expression, 67 Minn. L. Rev. 545 (1983). For a reduction of religious freedom commitments into equality values, see, for example, Ira C. Lupu, Keeping the Faith: Religion, Equality, and Speech in the U.S. Constitution, 18 Conn. L. Rev. 739 (1986). And see also chapter 1.

17. I have discussed these "reductionist" approaches to religious freedom at greater length in Steven D. Smith, The Rise and Fall of Religious Freedom in Constitutional Discourse, 140 U. Pa. L. Rev. 149, 196–223, 239–40 (1991).

18. John Locke, A Letter concerning Toleration, in John Locke on Politics and Education 21, 25 (Classics Club ed. 1947).

19. Id. at 35.

20. Id. at 52–53.

21. James 1:8.

22. "[A]s this life is common to both cities, so there is a harmony between them in regard to what belongs to it." City of God 19.17.

23. Id. (emphasis added).

24. Id.

NOTES TO CHAPTER 4

This chapter is adapted from a paper presented at a symposium on Religion and the Constitution at the University of San Diego in February 1996.

1. The Garden and the Wilderness 174 (1965).

2. Herbert Wechsler, Toward Neutral Principles of Constitutional Law, 73 Harv. L. Rev. 9 (1959).

3. Cf. Harvey Cox, The Influence of Religion in America—More, Less, or What? in An Unsettled Arena: Religion and the Bill of Rights 115–16 (Ronald C. White, Jr. and Albright G. Zimmerman eds. 1992) (noting "what appears to be a massive and unanticipated reentry of religious influence in the public domain," and observing that "some of this activity has definitely come in response to what its advocates define as an attack on religion by the courts").

4. Frederick Mark Gedicks, The Ironic State of Religious Liberty in America, 46 Mercer L. Rev. 1157, 1157–59 (1995).

5. Robert F. Nagel, Judicial Power and American Character 97 (1994).

6. Sanford Levinson, The Multicultures of Belief and Disbelief (review essay), 92 Mich. L. Rev. 1873, 1891 (1994).

7. I discuss this decision in more detail in the following chapter.

8. Zorach v. Clauson, 343 U.S. 306 (1952).

9. See Steven D. Smith, The Rise and Fall of Religious Freedom in Constitutional Discourse, 140 U. Penn. L. Rev. 149, 193–96 (1991) (arguing that Jefferson's statute, which as its basic premise begins by proclaiming that "Almighty

God hath created the mind free," plainly endorses religion in a way that recent decisions purport to forbid).

10. See Douglas Laycock, Equal Access and Moments of Silence: The Equal Status of Religious Speech by Private Speakers, 81 Nw. U.L. Rev. 1, 8 (1986) (arguing that in principle the names of cities like Los Angeles and Corpus Christi unconstitutionally endorse religion).

11. See Mary Ann Glendon, Law, Communities, and the Religious Freedom Language of the Constitution, 60 Geo. Wash. L. Rev. 672, 673 (1992) (describing survey evidence showing that the American public values freedom of religion highly, above freedom of speech).

12. 485 U.S. 439 (1988).

13. Id. at 451.

14. Id. at 452 (emphasis added).

15. Zorach v. Clauson, 343 U.S. 306 (1952).

16. 473 U.S. 373 (1985).

17. 473 U.S. 402 (1985).

18. *Aguilar,* 473 U.S. at 415 (Powell, J., concurring) (quoting with approval Circuit Court opinion by Judge Friendly).

19. In *Aguilar,* the Court also stressed the dangers of entanglement associated with the government's program for monitoring use of public funds.

20. *Aguilar,* 473 U.S. at 424 (O'Connor, J., dissenting).

21. *Grand Rapids,* 473 U.S. at 388–89.

22. Twelve years later, *Aguilar* was overruled in Agostini v. Felton, 521 U.S. 203 (1997).

23. See Erwin Chemerinsky, Federal Jurisdiction 77–84 (1989).

24. William P. Marshall, The Concept of Offensiveness in Establishment and Free Exercise Clause Jurisprudence, 66 Ind. L.J. 351 (1991).

25. ACLU v. Capitol Square Review Board, 210 F.3d 703 (6th Cir.), vacated and rehearing granted, 222 F.3d 268 (6th Cir. 2000).

26. For a critical assessment of this development, see Steven D. Smith, Symbols, Perceptions, and Doctrinal Illusions: Establishment Neutrality and the "No Endorsement" Test, 86 Mich. L. Rev. 266 (1987).

27. 515 U.S. 753 (1995), at 779–80 (O'Connor, J., concurring) and at 800 n. 5 (Stevens, J., dissenting).

28. Id.

29. County of Allegheny v. ACLU, 492 U.S. 573, 640 (1989) (Brennan, J., concurring and dissenting).

30. Facts similar to these were alleged in Bauchman v. West High School, 132 F.3d 542 (10th Cir. 1997), though the courts declined to give any relief.

31. 921 F.2d 1047 (10th Cir. 1990).

32. See id. at 1055–56:

The mere fact that the actions were aimed exclusively at Christian religious materials does not automatically mean the actions' primary effect was to send a disapproving message regarding Christianity. If we must draw any message from the actions, that message must be that the school district disapproves of the teaching of Christianity in the public schools. . . . Because Mr. Roberts chose to keep his Bible on his desk continuously and read it frequently, Ms. Madigan feared that Mr. Roberts was setting a Christian tone in his classroom. . . . Ms. Madigan's only stated reasons were that the Christian books and the Bible might violate "separation of church and state" and that "religion may not be taught in a public school." We discern no anti-Christian message here.

33. Id. at 1049.

34. Id. at 1060 (Barrett, J., dissenting).

35. Although the court's opinion seems on the whole to endorse the principal's overall position, some language in the opinion seems more qualified, suggesting that, *given her perception* of the situation, the principal was required to act as she did:

Because Mr. Roberts chose to keep his Bible on his desk continuously and read it frequently, Ms. Madigan feared that Mr. Roberts was setting a Christian tone in his classroom. *Having formed that impression,* Ms. Madigan had a duty to take corrective steps, and to do so in a religiously neutral manner.

Id. at 1055–56 (emphasis added).

36. See, e.g., Ronald Dworkin, A Matter of Principle 69–71 (1985).

NOTES TO CHAPTER 5

1. Lemon v. Kurtzman, 403 U.S. 602 (1971).

2. John Mansfield, The Religion Clauses of the First Amendment and the Philosophy of the Constitution, 72 Cal. L. Rev. 846, 848 (1984).

3. Douglas Laycock, A Survey of Religious Liberty in the United States, 47 Ohio St. L.J. 409, 450 (1986).

4. 494 U.S. 872 (1990).

5. See, e.g., Mark V. Tushnet, "Of Church and State and the Supreme Court": Kurland Revisited, 1989 Sup. Ct. Rev. 373, 379; Stephen Pepper, A Brief for the Free Exercise Clause, 7 J. Law & Rel. 323, 345 (1989).

6. See, e.g., James D. Gordon III, Free Exercise on the Mountaintop, 79 Cal. L. Rev. 91 (1991); Michael W. McConnell, Free Exercise Revisionism and the Smith Decision, 57 U. Chi. L. Rev. 1109 (1990). For my own two cents' worth, see

Steven D. Smith, The Rise and Fall of Religious Freedom in Constitutional Discourse, 140 U. Penn. L. Rev. 149, 231–37 (1991).

7. City of Boerne v. Flores, 521 U.S. 507 (1997).

8. See Ira C. Lupu, The Case against Legislative Codification of Religious Liberty, 21 Card. L. Rev. 565, 568–76 (1999).

9. Mark Tushnet describes the disagreement in degree in this way:

[Imagine] that we have developed a measure of the determinacy of a set of legal rules, the "determinile." A completely determinate legal system would measure 100 determiniles, while a completely indeterminate one would measure zero. CLS [Critical Legal Studies] adherents at present defend the position that the proper measure of legal systems is between five and fifteen. . . . Mainstream legal theorists at present defend the position that the proper measure of well-functioning legal systems like that of the United States is somewhere between forty and sixty.

Mark Tushnet, Critical Legal Studies: A Political History, 100 Yale L.J. 1515, 1538 (1991).

10. See, e.g., County of Allegheny v. ACLU, 492 U.S. 573, 655–79 (1989) (Kennedy, J., dissenting) (opinion joined by Scalia, J.).

11. See their respective opinions in Lee v. Weisman, 505 U.S. 577 (1992).

12. See their respective opinions in County of Allegheny v. ACLU, 492 U.S. 573 (1989).

13. Compare, for example, the majority opinion, in which Blackmun joined, with O'Connor's dissenting opinion in Aguilar v. Felton, 473 U.S. 402 (1985).

14. However, for exemplary instances of legal scholarship studying the cultural meaning and implications of constitutional doctrine and its effects on political discourse, see Robert F. Nagel, Constitutional Cultures: The Mentality and Consequences of Judicial Review (1989); Lee C. Bollinger, The Tolerant Society: Freedom of Speech and Extremist Speech in America (1986). A similar concern and emphasis are evident throughout the work of James Boyd White.

15. 374 U.S. 398 (1963).

16. See, e.g., Michael W. McConnell, The Origins and Historical Understanding of Free Exercise of Religion, 103 Harv. L. Rev. 1409, 1416–17 (1990); Ira C. Lupu, Where Rights Begin: The Problem of Burdens on the Free Exercise of Religion, 102 Harv. L. Rev. 933, 933–34 (1989).

17. 406 U.S. 205 (1972).

18. Tushnet, supra note 5 at 379. See also Ira C. Lupu, The Trouble with Accommodation, 60 Geo. Wash. L. Rev. 743, 756–57 (1992).

19. See T. Alexander Aleinikoff, Constitutional Law in the Age of Balancing, 96 Yale L.J. 943, 963–72 (1987).

20. 406 U.S. at 223–26.

21. See Aleinikoff, supra note 19 at 972–83.

22. "The essence of all that has been said and written on the subject is that only those interests of the highest order and those not otherwise served can overbalance legitimate claims to the free exercise or religion." 406 U.S. at 215. See id. at 214–15. Although these two pages contain the bulk of the opinion's balancing language, Stephen Pepper has pointed out to me that the opinion contains several other references to balancing or "weighing." Certainly there is enough such language to permit a lawyer to extract a "balancing" doctrine from the decision. Nonetheless, the muted character of the opinion on this point becomes evident upon comparing the majority opinion with Justice White's concurring opinion, in which the language of balancing is prominent and pervasive. Id. at 237–41.

23. 455 U.S. 252, 257–58 (1982) (emphasis added).

24. See, e.g., Hobbie v. Unemployment Appeals Comm'n, 480 U.S. 136, 141 (1987).

25. See O'Lone v. Estate of Shabbaz, 482 U.S. 342 (1987) (prison setting); Goldman v. Weinberger, 475 U.S. 503 (1986) (military setting).

26. 476 U.S. 693 (1986).

27. Cf. Bollinger, supra note 14 at 182.

28. Michael Perry observes that "[t]o practice such tolerance . . . is not to refuse to judge true from false, right from wrong, good from bad (or evil), moral from immoral. . . . To practice ecumenical political tolerance, rather, is to make such judgments, and sometimes to make them publicly . . . but to refrain from coercing others on the basis of the judgments." Michael J. Perry, Love and Power: The Role of Religion and Morality in American Politics 129 (1991).

29. Bollinger, supra note 14 at 11.

30. See Perry, supra note 28 at 132.

31. Thus, Harvey Cox asserts that "the Jesus of the Gospels . . . teaches us to expect to find God already present in the 'other,' . . . no matter how strange or unfamiliar that other's ideas or religious practices may seem." Harvey Cox, Many Mansions: A Christian's Encounter with Other Faiths 16 (1988). But Cox also observes that "Jesus was not a model of vacuous tolerance. He did make judgments about the faith of the people he met. In fact, he did so all the time." Id. at 14.

32. Charles Taylor, The Politics of Recognition, in Multiculturalism and "The Politics of Recognition" 25, 66–73 (Amy Gutman ed. 1992).

33. Id. at 72–73.

34. Id. at 73.

35. See, e.g., William P. Marshall, The Case against the Constitutionally Compelled Free Exercise Exemption, 40 Case W. Res. L. Rev. 357, 388–94,

398–400 (1989–90); Estate of Thornton v. Caldor, 472 U.S. 703 (1985) (invalidating mandatory Sabbath accommodation law).

36. See, e.g., Church of Jesus Christ of Latter-Day Saints v. Amos, 483 U.S. 327 (1987) (upholding statutory exemption of religion institutions from federal employment discrimination law).

37. McConnell, supra note 6 at 1109.

38. Goldman v. Weinberger, 475 U.S. 503, 528–33 (1986) (O'Connor, J., dissenting). See also Lyng v. Northwest Indian Cemetery Protective Ass'n, 485 U.S. 439, 458–77 (1988) (Brennan, J., dissenting).

39. 406 U.S. at 211.

40. Lemon v. Kurtzman, 403 U.S. 602 (1971).

41. 406 U.S. at 213, 221.

42. Id. at 224. See id. at 225, 235.

43. Id. at 210–11, 223–26.

44. Id. at 216 (emphasis added).

45. Id. at 223–24.

46. 406 U.S. at 246 (Douglas, J., dissenting).

47. Id. at 244–45.

48. Id. at 245–46 (emphasis added).

49. Id. at 245–46.

50. Taylor, supra note 32 at 63.

51. Id. at 72.

52. Id. at 73.

53. *Smith*, 494 U.S. at 879–80.

54. 406 U.S. 205, 215–16 (1972).

55. In this spirit, Taylor argues that what is granted under a regime of demanded recognition of equal value is not truly respect. On the contrary, "the giving of such a judgment [of respect] on demand is an act of breathtaking condescension. No one can really mean it as a genuine act of respect. . . . To be an object of such an act of respect demeans." Taylor, supra note 32 at 70.

56. See, e.g., County of Allegheny v. ACLU, 492 U.S. 573, 595–97, 625–27 (1989).

57. Cf. Bollinger, supra note 14 at 243 (observing, in the practice of tolerance, the "sheer impossibility of formulating in advance a rule for decision").

58. See, e.g., Epperson v. Arkansas, 393 U.S. 97, 103–4 (1969):

Government in our democracy, state and national, must be neutral in matters of religious theory, doctrine, and practice. It may not be hostile to any religion or to the advocacy of no-religion. . . . The First Amendment mandates governmental neutrality between religion and religion, and between religion and nonreligion.

59. See Antonin Scalia, The Rule of Law as a Law of Rules, 56 U. Chi. L. Rev. 1175 (1989).

60. Cf. Peter van Inwagen, The Nature of Metaphysics, in Contemporary Readings in the Foundations of Metaphysics 11, 13 (Stephen Laurence and Cynthia Macdonald eds. 1998):

> [A]ny "all" statement is in one sense "about everything." For example, the statement "All Greeks are mortal" is logically equivalent to "Everything is mortal if it is a Greek." (Every elephant and every neutron star and every non-Greek immortal is mortal if it is a Greek.) It is therefore not easy to say in any precise and useful way what it is for a statement to be "about everything."

61. See Philip Kurland, Of Church and State and the Supreme Court, 29 U. Chi. L. Rev. 1, 96 (1961).

62. See, e.g., Palmer v. Thompson, 403 U.S. 217, 224–25 (1971).

63. For a cogent judicial discussion of these difficulties, see Edwards v. Aguillard, 482 U.S. 578, 636–40 (1987) (Scalia, J., dissenting). For an academic discussion that uses speech act theory to reach similar conclusions, see Heidi Hurd, Sovereignty in Silence, 99 Yale L.J. 945, 968–76 (1990).

64. See generally William N. Eskridge, Jr. and Philip P. Frickey, Cases and Materials on Legislation 639–828 (1988).

NOTES TO CHAPTER 6

1. 393 U.S. 97 (1968).

2. 393 U.S. at 112–13 (Black, J., concurring).

3. See generally Phillip E. Johnson, Darwin on Trial (1991).

4. See Lucas A. Powe, Jr., The Warren Court and American Politics 213 (2000) (observing that "Fortas not only voted liberal but also did not have the slightest doubt about his own abilities or the efficacy of the Court acting as the engine of reform").

5. 393 U.S. at 106.

6. Id. at 108 n. 16.

7. Id. at 107–8 n. 15.

8. Id. at 108–9.

9. See Carol Iannone, The Truth about Inherit the Wind, 1997 First Things 28–33 (Feb. 1997).

10. 393 U.S. at 109.

11. Id. at 102.

12. 472 U.S. 38 (1985).

13. Id. at 57.

14. Id. at 58–59.

15. 472 U.S. at 87 (Burger, C.J., dissenting) (summarizing testimony of Senator Holmes).

16. 472 U.S. at 59.

17. For another, more recent instance of the same phenomenon, see Edwards v. Aguillard, 482 U.S. 578 (1987).

18. The facts reported here are taken from the Supreme Court majority opinion, 508 U.S. 520 (1993), and from the district court's opinion. 723 F. Supp. 1467 (S.D. Fla. 1989).

19. 508 U.S. at 535.

20. 936 F.2d 586 (11th Cir. 1991).

21. 508 U.S. at 533.

22. Id. at 542.

23. Id. at 521.

24. "In this case we need not define with precision the standard used to evaluate whether a prohibition is of general application, for these ordinances fall well below the minimum standard necessary to protect First Amendment rights." Id. at 543. This observation, by suggesting that the difficulty with a "general applicability" requirement is merely one of deciding how much generality is needed, provokes doubt about whether the Court perceived the conceptual difficulties that trouble the requirement, as discussed above.

25. Id. at 561 (Souter, J., concurring).

26. 508 U.S. at 521.

27. Id. at 523.

28. 723 F. Supp. at 1477, 1485–87.

29. Id. at 1479.

30. 508 U.S. at 536, 538, 544.

31. Id. at 538–39.

32. Id. at 532, 533, 540 (emphasis added).

33. Id. at 536.

34. 723 F. Supp. at 1472 n. 14.

35. 508 U.S. at 538–39.

36. 723 F. Supp. at 1473 n. 22.

37. Id. at 1470 n. 6.

38. 508 U.S. at 539.

39. Id. at 541.

40. Id. at 541–42.

41. Quoted in id. at 526 (emphasis added).

42. Id. at 557 (Scalia, J., concurring).

43. Id.

44. See, e.g., Lamb's Chapel v. Union Center Moriches Free School Dist., 508 U.S. 384, 397 (1993) (Scalia, J., concurring).

45. See Edwards v. Aguillard, 482 U.S. 578, 636–40 (1987) (Scalia, J., dissenting).

46. 508 U.S. at 558.

47. 508 U.S. at 559.

48. See Washington v. Davis, 426 U.S. 229 (1976).

49. See Romer v. Evans, 517 U.S. 620, 632 (1996) (arguing that the law "seems inexplicable by anything but animus toward the class it affects"). In attributing bad motives to Colorado voters, the Court echoed the sorts of charges that had been made in the state itself, both in court and in more general public debate. For a brief description, see Robert F. Nagel, Name-Calling and the Clear Error Rule, 88 Nw. U.L. Rev. 193, 193–96 (1993).

50. Id. at 199.

NOTES TO PART III: CAN FAITH TOLERATE?

1. Learned Hand, The Spirit of Liberty 72 (1952).

2. Stephen Macedo, Transformative Constitutionalism and the Case of Religion: Defending the Moderate Hegemony of Liberalism, 26 Pol. Theory 56, 61, 63 (1998).

3. Michael Walzer, On Toleration 66–67 (1997).

4. Stanley Fish, Mission Impossible: Settling the Just Bounds between Church and State, 97 Colum. L. Rev. 2255, 2256 (1997).

5. Id. at 2255.

NOTES TO CHAPTER 7

1. Thomas Jefferson, Notes on Virginia, in The Life and Selected Writings of Thomas Jefferson 187, 275 (Adrienne Koch and William Pedens eds. 1944).

2. Cf. Jay Newman, Foundations of Religious Tolerance 10 (1982) ("In considering the question of why men have so much trouble tolerating the religious 'believings' of other men, we must recognize that some of the sources of intolerance, such as superstition and ethnocentrism, are wholly irrational.").

3. The conversation is reported in a letter from Hand to Holmes, dated June 22, 1918, and reprinted in Gerald Gunther, Learned Hand and the Origins of Modern First Amendment Doctrine: Some Fragments of History, 27 Stan. L. Rev. 719, 755–56 (1975).

4. Holmes went on to explain that "[i]f you have no doubt of your premises or your power and want a certain result with all your heart you naturally express your wishes in law and sweep away all opposition. To allow opposition . . . seems to indicate that you . . . doubt either your power or your premises." Abrams v. United States, 250 U.S. 616, 630 (1919) (Holmes, J., dissenting).

5. For a discussion and criticism of Holmes's strategy of skepticism, see Steven D. Smith, Skepticism, Tolerance, and Truth in the Theory of Free Expression, 60 S. Cal. L. Rev. 649, 665–69 (1987).

6. Stanley Fish, Mission Impossible: Settling the Just Bounds between Church and State, Colum. L. Rev. 2255, 2256 (1997).

7. Id. at 2256, 2258.

8. John Stuart Mill, On Liberty 21 (Currin V. Shields ed. 1956) (first published 1859).

9. Cf. Newman, supra note 2 at 12 ("The altruistic bigots are the ones who want to save us. They cannot tolerate our doing ourselves harm. . . . They are worried about *us*, our souls, our spiritual lives.").

10. See Brian Tierney, Religious Rights: A Historical Perspective, in Religious Liberty in Western Thought 29, 32, 46–55 (Noel B. Reynolds and W. Cole Durham, Jr. eds. 1996).

11. See, e.g., John Locke, A Letter concerning Toleration, in John Locke on Politics and Education 21, 26–28, 41–42 (Classics Club ed. 1947).

12. Timothy L. Hall, Separating Church and State: Roger Williams and Religious Liberty (1998).

13. See id. at 48, 57, 61.

14. Id. at 59 (quoting John Cotton).

15. Waldron, supra note p. 147*, at 98, 120.

16. Brad S. Gregory, Salvation at Stake 81, 86 (1999).

17. See, e.g., Stephen M. Feldman, Please Don't Wish Me a Merry Christmas: A Critical History of the Separation of Church and State (1997). Writing from a Jewish perspective—the first paragraph of his text reads simply, "I am Jewish"—Feldman argues that modern attitudes toward "religious freedom" developed from "the emergence of Christianity as it contentiously separated from Judaism" and that "the separation of church and state stands, to a great extent, as a political and religious development that manifests and reinforces Christian domination in American society." Id. at 1, 5.

18. For a critical essay elaborating a largely unfavorable contrast between Christian practices of tolerance with those of many other world religions, see Gustav Mensching, Tolerance and Truth in Religion 11–99 (H. J. Klimkeit tr. 1955). Such comparisons are difficult and debatable, of course, in part because Christians and Christian institutions have a tremendously varied record with regard to tolerance and intolerance. For a useful history, see Henry Kamen, The Rise of Toleration (1967).

19. John Hick observes that "the idea of salvation . . . is absolutely central to Christian thought, both traditional and revisionary." John Hick, The Rainbow of Faiths: Critical Dialogues on Religious Pluralism 16 (1995).

20. For an argument that a variety of different religions, Christian and non-Christian, can all be considered to be exclusively "true" because they aim at

different kinds of "salvation," see S. Mark Heim, Salvations: Truth and Difference in Religion (1995). For a dissent from this view, see Hick, supra note 19 at 106–8.

21. Mark 8:36 (KJV).

22. Miguel de Unamuno, The Tragic Sense of Life 12 (J. E. Crawford Flitch tr., Dover ed. 1954).

23. A dated but nonetheless impressive compilation of creeds, both ancient and more modern, is Philip Schaff's three-volume work, The Creeds of Christendom (6th ed., Philip Schaff ed., revised by David Schaff, reprinted 1998).

24. The most distinctively American forms of Christianity during the founding period, suspicious of orthodox formulations, tended to favor the notion of "no creed but the Bible." Nathan O. Hatch, The Democratization of American Christianity 81, 179–83 (1989).

25. John 3:16 (KJV) (emphasis added).

26. John 6:28–29 (emphasis added).

27. For a useful historical overview of the varied and evolving Christian attitudes toward the idea that acceptance of true beliefs is necessary to salvation and toward the closely related notion that there is "no salvation outside the Church," see Jacques Dupuis, S.J., Toward a Christian Theology of Religious Pluralism 25–201 (1997).

28. Athanasian Creed, vs. 1–2, in 2 Schaff, supra note 23 at 66. The creed ends by repeating the warning: "This is the Catholic Faith: which except a man believe faithfully . . . , he can not be saved." Id. at 70. Writing in the nineteenth century and from a conspicuously Protestant orientation, Philip Schaff expressed a modern embarrassment about this warning:

> The damnatory clauses, especially when sung or chanted in public worship, grate harshly on modern Protestant ears, and it may well be doubted whether they are consistent with true Christian charity and humility, and whether they do not transcend the legitimate authority of the Church. . . . Creeds, like hymns, lose their true force and miss their aim in proportion as they are polemical and partake of the character of manifestoes of war rather than confessions of faith and thanks to God for his mighty works.

1 Schaff, supra note 23 at 40.

29. See id. at 39 (describing the Athanasian Creed's "contrast with the uncontroversial and peaceful tone of the Apostles' Creed").

30. See, e.g., Mark 16:16 ("He that believeth and is baptized shall be saved; but he that believeth not shall be damned."); Galatians 1:8 ("But though we, or an angel from heaven, preach any other gospel unto you than that which we have preached unto you, let him be accursed.").

31. Francis A. Sullivan, S.J., Salvation Outside the Church? Tracing the History of the Catholic Response 97–98 (1992).

32. Gregory, supra note 16 at 6, 18.

33. Id. at 12–13, 100, 106, 123, 124.

34. Id. at 17 (quoting Johannes Fabri von Heilbronn).

35. Id. at 79 (footnote omitted).

36. Deuteronomy 7:1–6 (KJV).

37. Peter L. Berger, Protestantism and the Quest for Certainty, 115 Christian Century 782 (Aug. 26, 1998). There is nothing especially distinctive about *religious* beliefs in this respect. As philosophers like William James have explained, it will inevitably be true for all human beings that only a small percentage of our beliefs will be consciously scrutinized and justified; of necessity, most will simply be taken over, with little examination, from our past and our surroundings. William James, Pragmatism, in Pragmatism and Other Essays 74–76, 109–12 (Washington Square Press ed. 1963).

38. Cf. Newman, supra note 2 at 13:

> Many people regard the religious "outsider" as a threat to the unity of their religious community. . . . When children see how the outsider behaves, their respect for the religion of their parents often wanes. They begin to grasp the concept of alternatives, to ask questions, to challenge authority. If the outsider quietly held to his personal beliefs but acted as everyone else does, he would not be a threat.

39. Martin Marty, North America, in The Oxford History of Christianity 396, 398 (John McManners ed. 1993).

40. Paul Badham, The Case for Religious Pluralism, in Many Mansions 82, 84 (Dan Cohn-Sherhock ed. 1992).

41. John Rawls, Political Liberalism xxvii (1996 ed.).

42. Sanford Levinson, Some Reflections on Multiculturalism, "Equal Concern and Respect," and the Establishment Clause of the First Amendment, 27 U. Rich. L. Rev. 989, 993 (1993).

43. Id. at 993–94.

44. Id. at 993.

45. Id. at 1020.

46. Nathaniel Ward, The Simple Cobbler of Aggawwam in America 12, 5 (1647).

47. Fish, supra note 6 at 2258.

48. Gregory, supra note 16 at 86.

49. The Emperor Phillip II asserted, for example, that he would prefer to lose "all my states and even a hundred lives, if I had them," rather than to become a "sovereign of heretics." Id. at 91.

50. See Alain Epp Weaver, The Religious Right's Future? Drop-out Christianity, 116 Christian Century 300 (Mar. 17, 1999).

51. See, e.g., Justice Stevens's separate opinion in Board of Education of Kiryas Joel v. Grumet, 512 U.S. 687 (1994), and Justice Douglas's opinion in Wisconsin v. Yoder, 406 U.S. 205 (1972).

52. See, e.g., Ward, supra note 46 at 8. As noted, Holmes's celebrated *Abrams* dissent suggests that "[t]o allow opposition . . . seems to indicate that you . . . doubt either your power or your premises." 250 U.S. at 630.

53. Michael P. Zuckert, Is Modern Liberalism Compatible with Limited Government? The Case of Rawls, in Natural Law, Liberalism, and Morality 49, 77–78 (Robert P. George ed. 1996).

54. See generally Rawls, supra note 41.

55. See id. at 243, 253.

56. See Edward P. Foley, Political Liberalism and Establishment Clause Jurisprudence, 43 Case W. Res. L. Rev. 963, 973–74 (1993):

> In short, the political philosophy of liberalism necessarily divides religions into two categories: (1) liberal religions, which are those philosophically reasonable religions that accept the liberal position that the government must be impartial among all philosophically reasonable religions; and (2) illiberal religions, which are those that deny this liberal position and insist, instead, that the government endorse or favor their particular creed as the one true faith. While the government can maintain a position of neutrality among liberal religions, liberalism itself necessitates that the government must disfavor and discriminate against illiberal religions.

57. Thus, noting Rawls's statement that "[w]e need not say that [illiberal] religious beliefs are not true," Foley responds: "I confess that I am not altogether sure about the meaning of this passage. It seems to me that illiberalism does reject as *false,* as well as *unreasonable,* the idea that the state should endorse a particular creed." Id. at 975 n. 40.

58. Id. at 976–78.

59. Fish, supra note 6 at 2262–63.

60. Id. at 2279–83.

61. Id. at 2282 (footnotes omitted). Fish asserts that "[a] fanatic in Thiemann's vocabulary is someone who holds to his position with an inappropriate 'degree of certainty.' A fanatic, in other words, is someone who believes something too strongly or, more precisely, someone who believes the wrong thing." Id. (footnote omitted).

62. Id. at 2284.

63. Ward, supra note 46 at 17–18.

64. For a scathing indictment by a leading evangelical theologian who sees

the apparent flourishing of religion in this country as largely a product of marketing techniques concealing a spiritual and theological emptiness, see David F. Wells, God in the Wasteland 60–87 (1994).

NOTES TO CHAPTER 8

1. For an overview of these and related efforts to provide "substitutes for the Gospel," see Jacques Dupuis, S.J., Toward a Christian Theology of Religious Pluralism 29–201 (1997); Francis A. Sullivan, S.J., Salvation Outside the Church? Tracing the History of the Catholic Response 97–98 (1992); Paul F. Knitter, No Other Name? A Critical Survey of Christian Attitudes toward the World Religions (1985).

2. Heiko A. Oberman, Luther: Man between God and the Devil 127 (Eileen Walliser-Schwarzbart tr. 1993).

3. The Augsburg Confession, prepared in 1530 with Luther's full approval by his close associate Philip Melanchthon, see 1 Philip Schaff, The Creeds of Christendom 226 (6th ed., Philip Schaff ed., revised by David Schaff, reprinted 1998), asserts that a "deep silence" had lately prevailed concerning the correct relationship between faith and works but that the Lutheran doctrine was fully supported by the New Testament and early church fathers. Augsburg Confession, Arts. XX, XXII, in 1 Schaff, id. at 20–27.

4. See Alister McGrath, The Intellectual Origins of the European Reformation 27 (1987).

5. For a discussion, see Oberman, supra note 2 at 199–206.

6. Id. at 299.

7. Luther declared the Athanasian Creed to be "the most important and glorious composition since the days of the apostles." Quoted in 1 Schaff, supra note 3 at 41.

8. Oberman, supra note 2 at 92, 124–45.

9. Id. at 127.

10. Alister McGrath, Luther's Theology of the Cross 96 (1985) (quoting Luther).

11. Oberman, supra note 2 at 128 (quoting Luther).

12. Id.

13. McGrath, supra note 10 at 96 (quoting Luther).

14. Id. at 96–97.

15. The Augsburg Confession explains that "men can not be justified . . . before God by their own powers, merits, or works; but are justified freely . . . for Christ's sake through faith, when they believe that they are received into favor, and their sins forgiven for Christ's sake, who by his death hath satisfied for our sins. This faith doth God impute for righteousness before him." Augsburg Confession, Art. IV, in 3 Schaff, supra note 3 at 10.

16. Oberman, supra note 2 at 165.

17. McGrath, supra note 10 at 97 (quoting Luther).

18. See Romans 3:7–8; 6:1–4, 15–18. The basic idea is that works are an *expression* of faith, and of the grace that comes through faith. See Martin Luther, The Freedom of a Christian, reprinted in Martin Luther's Basic Theological Writings 585, 611 (Timothy F. Lull ed. 1989):

> Since by faith the soul is cleansed and made to love God, it desires that all things, and especially its own body, shall be purified so that all things may join with it in loving and praising God. Hence a man cannot be idle, for the need of his body drives him and he is compelled to do many good works to reduce it to subjection. Nevertheless the works themselves do not justify him before God, but he does the works out of spontaneous love in obedience to God.

A contemporary Lutheran theologian explains the point in this way:

> I characterize the Christian life as one of faith that gives rise to faithfulness. Christians believe that in Jesus God has cared for us. Eternally secure, we are set free to be his agents in caring for others. Put simply, the grace of God frees us to love.

Gilbert C. Meilaender, Faith and Faithfulness: Basic Themes in Christian Ethics ix (1991).

19. John Calvin, Institutes of the Christian Religion, Bk. III, ch. XVI, p. 98 (Henry Beveridge tr. 1989).

20. It is often suggested that although Luther himself hardly believed in religious toleration or religious freedom in anything like a modern sense, he nonetheless helped pave the way for modern religious freedom by his emphasis on *individual judgment,* as opposed to submission to the creedal authority of the church. See, e.g., Henry Kamen, The Rise of Toleration 41, 54–55 (1967) Whether or not the point is correct, it is not this particular extension of Luther's ideas that I will be discussing here.

21. For a careful presentation of these developments and their effects on belief in this country, see James Turner, Without God, Without Creed 141–202 (1985).

22. Peter L. Berger, Protestantism and the Quest for Certainty, 115 Christian Century 782 (Aug. 26, 1998).

23. For example, he explains that his course of faith "is founded on faith in God who is truth." But of course belief in God is itself one of the tenets that, as he earlier indicates, is very much in question. ("God has not exactly made it easy for us to believe in him, and, it seems to me, a just God will not hold it against us if we don't manage the exercise."). Berger also indicates that "[a]s Christians we believe in the resurrection of Jesus Christ and in his glorious re-

turn," but it is not clear whether or how these beliefs should be included in the more minimalist faith that Berger recommends.

24. Cf. Gavin D'Costa, Christianity and Other Religions, in Many Mansions 31, 34 (Dan Cohn-Sherhock ed. 1992):

A God of infinite love, mercy and justice surely could not condemn the majority of humankind to perdition, most of whom have never even heard the gospel, let alone rejected it. Such a God could only be deemed an unjust tyrant.

25. Cf. Brian Tierney, Religious Rights: A Historical Perspective, in Religious Liberty in Western Thought 46 (Noel B. Reynolds and W. Cole Durham, Jr. eds. 1996) ("It would indeed be hard to discern any seeds of religious liberty in Luther's rantings against Catholics and Jews or in Calvin's grim-lipped defense of persecution after the execution of Servetus."). See also Steven Ozment, Martin Luther on Religious Liberty, in Religious Liberty in Western Thought 75, 77 (Noel B. Reynolds and W. Cole Durham, Jr. eds. 1996) (observing that "[i]n Lutheran lands, Christian freedom in the end meant the right to dissent from Rome and to agree with Wittenberg. . . . [I]t was . . . bondage to a new dogmatic creed"). For an overview of Luther's seemingly inconsistent pronouncements, see Kamen, supra note 20 at 30–42.

26. From the perspective of the "theology of religions," what I am calling ultra-protestantism might be viewed as a version of—or perhaps a variation on—a general approach often called "inclusivism." For a very helpful presentation of this position, see John Sanders, No Other Name: An Investigation into the Destiny of the Unevangelized 215–80 (1992). Sanders points out that "[i]nclusivism has its roots in the early church," and that "[t]oday it is the dominant view among Roman Catholic theologians" and enjoys growing influence "within evangelical circles." Id. at 216.

27. Cf. Daniel O. Conkle, Different Religions, Different Politics: Evaluating the Role of Competing Religious Traditions in American Politics and Law, 10 J. Law & Relig. 1, 14–16 (1993–94) (arguing that "fundamentalists"—that is, believers who "[w]hatever their particular faiths or denominations, . . . regard their religious text (or other religious authority) as a source of truth that is absolute, plain, and unchangeable"—are at odds with the democratic requirement of "dialogic decision-making").

28. John Knox, Limits of Unbelief 23 (1970).

29. Robert L. Wilken, Remembering the Christian Past 56 (1995).

30. Cf. Michael J. Perry, Love and Power 73–74 (1991) (arguing for a "distinction between religious faith and religious beliefs").

31. See, e.g., Vladimir Lossky, The Mystical Theology of the Eastern Church 25 (1957) ("It is by *unknowing* . . . that one may know Him who is above every possible object of knowledge. Proceeding by negations one ascends from

the inferior degrees of being to the highest, by progressively setting aside all that can be known, in order to draw near to the Unknown in the darkness of absolute ignorance.") See generally id. at 21–43.

32. Alasdair MacIntyre, The Debate about God: Victorian Relevance and Contemporary Irrelevance, in Alasdair MacIntyre and Paul Ricoeur, The Religious Significance of Atheism 24–29 (1969).

33. In Voltaire's story *Zadig*, the protagonist defuses an explosive dispute among adherents of a variety of world religions by convincing the disputants—in just a few sentences!—that their various deities are all images of "a superior Being on whom Form and Matter depend" and that in reality, therefore, they "all think the same thing, and consequently there is no reason for quarreling." Voltaire, Zadig, in The Portable Voltaire 329, 370–71 (Ben Ray Redman ed. 1949). The "unity of religions" theme has been taken up by numerous modern thinkers—usually at greater length—and has sometimes been promoted as the primary basis for tolerance or mutual respect. See, e.g., Gustav Mensching, Tolerance and Truth in Religion 155–63 (J. Klimkeit tr. 1955).

34. John Hick, The Rainbow of Faiths: Critical Dialogues on Religious Pluralism 27 (1995). In a number of works, Hick argues that "the ultimate ineffable Reality is capable of being authentically experienced in terms of different sets of human concepts, *as* Jahweh, *as* the Holy Trinity, *as* Allah, *as* Shiva, *as* Vishnu, and again *as* Brahman, *as* the Dharmakaya, *as* the Tao, and so on." Id. at 25. Though attempting to encompass all the major world religions, Hick's position arguably rejects all of them, so that "despite its seeming liberalism" his unity in plurality view "actually represents a rigid, self-contradictory position." Dupuis, supra note 1 at 192. See generally id. at 257–68. See also D'Costa, supra note 24 at 36–38.

35. Cf. D'Costa, supra note 24 at 37:

> Most religious and non-religious believers hold the conviction that what they are talking about is *true*; that their convictions actually relate to reality, the state of things as they are. The problem with the pluralist stance [of thinkers like Hick] is that it too easily bypasses the very genuine problem of conflicting truth claims.

36. See id. at 40:

> [I] am only arguing a theological case for the possibility of God's salvific activity throughout humankind. The implications of this case mean that theologically, a humanist who professes disbelief in God may be saved.

But cf. Sanders, supra note 26 at 228 (observing that "most inclusivists maintain that an 'act of faith' or a conscious decision for God is necessary for salvation").

There is an important qualification to this conclusion, but one that need not be explored at length here. Different religions will typically give instruction regarding the methods (careful scripture study, or prayer, or personal revelation) by which individuals can come to understand and be convinced of religious truths. Adherents to such religions may naturally wonder about the good faith of those who decline to employ such methods or to acknowledge the conclusions that are supposed to follow from those methods; they may regard others' persistent disbelief as among what is sometimes called "the noetic effects of sin." But this possibility provides no warrant, in an ultra-protestant frame at least, for intolerance, because the believer is also enjoined to recognize two additional truths: first, that *everyone* sins, and hence is subject to the noetic effects of sin, and second, that only God can discern what is in the heart. Consequently, believers are well advised to "judge not that [they] be not judged." Matt. 7:1. Cf. D'Costa, supra note 24 at 31, 40 ("Quite simply, only God can read hearts. It is impossible and absurd to say that this or that person is saved or lost.").

37. How much value one attaches to such pluralistic interchanges will depend in part on what we might call one's "epistemology of religious belief"—a complicated subject that is well beyond the scope of this book. See generally Keith E. Yandell, The Epistemology of Religious Experience (1993). In general, it seems that for those who view religious belief as a kind of rational inference to the best explanation and hence suppose a "unity of epistemology," discussion and reasoning ought to have the same value that these methods have in testing other kinds of beliefs. See Larry Alexander, Liberalism, Religion, and the Unity of Epistemology, 30 San Diego L. Rev. 763 (1993). But even for those who emphasize "revelation" or "inspiration" as the primary sources of religious belief, discussion and comparison can be valuable. That is because revelations and inspirations may be viewed as real but not self-authenticating or self-interpreting; and discussion can be an aid in assessing the genuineness and significance of such super-rational disclosures.

38. Niebuhr explained that "[e]xtreme orthodoxy betrays by its very nature that the poison of skepticism has entered the soul of the Church; for men insist more vehemently upon the certainties when their hold upon them has been shaken. Frantic orthodoxy is a method for obscuring doubt." Quoted in Marvin E. Frankel, Faith and Freedom: Religious Liberty in America 109–10 (1994).

39. The pluralism within American Protestantism is stressed in Hatch, infra note 40. More generally, Jon Butler emphasizes that American Christianity after 1700 was "so complex and heterogeneous as to baffle observers and adherents alike." Jon Butler, Awash in a Sea of Faith: Christianizing the American People 2 (1990).

40. See Nathan O. Hatch, The Democratization of American Christianity 9–10, 162 (1989).

41. See Robert H. Abzug, Cosmos Crumbling: American Reform and the

Religious Imagination 129–32, 142–62 (1994); Mark A. Noll, A History of Christianity in the United States and Canada 136–41 (1992).

42. Id. at 316.

43. See George M. Frederickson, The Inner Civil War: Northern Intellectuals and the Crisis of the Union 36–37, 42–43, 61, 81–85, 152–54 (1965).

44. Merrill D. Peterson, Lincoln in American Memory 217 (1994).

45. For a brief review of the claims, see William J. Wolf, Lincoln's Religion 201–3.

46. Allen C. Guelzo, Abraham Lincoln: Redeemer President 443 (1999).

47. Peterson, supra note 44 at 218.

48. David Herbert Donald, Lincoln 33, 49 (1995).

49. Guelzo, supra note 46 at 50–51, 80–81.

50. Donald, supra note 48 at 514.

51. A Yale-trained missionary to Illinois in 1829 found the local culture to be "a sea of sectarian rivalries . . . in constant agitation." Hatch, supra note 40 at 64.

52. A great deal of evidence of these practices is collected in Elton Trueblood, Abraham Lincoln: Theologian of American Anguish (1973). See also Mark A. Noll, One Nation under God? Christian Faith and Political Action in America 93–96 (1988). More recently, Allen Guelzo places Lincoln's serious turn to an austere religious faith at a later point in his presidency, and thus discounts (a bit too insistently, it seems to me) evidence of earlier religiosity. See Guelzo, supra note 46.

53. Trueblood, supra note 52 at 109–10.

54. Id. at 111 ("A creed is what a person *believes,* and Lincoln believed something very specific. His was not religion in general."), at 124 (describing the constant paradox in Lincoln's theological views). See also Wolf, supra note 45 at 75–78.

55. Trueblood, supra note 52 at 102.

56. Trueblood explains that Lincoln was "[d]eeply convinced of the reality of the divine will" but also "had no patience at all with any who were sure they knew the details of the divine will." Id. at 6. In similar vein, Reinhold Niebuhr remarked that Lincoln had "both faith and scepticism in the concept of providence." Reinhold Niebuhr, The Religion of Abraham Lincoln, in Lincoln and the Gettysburg Address 72, 74 (Allan Nevins ed. 1964). Tensions and vacillations may have been fed by ambiguities in the very notion of "providence." See Guelzo, supra note 46 at 318–20.

57. Trueblood, supra note 52 at 107.

58. Id. at 102.

59. Peterson, supra note 44 at 230 ("The fact that Lincoln never united with any Christian church undoubtedly contributed to the love American Jews felt for him.").

60. Trueblood, supra note 52 at 103.

61. As significant as the war was in provoking Lincoln to serious religious reflection, the devastating loss of his small son Willie, who died of sickness in 1862, was also a powerful inducement. See Donald, supra note 48 at 336–38.

62. Lincoln wrote to a newspaper editor that "[i]f slavery is not wrong, nothing is. I cannot remember when I did not so think, and feel." Wolf, supra note 45 at 176.

63. Trueblood, supra note 52 at 123 (describing Lincoln's "recognition of the universality of human fallibility").

64. Guelzo, supra note 46 at 327–45.

65. Id. at 327.

66. Quoted in Trueblood, supra note 52 at 8.

67. Id. at 126.

68. The full text of the brief address can be found at 8 The Collected Works of Abraham Lincoln 332–33 (1953).

69. Trueblood, supra note 52 at 135–37. See also Noll, supra note 52 at 100 ("It is no exaggeration to say that there is nothing like this address in the long, often tedious, and frequently hypocritical history of American political discourse.").

70. See generally McGrath, supra note 10 at 95–119.

71. Lincoln had earlier articulated this theme in a proclamation of a National Fast Day: "It is the duty of nations as well as of men to own dependence upon the overruling power of God, to confess their sins and transgressions, in humble sorrow, yet with assured hope that genuine repentance will lead to mercy and pardon." Quoted in Noll, supra note 52 at 98.

72. "Both parties deprecated war; but one of them would *make* war rather than let the nation survive; and the other would *accept* war rather than let it perish. And the war came."

73. Niebuhr, supra note 56 at 75.

74. Donald, supra note 48 at 566.

75. Trueblood, supra note 52 at vii (quoting Sperry).

Index

About the Author

STEVEN D. SMITH is the Robert and Marion Short Professor of Law, Notre Dame Law School. He is the author of *The Constitution and the Pride of Reason* (1998); *Foreordained Failure: The Quest for a Constitutional Principle of Religious Freedom* (1995); and, with Paul Campos and Pierre Schlag, *Against the Law* (1996).